The Other Pentecostalism
Alternative Themes in Contemporary Renewal Spirituality

Estrelda Alexander

Seymour Press *SP*

The Other Pentecostalism:
Alternative Themes in Contemporary Renewal Spirituality

ISBN 10: 1-938373-11-1
ISBN 13: 978-1-938373-11-4
LCCN: 2020930715

Printed in the United States of America

Unless otherwise noted, all biblical passages referenced are from the New American Standard Bible © the Lockman Foundation, 1995.

Copyright 2020 Seymour Press
Capitol Heights, MD

All rights reserved. No part of this publication may be reproduced, distributed, or transmitted in any form or by any means, including photocopying, recording, or other electronic or mechanical methods, without the prior written permission of the publisher.

Table of Contents

Dedication i

Foreword iii

Preface ix

Introduction 1

1. Ev'ry Time I Feel the Spirit: Pentecostal Retentions from African Spirituality 15
2. Faith of Our Fathers: Recovering Black Theology in Early African-American Holiness-Pentecostal Thought 65
3. Ecumenism of the Spirit: An Alternative Interpretation of Glossolalia 93
4. Limited Liberty: The Myth of Women's Freedom in Ministry in the Early Pentecostalism 139
5. From Azusa Street to Cleveland, Tennessee: The Shared Legacy of William Joseph Seymour and Ambrose Jessup Tomlinson 173
6. Without Form or Fashion: Liturgy in Non-Liturgical Classical Pentecostalism 203
7. Revisiting the "New Issue": Toward a Broader Conversation on the Godhead 247
8. What Doth the Lord Require: Toward a Pentecostal Theology of Justice 271

Bibliography 304

Index 312

Dedication

To all my students and the young scholars who have patiently listened as I have passionately expounded on these topics. You have always been the inspiration to keep my conversations open and truthful.

Forward

In western society, the "other" evokes images of a lesser, primitive being. The "other" is viewed with mild condescension often in need of investigation to locate points of similarities or points of divergence to establish a relational value. Simultaneously, the "other" in most American Protestant arenas historically placed Holiness-Pentecostalism in such a category within Christendom. In 1906 during its infancy, William J. Seymour and proponent of spirit-filled worship resulting from a Pentecostal experience were working-class, urban-dwelling, people of color, whose dress, nomenclature, and separation from mainstream society substantiated the stereotype of their otherness.

Unlike other Protestant denominations, Pentecostalism is a composite expression comprised of hundreds of independent denominational bodies that all subscribe to the divinity of Jesus Christ and His ever expected soon return. This salient point is often overlooked by academics who cluster all "Spirit-filled" faith groups into the catchall phrase Holiness-Pentecostals.

Within one hundred years, Pentecostalism has grown from a storefront mission into a fast-rising global expression of Christianity. Akin to its American antecedents, those espousing spirit-filled worship and a Pentecostal experience remain those on the fringes of society ethnically, economically, and politically. Concurrently, American Pentecostals since the 1970s developed and/or joined professional organizations and produced a corpus of scholarly literature to situate the socio-biblical legitimacy of spirit-filled worship and spirit-filled intellects as harmonious with those who adhere to the sovereignty of the Holy Spirit in all affairs of human activity. A fitting coda to the 20th century, Pentecostalism gradually moved from the periphery to the center in academic literature, musical expression, and Christian culture.

In the 21st century, Pentecostalism's external acceptance came at the expense of continued internal neglect. Issues of gender, oneness-trinitarianism, social justice, and history collided with myopia in denominational leadership of both clergy and academic circles that relegated some matters taboo or simply beyond the pale of relevance in part from increasing invitations to speak, publish, perform or participate in reality television all for pay. Subsequently, the Holiness-Pentecostalism preached by William Seymour, Ida Bell Robinson, Charles H. Mason, and others is now a feel-good experience no longer speaking or seeking to bring truth to power. Contemporary Pentecostalism is comfortable in the trappings of position and blessings, while those lacking within our sanctuaries are given scriptural pablum and social services to "fix" their problems and the larger worlds—both sacred and secular —fall deeper in love with their image like Narcissus seeking complete ecstasy in full union within itself, irrespective of that tragic outcome.

The current intellectual posture of Pentecostalism is problematic and troublesome but not sinful. It neglects the call to write the plain vision and strengthen our brethren in the movement's prophetic tradition. Estrelda Alexander's *The Other Pentecostalism: Alternative Themes in Contemporary Renewal Spirituality*, in full understanding of this lack, explores select internal fractures within the Pentecostal tradition and its continued wariness of academically trained intellectuals. Alexander's paradigm is filtered through a quintuple layer of otherness that informs her perspective. This spirit-filled, academically trained, African American woman scholar and minister provides an argus-eyed view on the strains and contradictions within the practice, social engagement, and historiography of a movement that often juxtaposes intellectual discourse against liturgical tradition, history, and now, social currency in a way that makes it spiritually irrelevant.

This series of eight essays examines Pentecostal history from its beginnings through its chief proponent, William J. Seymour, to the formation of Black theology expressed in the first generation of American Pentecostalism, to the theological fallout between oneness/trinitarian believers. Each essay examines a topic's origin while including the scholarship on the matter. Moreover, these entries question how succeeding generations of Spirit-empowered scholars can continue to press and push for greater intellectual and spiritual understanding; thus, bridging the prophetic aspect of Pentecostal faith and allowing it to resonate through the Church and into the larger society.

This work is especially valuable because it chronicles significant issues within Pentecostalism filtered through Alexander's activist scholarship. As an African American woman minister, the voices of Pentecostal African American foremothers are barely audible, in part, from the dearth of surviving documentary evidence. Their sermons, thoughts, and responses to issues of their day are rare finds, or, generally, relegated to brief quotations in larger works.

Divergent from other Protestant denominations, women were integral in the early years of Pentecostalism. As the fire cooled, women were relegated to auxiliary positions. In response, several women shook of second-class membership and established their own denominations in efforts to live out the words Galatians 3:28. Yet, all too often, women scholars in general, and Pentecostal woman s in particular, do not make do the hard work of preserving their voices. Their failure in continuing to mentor and produce scholarship gives little regard for how their authentic voice will be recalled when they are no longer around.

Alexander's work pays attention to the reality that Yes, proteges serve as evangelists, however, the documentary evidence in literal voice is invaluable without inadvertent filters. Alexander's determination to gather and publish her thoughts, however, provides an intellectual connection for future African American women scholars, theologians, and others about the how and what of the thoughts of a late 20th century Spirit-filled African American woman of her ilk.

Written in clear and direct language, this book will enrich the laity, clergy, academic and general readers who are concerned about race, gender, and renewal for humankind from a faith-based perspective. *The Other Pentecostalism: Alternative Themes in Contemporary Renewal Spirituality* covers issues of liturgy, oneness-trinitarianism, and social justice with erudition and Spirit-empowered intellect and sensitivity.

Alexander interposes her two-worlds faith and scholarship into one community populated with fallible people, potentially well-intentioned and in need of solutions. In essence, her other Pentecostalism insists that we must cease to ignore the benefits of Spirit-empowered intellectualism and embrace renewal as a method of effective witness and awareness of the larger world and they that dwell therein.

Ida E. Jones, Ph.D

Preface

In conversations with Pentecostal colleagues within the academy regarding the movement with which we hold a love-hate relationship, I often find that we are not discussing the same entity. The Pentecostalism I have loved is represented by an early prophetic movement that held in its bones the possibility of turning the world upside down. It sought to create a social culture that bore the visible marks of the Kingdom of God–racial and gender inclusiveness, lack of class distinction, and genuine regard for the least of these. It attempted to forge a climate of unity within diversity that treated intra-doctrinal differences as something that did not have to break the "unity of the Spirit" while it allowed for the maintenance of creedal distinction.

The Pentecostalism I have grown to dislike is one that, for much of the last half of a century, has been rigidly divided along racial, gender, and class lines. Further, while allowing itself to be segmented by internal squabbles, it has sought to cut itself off from the rest of the body of Christ, this Pentecostalism has often branded itself as holding to a superior spirituality that could not be sullied by intermixing with the wider Christian community and sought to cut itself off from the rest of the body of Christ.

My identity as a black woman intermingled with a spiritual identity as Pentecostal has been formative in shaping a theological identification and worldview. Though remaining, unashamedly, Pentecostal, theological education within the Wesleyan and Catholic traditions has provided tools for critically reflecting on a movement that has embodied life and identity as both participant and observer. My formal theological formation is colored by what has been gained from these training foci in ways about which I am not always conscious. Taken together, both my organic and formal formation have shaped conversations with colleagues in and outside the movement and determined the tenor and content of my scholarly endeavors.

This formation has engendered two felt needs. First, I sense the necessity to justify Pentecostalism, and my position within it, to outsiders, to rescue it from its reputation as an entirely otherworldly, cultic spiritual oddity and place it in the realm of Christian orthodoxy. But secondly, as one given the gift of intellectual acuity, I am compelled to offer an objective critique and/or corrective for problematic aspects of the movement to those within it.

As a Pentecostal woman, I, sometimes, am at odds with male colleagues regarding how the movement has treated gender issues. At the same time, I, often, find myself out of sync with white colleagues regarding how it has treated people of color. Further, I find myself in contention with various segments of the movement concerning how they have treated each other. Moreover, I am frequently disappointed with the movement at large and other segments of the body of Christ about how they have coexisted or failed to coexist with each other.

My unique posture, as a person informed by both sides, has forced me to look both ways and consider aspects of Pentecostalism that both its detractors and supporters tend to take for granted. The middle ground position allows me to see disparate sides of issues that many declare to have been settled, others find too unimportant or arduous to revisit, or that cause some scholars who have been nurtured by the movement to walk away from it, and, sometimes, from the church.

One promising sign is that as Pentecostalism has matured and become a more acceptable expression of orthodox Christian faith, some segments of the movement have sought to broaden the circle of conversation partners it engages. Hopefully, as Pentecostalism becomes less of an oddity relegated to the cult section of mainline libraries, and "Pentecostal scholarship" is no longer considered an oxymoronic term, colleagues on both sides will continue to engage in meaningful dialogue and find new ways to discuss what it means to be part of the inclusive body of Christ while maintaining Pentecostal identity.

Introduction

In 1906 in a little mission church in Los Angeles, California, a seemingly unimportant revival meeting began among a group that was, initially, composed mainly of African American household workers. The group was led by a self-educated son of former slaves who had migrated from the Reconstruction South on a journey that took several spiritual turns and eventually landed him at the head of what would become one of the most significant movements in global twentieth-century Christianity. *Life* magazine listed Pentecostalism as sixty-eighth among the top one hundred events of the second millennium,[1] while *The Dictionary of Christianity in America* asserts the movement is perhaps "the single most significant development of twentieth-century Christianity."[2] Within a few months, the revival grew enough to attract the attention of local and national newspapers and draw attendants from across the nation and around the world.

The "fire on Azusa Street" began as an ember that first burned in the hearts of the small group that gathered nightly to pray and tarry together and wait for what they hoped and expected would change their lives forever. They sought an infusion of God's Spirit that would imbue them with the power to live a more godly lifestyle but also empower them to win more souls for the Kingdom of God.

Not only did it change the lives of the few faithful who had gathered initially, but within a short period, the revival was the catalyst

---

[1] The Life Millennium: *The 100 Most Important Events and People of the Past 1,000 Years,* First Edition, Collingdale, PA Diane Publishing Company, 1998.
[2] Roger G. Robins "Pentecostal Movement," in Daniel G. Reid, ed.; *The Dictionary of Christianity in America*. Downers Grove, IL: InterVarsity Press, 1990, 885.

for the beginning of a movement that is among the fastest growing segments of Christianity. Worldwide, estimates of Pentecostal/Charismatic/Neo-Pentecostal adherents account for 600 million believers, and projection of yearly expansion is approximately twelve to fifteen million. Globally, many of the largest churches are classical Pentecostal, independent non-denominational congregations with a Pentecostal bent. Further, a substantial proportion of the growth is occurring among people of color in the two-thirds world.

Depending on who makes the assessment, reasons for growth include both the movement's perceived strengths and weaknesses. Explanations use a range of theological, historical, sociological, psychological, and economic lenses.

Proponents describe Pentecostalism as a reformation movement born of the Holy Spirit. They see its growth emanating from the potential for both personal and social transformation. For them, the explosive growth can be attributed directly to an evangelistic zeal in the hearts of those touched by the red-hot fires of Pentecost to win all the lost into the Kingdom before the Christ's "imminent" return.

Explanations of detractors range from its ecstatic attraction as a vibrant reformation movement born of the Holy Spirit with the promised potential for both personal and social transformation,[3] to its appeal to masses of marginalized persons discounted by more acceptable" Christian traditions in their attempt to escape the harsh realities of an often hostile world and form a haven of submerged religious protest.[4]

---

[3]For a discussion of this issue, see Steven J. Land, *Pentecostal Spirituality: A Passion for the Kingdom*. Sheffield, England: Sheffield Press, 1993.
[4] See Anderson, *Vision of the Disinherited: The Making of American Pentecostalism,* Peabody, MA: Hendrickson Publishers, 1992 for an exposition of

However, no single entity can be identified as Pentecostalism. Differences between classical Pentecostalism, Neo-Pentecostalism, and the Charismatic movement, the three major divisions within classical Pentecostalism (Holiness/Pentecostals, Finished Work and Oneness), along with over 200 denominations and smaller bodies, making it difficult to characterize the movement. According to some estimates, there are at least thirty-eight major categories of Pentecostalism with their sacramental, ecclesiological, and practical particularities, as well as doctrinal and theological distinctions.

Defining Pentecostalism

The often-repeated question is, "what is Pentecostalism?" or "what does it mean to be a Pentecostal?" Though a definition has evolved over its little more than one-hundred-year history, no singular agreement has emerged as to what the term means. The distinguishing feature of Pentecostalism is the belief that the "baptism" or "outpouring" of the Holy Spirit on the Christian believer is an essential aspect of Christian experience that is understood to be a direct fulfillment of the prophecy of the Old Testament book of Joel. To Pentecostals, this "in-filling" of the Holy Spirit endows believers with supernatural empowerment to both live a "holy" life and to accomplish "works of righteousness" on behalf of the Kingdom of God. Adherents seek to establish a personal communion with God through ecstatic religious experience, including glossolalia, or speaking in tongues, as initial objective evidence of that outpouring and in-filling.

There is no Pentecostalism with a central governing body or one form of government. Rather, the movement is made up of numerous,

---

this view.

variably sized denominations and independent groups that subscribe to doctrinal convictions relating primarily to the person and work of the Holy Spirit in the life of the believer and the church. Outside these essential tenets, however, groups differ regarding whether speaking in tongues is "the" or "an" initial evidence of Holy Spirit baptism and the subsequent nature and place of glossolalia in the believer's life and ministry of the and the church's worship. Additionally, no movement-wide consensus exists regarding the nature of biblical inspiration, the nature of the Godhead, the reality and mode of sanctification, or the appropriate means of receiving Holy Spirit the baptism. Divergence also exists around such practical matters as the relationship of inward spirituality to outward dress, participation in secular entertainment, the nature of church government, sacramental formulas and protocol, and the appropriate level of participation of women and laity in the ministry and leadership of the church.

Pentecostal groups include all who accept this self-identification (or that of Neo-Pentecostal, Charismatic, Full-Gospel or Third-Wave)[5] and whose members seek or manifest (speaking in) tongues and other 'charismatic' gifts recorded in the Scripture as accompanying the emergence of the early church.[6] These gifts are understood to be for

---

[5]Though scholars define the terms differently, Charismatic most often refers to non-denominational churches or smaller groups within existing congregations (especially Catholic parishes) who experience tongues and who place emphasis on the use of spiritual gifts (or charismata) but have fewer social restrictions than classical Pentecostals. Neo-Pentecostal (or third-wave) includes individuals who report having the Pentecostal experience who remain in mainline congregations and who prefer to maintain their denominational affiliation but who are essentially Pentecostal or charismatic in their beliefs and style of worship.

[6]Luther P. Gerlach, "Pentecostalism: Revolution or Counter-Revolution" in Irving Zaretsky and Mark Leone, eds., *Religious Movements in Contemporary America,* Princeton, NJ: Princeton University Press, 1974, 675.

the edification of the individual, their particular faith community, and the body of Christ. However, considerable disagreement revolves around the freedom believers have in the operation of these gifts in public worship. More charismatic groups promote the freer operation of a variety of gifts while traditional Pentecostals are more restrained in this area, opting for a more central focus of gifts in ministers and leaders.

Beyond these basics, Pentecostals have generally held that individuals, as well as the corporate body of believers, should seek for and submit to the leading of the Holy Spirit for direction in one's spiritual and practical life, that there should be a return to apostolic simplicity in worship, and the restoration of spiritual gifts (particularly divine healing) to the church, that baptism should be reserved for believers as a sign of obedience to the command of Christ, and that the visible return of Christ is imminent, after which He will set up His millennial reign on the earth.

A common misconception characterizes Pentecostalism as an escapist movement. In part, this stems from many Christians' lack of exposure to the broad Pentecostal spectrum, including some segments' historic engagement with their communities' socio-political realities. It also stems, in part, from Pentecostals failure to document their history and theological musings in generally accessible media and, instead, burying explanations of themselves in inaccessible media such as tracts, sermons, and in-house periodicals circulated within the community.

Misconceptions also stem from the over-exposure of charismatic, "super-star," televangelists and mega-churches that focus the majority of their ministry on personal prosperity and the well-being of individual believers. The "word-faith" or "name-it-and-claim-it" movement accounts for only a small, though growing, and highly visible sector of global Pentecostalism. Social and traditional media has brought a variety of Pentecostal/Charismatic experiences (though not the most representative) ton our attention. Yet, charismatic personalities with mega-ministries and emphasis on prosperity and material gain for faithful supporters provide a distorted picture of the whole of Pentecostalism.

The Pentecostal landscape is dotted with small to moderate size, lower to middle-class congregations. It is housed in inner-city storefronts on thoroughfares and streets of urban communities, renovated former synagogues and mainline churches, as well as upper-middle-class, modernistic suburban complexes. Further, a significant segment of the movement exists in third world populations who regularly subsist at or near poverty levels.

Another popular misconception characterizes Pentecostals as part of the fundamentalist or "Christian Right" movement. While some Pentecostals align themselves with ultra-conservative politics squarely with the evangelical camp, most have never been an integral part of the fundamentalist party, and mostly, until recently, have shied away from the fundamentalist-liberal controversy for several reasons. First, true fundamentalists generally denounce Pentecostals along with liberals and Catholics. Second, while fundamentalism primarily falls into the Calvinist camp, Pentecostal doctrine is generally Arminian. Third, the close alliance that has developed over the years between Evangelicals and Pentecostals came about only as Evangelicals began to distance themselves from the fundamentalist camp during the World War II period.[7] More importantly, some of this misunderstanding stems from prejudice on the part of more liberal Christians who succumb to the

---

[7] See James D. Hunter, *American Evangelicalism: Conservative Religion and the Quandary of Modernity.* New Brunswick, NJ: Rutgers University Press, 1983.

temptation to cast even moderate theological positions that are right of liberal as fundamentalism.

Pentecostals and fundamentalists hold some basic beliefs in common, including the verbal inspiration of Scripture and the virgin birth and deity of Christ and His atoning work on the Cross. They differ, though, about practical aspects such as the place of women in the home and church, the cessation or perpetuity of tongues and spiritual gifts, and biblical literalism. Further, though most Pentecostal adherents are comfortable in the theologically conservative camp, many stay away from extreme conservative theological pronouncements. As relates to political affiliation, Pentecostals can be found on either side of the political spectrum and at all points in between.

The year was 1906 when in a little mission church in Los Angeles, California, a seemingly unimportant revival meeting began among a group that was, initially, composed mainly of African American household workers. The group was led by a self-educated son of former slaves who had migrated from the Reconstruction South on a journey that took several spiritual turns and eventually landed him at the head of what would become one of the most significant movements in global twentieth-century Christianity. Life magazine listed Pentecostalism as sixty-eighth among the top one hundred events of the second millennium, while The Dictionary of Christianity in America asserts the movement is perhaps "the single most significant development of twentieth-century Christianity." Within a few months, the revival grew enough to attract the attention of local and national newspapers and draw attendants from across the nation and around the world.

The "fire on Azusa Street" began as an ember that first burned in the hearts of the small group that gathered nightly to pray and tarry together and wait for what they hoped and expected would change their lives forever. They sought an infusion of God's Spirit that would imbue them with the power for a godly lifestyle but also empower them to win souls for the Kingdom of God.

Not only did it change the lives of the few faithful who had gathered initially, but soon the revival was the catalyst for the beginning of a movement that is among the fastest growing segments of Christianity. Worldwide, estimates of Pentecostal/Charismatic/Neo-Pentecostal adherents account for 600 million believers, and projection of yearly expansion is approximately twelve to fifteen million. Globally, many of the largest churches are classical Pentecostal, independent non-denominational congregations with a Pentecostal bent. Further, a substantial proportion of the growth is occurring among people of color in the two-thirds world.

Depending on who makes the assessment, reasons for growth include both the movement's perceived strengths and weaknesses. Explanations use a range of theological, historical, sociological, psychological, and economic lenses.

Proponents describe Pentecostalism as a reformation movement born of the Holy Spirit. They see its growth emanating from the potential for both personal and social transformation. For them, the explosive growth can be attributed directly to an evangelistic zeal in the hearts of those touched by the red-hot fires of Pentecost to win all the lost into the Kingdom before the Christ's "imminent" return.

Explanations of detractors range from its ecstatic attraction as a vibrant reformation movement with the promised potential for both personal and social transformation, to its appeal to masses of marginalized persons discounted by more acceptable" Christian traditions in their attempt to escape the harsh realities of an often hostile world and form a haven of submerged religious protest.

However, no single entity can be identified as Pentecostalism. Differences between classical Pentecostalism, Neo-Pentecostalism, and the Charismatic movement, the three major divisions within classical Pentecostalism (Holiness/Pentecostals, Finished Work and Oneness), along with over 200 denominations and smaller bodies, making it difficult to characterize the movement. According to some estimates, there are at least thirty-eight major categories of Pentecostalism with their sacramental, ecclesiological, and practical particularities, as well as doctrinal and theological distinctions.

Significantly, African American Pentecostals (whom much of this book is about) tend to be more inclined toward a more progressive stance on socio-political issues. And, often the political divide within the movement is a racial divide such that the same issues that continue to divide white and black America, continue to divide the Pentecostal movement.

The racially inclusive ideal of Pentecostalism memorialized by the phrase, "the colored line was washed away in the blood [of Jesus]" soon gave way to the reality that this line had been indelibly etched into the psyche of American society. The playing out of this reality has left a movement that remains largely divided along racial lines. Each side views the beginning of the movement through a lens colored by their racial identity.

Black Pentecostals quickly and eagerly point to Azusa Street as the progenitor of the entire movement and see Seymour as one of the most important leaders–black or white–of this era. On the other hand, their white counterparts, in many cases, are just as quick and easy to move the spotlight, suggesting that there are several starting points.

Concomitantly, black Pentecostals can be characterized, out of necessity, as more socially progressive. While they maintain rigid personal piety, they tie this to ensuring racial uplift and economic and social survival in this world at the same time as they are ensuring spiritual reward in the hereafter.

In sum, the variety of its expressions can characterize the Pentecostal movement in the United States. This characterization, spawned by the many schisms, has hallmarked the movement since its inception. One reason is adherents' openness to continuing revelation that sees the canon as always subject to enlargement and allows leaders to see their "God-given" truth as the corrective to spiritualities that fail to provide the "full Gospel." This posture makes it difficult to develop a systematic Pentecostal theology or determine what it means to do justice or, simply, to agree on what it means to be Pentecostal.

Since there is no one Pentecostalism or Pentecostal movement and no one speaks for the entire group that self-identifies as Pentecostal. Rather, many speak for it, or, at least, for their little corner. Those that stand at different points within the movement involve themselves in dialogue regarding how to account for its roots and its practical, doctrinal, cultural, and racial diversity found in it. This work deals with these questions and the larger conversation from the vantage of an African American Pentecostal scholar whose involvement outside of the movement has been forced this broader dialogue.

Can we legitimately recover elements of African spirituality that informed early Pentecostalism and that remain embedded (though often unacknowledged) within the fabric of the movement? How are they incorporated and how do adherents interpret these elements within the contexts of Christian orthodoxy?

It is evident that, at least within the African American community, ideas of social justice infused Pentecostal sensitivities and spirituality. Moreover, it did so in such a way that leaders of this branch of Pentecostal were outspoken critics of racial injustice within the broader society as well as the complicity of Christians in not doing more to break the back of injustice.

At least in one instance, black Pentecostals did not stand alone in attempting to garner support. As the narrative regarding Ambrose J. Tomlinson attests, some sympathetic white Pentecostals drew on their radical holiness leanings and their convicting sense of the unifying work of the Holy Spirit.

What to do with the women within Pentecostal want? To answer that question, we have to examine the experience of Pentecostal women throughout the life of the movement. If we start with the earliest days when its evangelistic zeal and radical inclusiveness provided women with a sense that they had found a place where they could be all that God ordained for them. This quickly gave way to a more restricted role.

What do we do with theological differences that arise within the movement and between the movement and other parts of the Body of Christ? Can these differences be reconciled by a deeper exploration of their roots and what is at stake when we remain fractured?

What is the place of glossolalia (speaking in tongues) in the congregation's and the believer's life? Can Pentecostals embrace an understanding of the phenomenon as more than the initial biblical evidence of Holy Spirit baptism or even as a personal prayer language?

Further, what would such a broadened understanding do to further the ecumenical project of increased unity within the body of Christ?

Does a difference of understanding of the nature of the Godhead have to lead to a divided movement? Or does it mean that an entire faction of this movement has to be cut off from meaningful interaction and theological dialogue with its other members or other members of the body of Christ? What is really at stake in this centuries-old revision of the early church argument?

Despite protestations to the contrary, there have been perceptible elements of ritual and liturgy within Pentecostalism. Self-definitions as non-liturgical notwithstanding, there are recurring practices that can be found throughout the breadth of Pentecostal worship that brand it as a particular type of spirituality.

Finally, is there the issue of whether a genuine theology of social justice is possible within the Pentecostal framework? Its beginnings and history suggest that elements of such theology have always been present. Yet, can we build on these to craft a sustainable response to the significant issues that increasingly challenge brokenness, economic inequality, poverty, health care, family, and social concerns?

To answer these issues, requires a broader conversation among the various groupings of adherents as well as between Pentecostals and the broader body of Christ. We need common ground on which to base these discussions and need to hear alternative interpretations of the movement as well as its ecumenical contribution. A deeper examination suggests that there is more to the contemporary Pentecostalism than is casually observed and helps us see what the movement—again, the fastest growing segment of the Christian tradition—has added to the body of Christ.

My intent has not been to speak for the entire movement. For, though I have often served within multi-cultural contexts, I am unashamedly an African American woman and can best speak from within that context. Nor do I posit that there always is or should be a winning side to multifarious schisms that have shaped the movement. My sole intent is to foster critical dialog that could strengthen the contribution Pentecostals can make to ecumenical dialog over the next decade and thus broaden the mutual appreciation between the movement and the broader body of Christ.

Ev'ry Time I Feel the Spirit: Pentecostal Retentions from African Spirituality

> *For as I was... considering the objects of your worship, I even found an altar with this inscription: TO THE UNKNOWN GOD. Therefore, the One whom you worship without knowing, Him I proclaim to you. (Acts 17:23)*

Shortly after the Azusa Street Revival moved into full gear, William Seymour invited his mentor and colleague, Charles Fox Parham, to see for himself how the Lord was using his student to continue his vision for an end-time revival. Seymour expected Parham to be excited that his vision of believers embracing the understanding of Holy Spirit baptism with tongues was being lived out, validating the doctrine of initial evidence with proof that God was pouring out His Spirit "on all flesh." As pastor of the small mission, Seymour believed Parham approved God's marvelous use of his former student.

Parham, on the contrary, was repulsed by the assorted assembly's scandalous, unrestrained, and disorderly race-mixing and the "Africanisms" they displayed. He was sickened by the sight of white people freely associating with black and Latino believers and engaging in what he saw as "crude negroisms."[8] Parham left the revival, insisting that most of those claiming the Holy Spirit's baptism, merely, were subject to "animal spiritism."[9] He called the famous "heavenly choir"— the singing in tongues about which many raved—a form of "Negro chanting," declaring it had nothing to do with Pentecostal Spirit baptism.[10]

---

[8]Parham, *The Apostolic Faith* (Baxter Springs, KS.) 1:8 (October 1912), 6.
[9]Ibid.
[10]Parham, New Year's Greetings," *The Apostolic Faith* (Baxter Springs,

Parham's sentiments toward what he saw as "heathenish" elements were echoed by other white religionists as well as members of the secular press. A Los Angeles Times article, for example, referred to speaking in tongues as "weird babel."[11] Leading white fundamentalist pastors, unsympathetic to both emotive worship and racial mixing, derided the revival in their sermons. One called it a "disgusting amalgamation of African voodoo superstition and Caucasian insanity."[12] Others used similar epithets to link its perceived strangeness to a variety of causes. Early mainline black religionists were no less caustic in critiquing the revival's primitive folk elements.

Religious scholarship is replete with denigrating references to practices found in lower-class black religion into which they categorically characterized Pentecostalism. In *The Small Sects of America*, written forty years after the revival, Elmer Clark insisted that all African American worship (not derived from a white Christian tradition) was tainted by roots in African spirituality, characterizing emotive exercises, shouting, trances and bodily movements that blacks attributed to the Holy Spirit as "primitive traits."[13]

These "negroisms"—shouting, dancing, jerking, Spirit possession, falling, visions and trances—have been a part of black and white revivalist worship for decades. Certainly, many behaviors identified as retentions (or survivals) were also found among predominantly white

---

KS.) (January 1912), 6.

[11] "Weird Babel of Tongues," *Los Angeles Daily Times*, (April 18, 1906), 1.

[12] "New Religions Come, Then Go," *Los Angeles Herald*, September 24, 1906, 7, cited in Cecil M. Robeck, "The Past: Historical Roots of Racial Unity and Division in American Pentecostalism," *Cyberjournal for Pentecostal-Charismatic Research* 14 (2005) <www.pctii.org/cyberj/cyber14.html>.

[13] Elmer T. Clark, *The Small Sects in America* (Nashville: Cokesbury Press, 1949), 142.

nineteenth-century camp meetings and the bodies that sponsored or grew out of them. The worship of the Great Awakenings—especially extraordinary meetings such as the Cane Ridge Revival—though they were largely led by whites, attracted blacks precisely because they exhibited behaviors common in the worship of African Traditional Religion.[14]

Any discussion of African religious retentions within African American Christianity must consider several mitigating factors that diminish the ability to discern direct connections between the traditions. First, there is no one African religious tradition, just as there is no single African culture. The vast continent of Africa is the second largest, spanning 11,725,385 square miles. Then, as now, the continent had numerous distinct political divisions and cultural systems. African people were further clustered by tribal affiliations with significant variety in cultural development and worldviews. There are over one thousand ethnolinguistic communities in black (sub-Saharan) Africa, each with its socio-cultural heritage, yielding various national, regional, and religious traditions from which New World expressions arose.

Most slaves came from the western coast of the continent: Gold Coast (now Ghana), Sierra Leone, Benin, and Dahomey. There was also a considerable number from Cameroon, Gabon, Ivory Coast, the Congo, Angola, Mozambique, and Madagascar.[15] Each region had its cultural and religious customs. Yet, when viewed holistically, these traditions evidence common elements that support a generically

---

[14] Richard D. Shiels "America's Pentecost," *Cross Currents* 42, no. 1 (1992), 90.

[15] For a discussion of the impact of each country see, Hugh Thomas, *The Slave Trade, The Story of the Atlantic Slave Trade: 1440-1870* (New York: Simon & Schuster, 1997).

African understanding of reality, that, at its root, is ontologically different from the Western worldview.

Second, for several reasons, nothing from Africa survived the middle passage without substantial transformation. The social context of U.S. blacks demonstrated the least degree of African retentions of all the slaves imported into the New World.[16] Further, no segment of Christianity among African Americans in the United States displays direct importation of African spirituality as found in Caribbean traditions as Haitian Vodun, Brazilian Contomblé, or Cuban Santeria. For, the Spanish and French slaveholders who controlled the Caribbean were much more open to slaves retaining some form of their religious identity and were not averse to the expression of that spirituality. They, therefore, felt no need to replace it with a "purer" Christian spirituality.[17]

---

[16] In *The Myth of the Negro Past*, Herskovits, centered his study on the Caribbean and South America. Between 1619, when the first slaves were introduced onto the mainland at Jamestown, Virginia, and 1865 when the Emancipation Proclamation ended legal slavery, twelve million black Africans were shipped to the Americas. The majority were shipped to Brazil; less than 600,000 were transported to North America, though several hundred thousand were born here. This is a relatively insignificant number compared to those imported to the Caribbean and South America, since only five to ten percent of those brought to the new world came to the United States. Individual plantations had relatively small numbers of slaves in comparison to those in other countries. The average number of slaves on these plantations was twelve, while in Brazil, for example, the average was one hundred. Slave importation in this country ended comparably early and the increase in the population coming mainly through rapid reproduction. So, while growth in the U.S. slave population kept pace with that in other regions, it did not involve newly captured peoples coming from the homeland with cultural identities still intact in their souls and spirits.

[17] Albert J. Raboteau, Slave Religion: *The "Invisible Institution" in the Antebellum South* New York: Oxford University Press, 1980.

African Spirituality

The disparate cultures that informed traditional African spirituality ensured that no one cohesive system of belief characterized the religion of all of Africa. Several threads running throughout the African religious cosmos found their way into slave worship and through it, into black Christian faith. These elements came through the Middle Passage embedded, in some shape, in the slaves' psyche so that decades of unimaginably inhumane treatment could not completely erase them. Attempts to divorce the slaves from "primitive" understandings of reality proved less than successful. Each element—universal belief in a supreme being; a pervasive sense of the reality of the spirit world; blurring of lines between the sacred and profane; practical use of religion in all of life; surrender of excessive individualism for community solidarity; reverence for ancestors and their symbolic communal presence; creative use of rhythm, singing and dance in life and worship; and greater involvement of women in ritual and community leadership—has implications for African American spirituality and variously display themselves in African American Pentecostalism.

The slaves who came to the New World were not, totally, uncivilized, irreligious, heathens. Rather, their religious heritage incorporated facets that resonated with Christian faith. Among the most relevant was the universality of belief in a supreme being—the Great Spirit or holy God. This God was not one among many or chief among equals, but the eternal Creator of every other being, including lesser gods created for his bidding, other spirits, the universe, humanity, and every animate or inanimate thing that exists. As in the Judeo-Christian tradition, this transcendent Creator deity is the sustainer and controller of the universe. This God is omnipotent, omnipresent, omniscient, and sovereign.

As omnipotent, this supreme God originates and sustains all creation; every other thing that exists is subject to the one God. Any power exercised by another being, individual, or community has its source in God and cannot be exercised without God's enablement. Since God is omnipresent, one need not erect buildings to confine worship. Everything God created is sacred and worship can take place anywhere: at the mountain, at the river, beside a tree, for God's presence and majesty can be seen in these things. Western missionaries, unfamiliar with this worldview, generally, mistook the African marvel at God's creation and apprehension of God within it as idolatry—worship of that creation. Within African cosmology, however, God is not, pantheistically or panentheistically, part of everything. God's presence is in everything. God's omniscience is understood as possessing the highest possible level of wisdom, including knowing the secrets and intent of the hearts of men and women. Nothing is hidden from God.

As sovereign God of the universe, the Supreme God is not part of the pantheon of divinities but holds a position unique to himself. God is not an ancestor or chief among ancestors, but the "great other, beyond, yet at the center of, all human understanding and actions."[18] Not just a god of power and wisdom, this God is, most of all, a personal being, helping to defeat enemies and interjecting Godself into peoples' lives. This God is known by a variety of names Oladumare or

---

[18]Eunice Kamaara, "The Influence of Christianity on African Society's Concept of God," African Ecclesiastical Review 40:1 (1998), 48.

Olorun among Yoruba in Nigeria, Imana in Ruanda, Onayeme or Nyame among Ghanaian Ashanti, and Mwari in Shona or Bantu.[19]

A host of lesser, immanent gods serves this supreme God. These beings function similarly to the angelic realm in Western religious conceptions. They stand between God and the rest of created reality, mediating God's power to the world and doing God's bidding. They do not carry out their will, but God's. Within this cosmology, a personal devil is no less real than the supreme God and is associated with bad magic. No dualistic or polytheistic equality exists between the forces of good and evil, however. The devil's power is not equal to that of God, for the devil is a created being. While he is respected for his power, the ultimate mediator of justice remains the supreme God.

The African worldview is open to the supernatural in all of life. The African prays for and expects God's necessary, supernatural intervention in all of his or her affairs. The entirety of existence —from birth to death, the religious and non-religious—therefore, is infused with both wonder and fear. No word exists for religion because religious affections permeate all other aspects of life. God is involved in all of human reality, and the line between that which is devoted exclusively to one's service to God or the worldly and temporal realities is blotted out.

All of life has a sacred element. For this reason, Arthur Fauset's observation that to the casual eye, the appeal of religion to the black person is as natural as the appeal of water to fish belies several misunderstandings about the black religious context.[20] Within this

---

[19]See, for example, William A. Brown, "Concepts for God in Africa," *Journal of Religious Thought* 39:2 (1982-1983), 5-16.
[20]Arthur H. Fauset, *Black Gods of the Metropolis Negro Religious Cults of the Urban North*, (Philadelphia: University of Pennsylvania Press, 1970), 1.

context, we must reexamine the charge of animism. Africans do not worship nature as God; rather, God indwells all of nature. They do not worship the tree; the tree is a beautiful manifestation of God's handy work to be deeply admired. They do not worship the lion; the majestic lion epitomizes the grandeur of God's creative power.

Further, African spirituality infuses all of life with a ritual component. It not only considers the well-being of the eternal soul but the totality of temporal experiences. Still, all religious practice contains a profanely secular element; and nothing is done purely for the sake of ritual. Every ceremonial act has practical implications, and every secular, life-sustaining act has a religious aspect. God's name is invoked in everyday situations, not just reserved for worship, ritual, or prayer. What white missionaries saw as taking God's name in vain was, for the African, invoking the name of God in lived reality.

Rugged individualism is strange to the African mind, that surrenders rigid individualism—excessive egoism—for solidarity with the community and all of nature. African intercourse is concerned with interrelationships between the individual, God, spirits, ancestors, and the living community. Life centers on the entire society's needs, and sin is, first, that which breaches community—between the individual and God, one's fellow person, family, tribe, nation, and with the rest of creation. Each person is implicitly related to every other member of the community—the living and the dead, the animate and the inanimate. The well-being of the individual is intimately connected with the well-being of all of creation.[21] When any part of that connection is out of balance, broken or distorted, it does not bode well for the individual or community since "to be human is to belong to the

---

[21]John Mbiti, "Christianity and African Culture," *Journal of Theology for Southern Africa* 20 (1977), 26.

whole community... participating in (its) beliefs, ceremonies, rituals, and festivals."[22] The idea of covenant is taken seriously, and breaking covenant is an egregious sin. In keeping with the orality of the community, no formal written agreement is necessary. A spoken covenant is a good as a written contract and a person's word is his or her bond. Yet rituals and ceremonies are built around the making of covenant. Salvation within African traditional religion is a holistic concept. God, the creator of everything, is capable of redeeming everything. That redemption, however, relates as much to the present physical reality as to the afterlife.

Ancestor veneration—the real/symbolic presence of ancestors among the living to guide and inspire is a central focus of African spirituality. Not every deceased person is venerated; only those whose morally exemplary lives have significantly contributed to the entire community's survival are given this honor. Expressions of veneration range from pouring memorial libation to prayers or sacrifices offered to particularly pious deceased in the belief they may ascend to becoming minor deities. Within this continuum, distinctions between veneration and worship are not always clear. Worship ascribes deity to a being as the object of adulation, investing that being with salvific capacity, while veneration is reverential respect for a being because of their wisdom and dignity, without ascribing supernatural power except as that derived from a supernatural deity.

Honor is given on behalf of the ancestor, not to the ancestor. Libation is poured for the ancestor, not to the ancestor. Such honor carries the understanding that "God will witness your action and accept

---

[22]John Mbiti, *African Religions and Culture.* Oxford, GB: Heinemann, 1990, 106.

it," and the expectation that, "as you do for your parents, your children will do likewise for you."[23]

The ancestors, like all human beings, have an essentially spiritual essence. They are not dead, or annihilated, but are living spirits (not deities) who bind the present generation to the past, intermediating between the natural realm and God. Like the Catholic saints, they serve as intercessors. When prayer or libation was offered, the ancestors were not the intended end. These acts were offered to them so they could offer them to God. They were not deified or divinized. Ancestors or clan-founders, as well as tribal spirits, were never mistaken for gods, but seen as human spirits of human beings created by God and. were limited in power.[24]

Ancestral beliefs act as a social control to regulate the moral behavior of individuals as well as the entire community. Rites to honor ancestors, that take place in private settings such as intimate family meals or large public gatherings such as religious ceremonies, remind the community of those collective traits that are esteemed. Their deeds are recounted through song, story, myth, folklore, and proverbs, and the understanding that these ancestors are aware of one's actions restrains antisocial behavior.

While within the African cosmology, ancestor veneration serves as a source of restraint, music served as a source of release. All of African life and every ritual is infused with music and rhythm—singing and dancing. Not to sing or dance is not to be African. Africans sing while they work, while they pray; they sing to give and receive

---

[23]Karenga, M. *Kwanzaa: A Celebration of Family, Community and Culture* Los Angeles: University of Sankore Press, 1997, 80-81.
[24]Ignatius M. Zvarevashe, "Shona (Bantu) Traditional Religion," *African Ecclesial Review* 22:5 (1980), 295.

instruction. Music is essential to African spiritual reality. In the African context, spirit possession occurs when the music is at its highest pitch—when drumming, singing, and dancing are most intense and the participants become completely absorbed. The deities will not come unless they are implored. They will not come without song and rhythm.

Dancing is as important as singing. It permeates African ritual. Africans dance not only for social gatherings; they dance in worship; they dance before going to war, and to celebrate the victory of war. No one is too young or too old to dance. Not only the feet and the legs, but every part of the body dances—the arms, the hand, the shoulders, and the head. The dance, as does the song. conveys the community's stories. For dancing, like almost everything else in African culture, is communal. It is an expression of the collective narrative. No one is purely a spectator; everyone has a role to play.

For everyone—both men and women—are part of all African ritual life. The cosmology of African traditional religion is less male-dominated than the Western context. Women, as well as men, have historically played significant roles in African traditional religion. They served as priestesses, performing sacerdotal functions in worship, including admonishing, praying, and leading in the worship of deities. They were called on as healers, especially when those experiencing sickness were other women or children.[25] Women, often, maintained the sacred objects of worship. Outside of formal rituals, they were prophetesses and seers, given to visions that guided a community's decision making.

---

[25]For a full discussion of women's involvement in Traditional Religion see, John Mbiti, "The Role Of Women In African Traditional Religion" *Cahiers des Religions Africaines* 22 (1988), 69-82.

Gender has a different connotation within the African context. Both genders play a role; each is important for the maintenance of the community and its religious tradition. There are both male and female images of the one Supreme God.[26] And God has male and female names. God, unashamedly, has male and female qualities.

Slave Christianity

The Africans who came to the New World were as strange to their captors as their captors were to them. Many who later owned these men and women had never been in contact with an African and knew little of them as human beings. Though some had read descriptions of the people of the "dark continent," depictions of these exotic creatures were less than exemplary, casting them as savage, illiterate, and, largely, unteachable. Some depicted both men and women as voraciously sexual beings with inordinate libidos and lacking the requisite soul to be fully human receptacles for salvation.

Though Christian slaveholders treated their slaves more humanely than others, slavery was dehumanizing. Legally, they considered slaves as nonpersons, except when they committed crimes. An Alabama court asserted, for example, that slaves "are rational beings,… capable of committing crimes; and in reference to acts that are crimes… regarded as persons. (But) because they are slaves, they are incapable of performing civil acts, and, in reference to all such, they are things, not persons."[27]

---

[26]J. Akinyele Omoyajowo, "The Role of Women in Traditional African Religions and Independent Church Movements," *Dialogue & Alliance* 2:3 (1988),78.
[27]Helen T. Catterall, ed., *Judicial Cases Concerning Slavery and the Negro.* Washington, DC: Carnegie Institute, 1926, 247.

At least at first, the recent arrivals retained much of their African spiritual sensitivities within their bosoms. Though slaves, they still believed in a supreme being who was intimately concerned about them and reigned over a spirit world that, at God's bidding, was able to assist them. They made little distinction between what was sacred and profane, for all of life held both elements; religion was a practical help in all of life, and all of life was religious. Their sheer survival depended on preserving the community solidarity that was threatening to slave masters. Reverence for ancestors' symbolic communal presence was considered a component of that survival. Music—rhythm, singing, and dance—was an ever-present component of their lives. Their survival as a people demanded that the ablest among them—women, as well as men—be involved in ritual and community leadership.

The slaves and masters saw contradictions in each other's religions. Missionaries and slaveholders misunderstood many of the ritual practices that the slaves incorporated into everyday life and critiqued the slaves as severely superstitious and resorting to ignorant and uncivilized conjuring and nature worship. Masters ascribed reverence of the natural world to pagan witchcraft. They were threatened by practices perceived as giving slaves a sense of empowerment, potentially inciting them to aggressive, defiant behavior. These masters sought to eradicate these practices and erase them from the slaves' individual and collective memory to keep them docile and weaken communal bonds so vital to African spirituality. Individuals were separated from those of the same culture, language, or dialect. Families were broken apart, and not only were husbands separated from wives, but parents, children, and siblings were sold to different masters—sometimes on adjoining farms, but, often, miles, or even states away.

While loathing heathen tendencies they perceived in their religion, their doubts of the slaves' full humanity meant that masters, initially, made little attempt to convert their chattel. Moreover, some masters felt that, were slaves to be converted, they would, by conscience, be forced to treat them more humanely or free them. When masters began to acquiesce to slave conversion, the Christian religion served different purposes for them than for their slaves. For the master, it bolstered an economic system and way of life by providing a biblical warrant for slavery under the context of the God-ordained social order. Within that order, the slave remained at the bottom to assure that the structure would be sustained.[28]

According to Peter Paris, the Christianity offered to slaves had a fivefold utilitarian goal. White preachers used carefully selected passages to teach slaves that the lot they endured was part of that order, to admonish "biblical" obedience to masters, to convince slaves their desire for freedom was a satanic temptation, to convince them that patient diligence in work and punishment of laxity were within God's design, and to exhort them that forgiveness for wrongdoing was in the hands of God and the master.[29] Masters were more interested in religious indoctrination as a civilizing measure for the temporal sphere than in evangelism that offered salvation and made the slave a spiritual brother or sister with an equal stake in eternal reality. In almost every sermon, they attempted to entice slaves to patiently and humbly abide

---

[28] For an excellent discussion of these tactics, see, Elizabeth Fox-Genovese and Eugene D. Genovese, "The Divine Sanction of Social Order: Religious Foundations of the Southern Slaveholders' World View," *Journal of the American Academy of Religion* 55, no. 2 (1987), 211-33.

[29] See, for example, Peter J. Paris, "The Christian Way through the Black Experience," *Word & World* 6:2 (1986), 125-31; and Fox-Genovese and Eugene Genovese, 211-233.

their present, God-ordained lot to ensure their future betterment, but such tactics did little to assuage emotional and spiritual angst over the present misery of slave existence.

For slaves, the Christian faith was a source of comfort, providing affirmation of their dignity as children of the one supreme God, while reinforcing hope of either divine intervention in this life or a better existence and divine retribution in the life to come. They drew liberative elements from the biblical narrative and found comfort in the familiar African rituals that were played out in appropriations of that narrative that resonated with their status as captives in a strange land awaiting rescue by the great emancipator. Though early missionaries (who themselves were sometimes slaveholders) sought to placate audiences and make them malleable by holding out the promise of heaven for quietly and patiently enduring their humiliating lot on earth, objects of their evangelism were quick to discern inconsistencies in their conception of the Christian faith. They understood intrinsically what African American churchmen and scholars have often highlighted as the contradiction between the biblical Christianity that promotes equality of all humanity before God and the wanton disregard for black personhood encountered in their masters' definition of them as less than fully human.[30]

Some slaveholders, however, could see the humanity of their slaves and were genuinely concerned for their authentic spiritual needs. Yet early efforts by sincere Christians to convert slaves[31] met with only

---

[30] For example, the Three-Fifths Compromise struck during the 1787 Philadelphia Convention between Southern and Northern states stipulated that three-fifths of the slave population would be counted for purposes of distribution of taxes and the apportionment of the members of the House of Representatives.

[31] Such as those of the Society for the Propagation of the Gospel in Foreign Parts established by the Episcopal Church in 1701 to evangelize slaves and

limited success since they employed an evangelism strategy focused on instruction by catechesis and slaves' acceptance of formal religious propositions. They also fell short because they fail to critique the system of enslavement that was so abhorrent to their hearers.[32] By and large, the slaves rejected this Christianity as disingenuous and rejected the God of the slave masters, who condoned their inhumane treatment, as a false god. It did not make it more attractive that whites contended heaven would be as segregated as their earthly existence. While blacks would no longer be subjugated, they would not be housed in the same compartment as whites. There would be a Negro or "kitchen" heaven where slaves would be housed. Though it too would be glorious, it would be completely separate from where whites would be lodged.[33]

Slaves did not wholeheartedly embrace the Christian faith in this form. Neither did they flatly reject it. Though they saw hypocrisy in their masters' distorted belief system that offered them a "loving" God who subjugated them to slavery and denigrated their humanity, they could glean a kernel of truth to which they could hold. For them, the Jesus of the Bible was a different person than the harsh God the master declared required their subservience. This Jesus was as concerned about their welfare as that of the master. The God they embraced was an emancipator, like the God of their African faith, ready to deliver them from slavery's cruelties.

---

native Americans.

[32] See, for example, "250 Years of the SPG" *International Review of Mission* 40.3 (July 1951), 331-336. The society itself owned slaves in the West Indies.

[33] Lewis V. Baldwin, "A Home in Dat Rock: African American Folk Sources and Slave Visions of Heaven and Hell," *Journal of Religious Thought* 41, no. 1 (1984), 40.

As in Africa, religion was an ongoing part of the life of the slaves, and they practiced it openly. Slaves stole away during their free time in brush arbors and fields to practice their "invisible religion," where, far from the master's disdaining eye, they could give vent to a deeper spirituality. These practices ensured that despite attempts of slavers to suppress elements of traditional spirituality, many such as openness to the engagement of the supernatural, communal participation in ritual practices, reverence for ancestors, creative use of music and freedom for women to participate in ritual leadership, survived in the vivid memories of their psyches, and reappeared in whatever context they found themselves.

The significance of African survivals in black religion has been debated by anthropologists, sociologists, and historians. In the 1940s, renowned black sociologist, Franklin Frazier, contended that slavery destroyed any connection with an African past, stripping slaves of their social heritage so that African American culture developed independently of its influence.[34] Contrarily, white anthropologist, Melville J. Herskovits, countered that there was cultural continuity from Africa to the New World that influenced African American worship as well as the Southern white camp meeting religion.[35] According to ethicist, Leonard Lovett, famed historian, Carter G. Woodson, suggested that the affinity between African religion and the Christian tradition allowed slaves to re-label elements that had been practiced in Africa for centuries as Christian.36 For example, he

---

[34] See E. Franklin Frazier, *The Negro Family in the United States,* Chicago, University of Chicago Press, 1968.
[35] See, Melville J. Herskovits, *The Myth of the Negro Past;* New York: Harper & Brothers, 1941.
[36]

pointed out parallels between African belief systems and the Jewish background of Christianity exemplified in parallels between creation myths in both traditions.[37]

More recently, John Mbiti supported Herskovits' contention that there are "parallels from the life of the African peoples who were casts into the Diaspora in the New World... in spite of their loss of languages and... traditional setting," he contended, "African religion... remained in their blood."[38] Historian John Blassingame echoed this sentiment in contending that slaves hung on to their religion as a form of resistance. He insisted that many of the earliest black ministers in the missions of the Baptist churches, for example, were former river-cult priests from traditional religions of Africa.[39]

Once masters overcame their reluctance to accept slaves into the Christian faith, they determined to stamp out any vestiges of heathen religions that might intrude into true worship. Under the watchful eye of the master or overseer, slaves mimicked the white Christianity of their white owners and participated in emotionally restrained worship that made no room for elements retained within their bosoms. Attendance at the masters' worship services, however, was not their only religious experience.

Survivals were so intricately woven into the slaves' psyche that these elements found tacit or explicit expression in whatever religious tradition they were attracted to. Their influence was so ingrained into slave sensibilities that some black mainline leaders objected to their

---

[37]Carter G. Woodson, *The Negro in Our History*, Washington, DC: The Associated Publishers, 1941, 35.

[38] John Mbiti, "God, Sin and Salvation in African Religion" *Journal of the Interdenominational Theological Center*, 16:1-2, (1988-1999), 60.

[39] Ibid., and Melville Herskovits, "Social History of the Negro," *A Handbook of Social Psychology*. (Worcester: J. Clark Press, 1935, 256.

presence and took steps to eradicate them to infuse a measure of respectability into the black church. These leaders put as much distance as possible between themselves and anything that reminded them, and their white antagonists, of what was perceived as the slaves "uncivilized" past.

In the North, independent African Baptists and Methodists patterned worship after the white churches out of which they emerged. Richard Allen, founder of the African Methodist Episcopal Church, for example, denounced emotional displays in worship and ensured that emotive forms were excluded from the liturgy and worship of his nascent denomination.[40] Earlier, African Methodist Episcopal bishop, Daniel Payne, had condemned all forms of religious dance, including the ring shout. He reflected the attitude of many of his followers regarding what they consider the worship of "lower class" blacks, that "many... old churchgoers still cling to these heathenish habits... thinking that the more noise and motion they have, the better Christians they are."[41]

Despite these contradictions, slaves found much within the Christian faith with which they resonated. They were already open to belief in the supernatural, so evil spirits and the devil, as well as the angels and Christian God, made sense to them. Within slave culture, however, Christian faith existed side by side with other supernatural expressions such as conjuring and magic. Further, while some slaves came to denounce traditional African religious practices as evil, others

---

[40] Melva Wilson Costen, *African American Christian Worship*. Nashville: Abingdon Press, 1993), 95.
[41] Joe M. Richardson, "Christian Abolitionism: The American Missionary Association and the Florida Negro," *The Journal of Negro Education 40*:1 (Winter, 1971), 43.

embraced elements of both traditions—sometimes forming entirely new quasi-Christian traditions.

Conversion rituals paralleled communal rites of passage in African traditional society. Like these rituals, conversion was a communal affair—with both a private and a public element. Baptism paralleled African water rituals. The secretive and largely oral nature of slave religion means that little written detail of actual slave practices is extant. Fragments from slave narratives and oral histories of their descendants provide some indication of the content of that worship.

Music was a constant component of slave religion, and the extraordinary repertoire of Negro spiritual attests to its significance. The slaves sang to communicate messages of hope and endurance to each other. They sang encoded messages of defiance against an unjust system of servitude. They sang to reassure each other of ultimate emancipation from their dire situation. They sang to give and receive instruction. They sang to themselves (often silently) as they ran away. They sang for every occasion and about everything. Rhythm was an outstanding feature of slave music and the drum a central element in making that rhythm. David Daniels contends that "drums are the heartbeat of African music"—even within the new context of American religion.[42] The importance of this truth did not escape even the slave masters, who feared and outlawed drums in worship and social intercourse because of the perceived power their rhythm held over the slave. Where there was no drum, however, any item could be improvised to produce rhythm, the stump or bark of a tree, the ground,

---

[42] See, David Douglas Daniels, The Cultural Renewal of Slave Religion: Charles Price Jones and the Emergence of the Holiness Movement in Mississippi. PhD dissertation. Union Theological Seminary. New York, NY, 1992.

the floor of the praise house. And when there was no external rhythm, the slaves sang in rhythm. Their black bodies swayed, bowed, and moved in every direction as if controlled by an inner mechanism that needed no outside source to keep in perfectly in step with the tenor of the moment and the situation.

In a largely oral religious tradition, there was no Bible or holy books, no Book of Common Prayer with written creeds and liturgies, no polity, or hymnals to transmit the tradition or out of which to conduct worship.[43] Instead, salient elements were handed down through the generations in song, riddles, proverbs, and dance. For, as Joseph Washington asserts, "religion in African communities (was) written in the members' hearts, minds, histories, (and) rituals."[44] This orality held important implications for the development and spread of Pentecostalism, that for most of its history has been conceived of as a largely oral tradition. Even today, the global Pentecostal movement has seen its greatest growth within cultures that incorporate an oral communication mode.

Illiteracy or semi-literacy, however, did not reduce the importance of the "sacred book" within the community. Many black preachers learned long passages by heart. Those who could not read listened to those who could or others who had committed passages to memory. But the stories they encountered there were reinterpreted and contextualized within their struggle. The extent to which masters went to squelch teaching slaves to read has been often overstated. Yet, many slaves remained illiterate, semi-literature, or, at least, unable to read

---

[43] Iain, MacRoberts, *The Black Roots and White Racism of Early Pentecostalism.* New York: St. Martin's Press, 1988, 11.
[44] Joseph R. Washington, *Black Sects and Cults*, Garden City, NY, 1972, 25.

their master's language. The oral tradition of the African cult provided the slaves with a reliable means of communication. Some especially gifted slaves were able to commit entire biblical passages, sermons or hymns they had heard in white church services to memory. The most gifted among them could imbue these elements with remembrances from African culture or incidental anecdotes derived from their enslavement. What they crafted bore the unique character of slave sermons full of hope for ultimate emancipation that they could repeat with embellishment to a gathering of their peers.

Prayer was another constant of the slaves' religion, and slaves prayed about everything. They prayed for protection from the evil magic of the conjurer. They prayed for healing from the variety of physical, mental, and emotional diseases that afflicted them. They prayed for respite from the master's inhuman demands and the equally inhumane consequences of failing to meet even the harshest or most demeaning of these demands. In these prayers, they implored God to soften the master's heart. Mostly they prayed for emancipation and that God would avenge the injustice they suffered at the master's hands. Many of the slaves' prayers were communal, unlike the formal prayers of their masters. But there were also impromptu, individual prayers throughout the day—long and short conversations with God about everything. Their songs were prayers, their communications with each other were prayers, their thoughts were prayers, and their moans and shouts were prayers. For the supernatural God was never perceived to be far away. And sometimes the prayer was only the invocation of the name of his son—Jesus![45]

---

[45] For a deeper discussion, see James M. Washington, *Conversations with God: Two Centuries of Prayers by African Americans,* San Francisco: Harper Paperbacks, 1995.

African Spirituality within Pentecostalism

By the time the Azusa Street revival erupted in 1906, the blacks who made up a substantial portion of the congregation were like other descendants of slaves, heir to three hundred years of harsh subjugation and discrimination that might have destroyed a lesser stock of people. Through, like the rest of the African American community, they had endured extreme hardship, they retained belief in one supreme God who they were convinced was involved in every aspect of their lives. They also retained an appreciation for the pervasiveness of the spiritual realities that surrounded them. For them, religion was a mainstay. It was not just something practiced in church on Sunday, but the resource that sustained everyday lives.

Their communal solidarity was stronger than ever because their individual, as well as, collective, survival depended on it. They still gave great honor to their forebears and retained a place for women in ritual and community leadership. Music was an integral part of who they saw themselves as a people both in worship and in life.

Individual elements of African spirituality can be singularly found in all African American Christian expressions. Yet, in African American Pentecostalism these elements, collectively, tie the movement to its African roots, infusing it with a quality different in degree, if not nature, from traditions that had distanced themselves from such "heathenish" and uncouth origins. Further, contemporary scholars contend that not only black Pentecostals, but the entire Pentecostal movement was influenced by African spirituality through the Azusa Street Revival, since its leader, Seymour, and many who made up that congregation were products of this heritage.[46]

---

[46]Political scientist, James S. Tinney, theologians Steven J. Land and Allan Anderson, missiologist, Walter Hollenweger, and religionists Iain MacRoberts,

James Tinney agreed that the entire Pentecostal movement has roots derived from African sources, though he contended that it "thrives best among persons in the African Diaspora (or those who have come into contact with persons of African descent)."[47] For Tinney, the "truly African" nature of Pentecostalism is visible in its worship style, philosophy of faith, practices, and an organizational structure embodying three African themes: spirits, magic, and eschatology.[48] Tinney saw the persistence of song, dance, percussion, and tongue-speaking in Pentecostal worship as representative of this spirituality.[49] For him, Pentecostal theology, as primal as scholars might perceive it, was tied directly to African philosophy.[50]

Without linking Pentecostalism directly to Africa, Steven J. Land lists African American and Wesleyan religious ideologies as the two most important sources underlying the formation of early Pentecostalism.[51] He suggests the "spirituality of former slaves joined with the specifically Catholic spirituality of John Wesley to produce the movement's distinctive spiritual tenor."[52] Land contends that black spirituality was the immediate mediator of (the Azusa Street Revival) in the person of Seymour.[53] British theologian, Alan Anderson, concurs that "the African roots of Pentecostalism help explain its

---

and Roswith Gerloff see an African link to black Pentecostal spirituality, attempting to frame discussions which take this influence seriously.

[47]James S. Tinney, "The Blackness of Pentecostalism," *Spirit* 3: 2 (1979), 27.
[48]Ibid., 28.
[49]Ibid., 31.
[50]Ibid.
[51]Ibid., 47.
[52]Stephen J. Land, *Pentecostal Spirituality: A Passion for the Kingdom*. Sheffield, U.K.: Sheffield Academic Press, 1993, 35.
[53]Ibid., 52.

significance in the Third World today."⁵⁴ Sociologist, Walter Hollenweger lists orality as a main feature of Pentecostalism and insists that the movement owes its initial growth to oral modes of transmission such as those found in African Traditional Religion. For him, this movement's oral tradition and the narrative theological witness are embodied in the testimony for which decades were a central element of Pentecostal worship.⁵⁵ Iain MacRoberts asserts that the common Pentecostal practices of rhythmic hand clapping, the antiphonal participation of the congregation in the sermon, the immediacy of God in the services, and baptism by immersion are all "survivals of Africanisms."⁵⁶

Mainline black church leaders' denunciation of African survivals as vulgar and heathenish did not deter working and lower-class people who filled Holiness and Pentecostal pews. They not only held on to these remnants, but imbued them with Christian understandings, while incorporating them into their lives and worship. They were unashamedly emotive and exuberant in their use of music and rhythm. They were open to supernatural encounters with God through the Spirit. And, they understood all they did as somehow having sacred significance. Further, their unorthodox inclusion of all classes at every level of the community, and their inclusion of women at each level was scandalous, though very African.

The idea of sanctification in which every part of a person's being was set aside for God's use, not only in sacred ritual, but in the

---

⁵⁴See Allan Anderson, *The Origins, Growth and Significance of the Pentecostal Movements in the Third World*, Paper presented to the Post-Graduate Seminar, University of Leeds, November 1997.

⁵⁵Walter Hollenweger, *Pentecostalism: Origins and Developments Worldwide*, Peabody, MA: Hendrickson Publishers, 1997, 25.

⁵⁶MacRoberts, *Black Roots and White Racism*, 29.

mundane living of everyday life, resonated with the African blurring of lines between the sacred and profane, as well as the practical use of religion in all of life, and made both the Holiness and Pentecostal movements attractive to blacks. Even more importantly, the God that Pentecostalism offered to blacks was the God of power who was intimately interested in their personal as much as their spiritual well-being. Religion, then, was much more than a Sunday-go-to-meeting experience. It permeated all of their commonplace reality, imbuing it with since of sacred attachment.

Africanisms at Azusa Street

According to Douglas Nelson, whose seminal dissertation reintroduced Seymour as a prominent early Pentecostal leader, the Azusa Street pastor was among those who separated himself from the slave spirituality he experienced as a child in Louisiana.[57] Since the revival began only forty years after Emancipation, many blacks in attendance were either former slaves or children or grandchildren of slaves. Those who had not, personally, experienced slavery inherited at least a reminiscence of the "invisible religion" from their forebears. Lucy Farrow, for example, had either been born as a slave or was sold into slavery. Though we do not know the time or place or her birth, we can conjecture from her seeming age during her involvement at the revival that mother Prince had been born during slavery. Julia Hutchins, J. A. Warren, and other leaders in the revival were from the same era.

---

[57]J. Douglas Nelson, *Such a Time as This: The Story of Bishop William J. Seymour and the Azusa Street Revival, a Search for Pentecostal/Charismatic Roots.* (Ph. D. Dissertation, University of Birmingham, U.K., 1981, 157-158.

Their openness to the Spirit of God and an inclusive ecclesiology created scenes such as those Parham encountered at the Revival, and that, without the obvious interracial element, would characterize much of African American Pentecostal worship for decades. Surely, Parham's characterization of the meetings' "crude negroisms" and unsightly "animalisms" was colored by racial bias, but he was not the only critic who found the cultural undertones of the saints' behavior reprehensible. Newspaper articles quickly pointed out similarities between worship at Azusa Street and "pagan" rites.[58] Critics within the broader church also objected to aspects of the worship that they compared to "heathen" ritual.[59]

In essence, the most visible element of African religion within the revival was this spiritual openness. People of every race, culture, and age yielded themselves to the intense engagement with the Spirit of God that displayed itself in manifestations many other Los Angeles congregations would have considered strange. When the Spirit came, they danced the holy dance reminiscent of the ring shout, ran, jumped, fell, rolled, and exhibited other physical gyrations. Men, women, and children had trances and visions, and spoke prophetic orations as well as in "strange tongues."

As in African spirituality, music was a constant in the revival. The saints sang the hymns of their Holiness forebears that told of expectation of the coming Spirit and testified to their newfound piety and fervor. They also sang the Negro spirituals that had been fused

---

[58] For example, just as the revival got underway, a *Los Angeles Times* article of April 18, 1906, touted the headline, "Weird Babel Tongues."

[59] Besides Parham, this complaint was lodged by such notables as Greek scholar, W.B. Godbey; Alma White, founder of the Pillar of Fire; biblical scholar, Harry Ironsides; and R.A. Torrey of Moody Bible Institute.

from the meeting of African spirituality and Christian hope amid continued discrimination.[60] No longer under the master's whip or the threat of imminent harm or total deprivation of their rights and dignity, however, they imbued the spirituals with new meanings, out their experience of hope within this different, but continued oppression. And they sang new songs given to them by the Spirit that spoke of their new experience with God. Many of these songs would go into mainline collections, but several made their way into Pentecostal hymnody that has enriched the movement for generations.

They sang in English and they sang in known and unknown tongues. And when words were not enough to give vent to their spiritual longing or exhilaration, they hummed, moaned, or yell out wordless melodies. Such singing was always communal—African style. There was no robed, trained choir; there were no hymnals. The leader of the moment lined out the song and the congregation joined in an antiphonal symphony. And that singing was not accompanied by sophisticated, manufactured instruments, but whatever implement was on hand—tambourines, maracas, or washboards.

Healing rituals took a variety of forms: anointing with oil, laying on of hands and praying over material objects such as prayer clothes as points of contact to release faith for those in distress paralleled the use of artifacts in African traditions. Christian faith healers took the place of medicine men and women, using their supernatural power for the communal good. In either tradition, neither sickness nor death was understood, simply, as a natural matter. They were given spiritual connotations. Demonic roots were often ascribed to physical, mental,

---

[60]Spirituals such "Swing Low Sweet Chariot" and "Ev'ry Time I Feel the Spirit," for example, became of regular part of the African American Pentecostal repertoire.

or emotional illnesses. Prayer was offered as much for deliverance from the internal forces of evil plaguing them as for recovery from the outward symptoms of the distress.

The unusually heavy involvement of women in the revival led some observers to characterize early Pentecostalism as essentially "women's religion."[61] While such a characterization is exaggerated, the prominence of women at Azusa Street was tied to both biblical sanction and African cosmology. The biblical warrant drew on the Joel passage that speaks prophetically of an outpouring of the Holy Spirit on all flesh—both men and women—to usher an end-time harvest of lost souls into the kingdom. Those at the revival saw it being part of the last days' prophecy such that women, as well as men, were able to speak on God's behalf. Yet, it was not merely women's involvement, but their participation in every aspect of the congregation's worship and life that harkened back to women's involvement in African ritual. Because of this, some of the earliest and harshest criticism of the revival and the movement was lodged at the openness women enjoyed in keeping with African spirituality and communal life.

Yet, Parham's and others' criticism of the revival noted elements that a non-African observer might have viewed as out of place with Christian decorum between genders. The way men and women openly embraced each other or "inappropriately" approached each other to lay hands and pray for healing and deliverance. Women led worship, preached, and exhorted the entire community. They gave prophetic

---

[61] Ethnographer Elaine Lawless is one scholar who uses the characterization in her introduction to *God's Peculiar People: Women's Voices and Folk Tradition in a Pentecostal Church.* Lexington, KY: University of Kentucky Press, 1988, 6.

utterances, spoke in tongues, and interpreted, and prayed with and for others.

Such openness to women's involvement was entirely consistent with African communal understandings that valued their contribution to the community. Ithiel Clemmons contended that this characteristic communal aspect of African American spirituality made the Azusa Street revival different from earlier Evangelical revivals. He asserted that this communal sense (rather than speaking in tongues) even today, is what makes Pentecostalism—especially African American Pentecostalism—so significant.[62]

Africanisms in Developing Denominational Structures

The influence of African spirituality did not wane with the drawing to a close of the Azusa Street Revival. Instead, later black Pentecostal leaders picked up on the themes of this spirituality and incorporated them into the fabric of the numerous denominations that developed throughout the movement's one-hundred-year history. Some leaders were both deliberate and vocal in their support of African spirituality, others less so, but no less resolute in incorporating these elements into their context.

The earliest vestiges of African spirituality were visible in the denominations that developed with the antecedent Holiness Movement. Though he and his colleague later would disagree on the necessity of glossolalia as evidence of Spirit baptism, Charles Price Jones was as adamant as Charles Harrison Mason about incorporating Africa in the heritage of black Christians. In his 1902, poetic volume,

---

[62]Ithiel Clemmons, "New Life through New Community: The Prophetic Theological Praxis of Bishop William J. Seymour of the Azusa Street Revival," address delivered at Regent University School of Divinity, April 18, 1996.

Appeal to the Sons of Africa, he recalled the linkage of blacks in the United States to the motherland and called for his community to live out that heritage in the ethical and social structures of their lives.[63] Another Holiness leader, William Christian, made explicit claims about the value of African spirituality in the catechism of his denomination, the Church of the Living God (Christian Workers for Fellowship). In these, he went as far as asserting that "the saints of the Bible," including Jesus and David, "belonged to the black race."[64]

Mason, the founder of the Church of God in Christ (COGIC), was adamant that black Christians should acknowledge their African heritage and took pains to provide biblical sanction for its rudiments within COGIC culture. His passionate efforts imbued the denomination's worship with a character that found as much foundation within African and slave religion as Scripture—a distinction Mason found unwarranted.

In 1915, William T. Phillips left the Methodist Episcopal Church to find the Ethiopian Overcoming Holy Church of God, expressing within the organization's name, his pro-African sentiments. Though he was to later change the designation from "Ethiopian" to "Apostolic" to reflect a more inclusive ecclesiology, Phillips's denomination earlier constituted itself as a religion to meet black folk's spiritual needs within the segregated American South. After World War I, Elias Dempsey

---

[63]Charles Price Jones, *Appeal to the Sons of Africa: A number of Poems, Readings, Orations and Lectures, Designed Especially to Inspire Youth of African Blood with Sentiments of Hope and Nobility as well as to Entertain and Instruct All Classes of Readers and Lovers of Humanity.* Jackson, MS: Truth, 1902.

[64]"A Catechism: The Church of the Living God," <www.mc.maricopa.edu/~kefir/club/african_ american/index.html>. See also Walter Hollenweger "Black Pentecostal Concept," *Concept* 30. Geneva, Switzerland: World Council of Churches, 1970, 16-19.

Smith, founder of Triumph the Church and Kingdom of God, became enamored with Ethiopianism and Marcus Garvey's Back to Africa movement incorporating elements of the former into his ecclesiology. In 1920, he made a pilgrimage to that nation, where he was given a traditional royal reception, including a lavish banquet.

Scandrett-Leatherman makes the contention that black Pentecostalism provides "space" for continuities of African spirituality where "the feeling of being touched by the Holy Ghost, finds its fullest joy and bodily expression."[65] He, James Tinney,[66] and David Daniels[67] see the creative use of rhythm and drums as a key experience of Pentecostal worship. As in African spirituality, in the religion of the slaves and at Azusa Street, worship music remained a constant in Pentecostal worship. It accompanies the individual and congregational singing, it is played during prayer, as the offering is collected, and punctuates and emphasizes strategic points in the sermon and is an integral part of the altar ministry.[68] Kinetic spirituality—the body and movement—stands as a central symbol in these contexts.[69] Not to

---

[65] Craig Scandrett-Leatherman, "African Roots and Multi-Cultural Mission of Afro-Pentecostalism: Bishop Mason's Desk of Roots" in Raynard D. Smith, ed., *With Signs Following: The Life and Ministry of Charles Harrison Mason*, 2015, 29-42.

[66] James S. Tinney, "The Blackness of Pentecostalism" *Spirit* 2:2 (1979).

[67] See, David D. Daniels, "'Gotta Moan Sometime': A Sonic Exploration of Earwitnesses to Early Pentecostal Sound in North America" *Pneuma* 30:1 (Jan 1, 2008), 5–32.

[68] In the Pentecostal tradition, altar ministry is not a celebration of the sacraments, but rather is prayer conducted with individuals or the gathered congregation in front of the altar railing. In the Pentecostal understanding, the altar is a place of prayer rather than sacrifice.

[69] John Wilson and Harvey K. Clow. "Themes of Power and Control in a Pentecostal Assembly," *Journal for the Scientific Study of Religion* 20: (1981), 242.

move—to raise one's hands, to clap or to sway—in some visible way indicates that a person is not part of what the community is experiencing and signals a lack of spirituality. It gives evidence that he or she is an outsider and might be a candidate for conversion.

Another persistent element of African spirituality in Pentecostalism is dance. Dancing is conceived of as both a release of spiritual energy and an invitation for the Spirit to take control of the worshiper. For where rhythm is present, there is this common element. In one tract, Mason questioned rhetorically, "Is it right for the saints of God to dance?" He answered with a resounding, "Yes," and insisted that while shouting, or the holy dance, descended from the slaves' "ring shout," at the same time, it is an authentically biblical form of worship.[70]

Zora Neal Hurston, noted African American anthropologist, saw the significance of the influence African spirituality in combined elements of openness to the Spirit and the creativity that shouting (dancing) represents, commenting that,

> (t)here can be no doubt shouting is a survival of African 'possession' by the gods... (and is) a sign of special favor from the spirit that chooses to drive out the individual consciousness temporarily and use the body for its expression.[71]

---

[70] C.H. Mason, "Is it Right for the Saints of God to dance?" in In James Oglethorpe Patterson, R. Ross German and Julia Mason, eds., *History and Formative Years of the Church of God in Christ with Excerpts from the Life and Work-Bishop C. H. Mason.* Memphis, TN: Church of God in Christ Publishing House, 1969, 36.

[71] Zora Neale Hurston, *The Sanctified Church* Berkeley, CA: Turtle Island, 1981, 91.

Hurston further saw the communal importance of shouting within Pentecostal worship services, contending that it was,

> ... a community thing. It thrives in concert. It is the first shout that is difficult for the preacher to arouse. After that one, they are likely to seep over the church. This is easily understood, for rhythm is increasing with each shouter who communicates the fervor to someone else.[72]

Healing ritual remains a constant element of Pentecostal piety. Anointing with oil, the laying on of hands, and the use of prayer cloths and other objects are likely to happen in public worship as in private settings. The communal element of healing involves subjects being ringed by other believers or hand layered on the individuals as corporate prayers are uttered in each prayer's own words.

One of the most pronounced healing retentions within COGIC's worship remained the ceremonial healing ritual Mason promoted among the saints. Scandrett-Leatherman points out that in both African spirituality and COGIC culture, health is both physical and social; restoration is enacted in the corporate ritual that invests symbolic-medicine with the strong power to heal. While he concentrates on the vital role plants and gourd roots played for Mason, he contends that the COGIC founder continued many ritual healing practices begun at Azusa Street, such as laying on of hands, prayer cloths, and anointing with oil. Scandrett-Leatherman also contends that, for Mason, who unashamedly displayed his collection of healing

---

[72]Ibid.

roots he described as "mystical wonders of God,"[73] these had as much relevance in African traditional religion as in Scripture. Though criticized by some for bringing "magic" into the church by using these tactics, Mason consistently insisted that COGIC spirituality kept its allegiance to African and slave religion intact and prominent.

Though the early involvement of women in all levels of Pentecostal ministry and the distinctive COGIC structure for ministry roles for men and women may be seen as inconsistent with each other, both are structured elements within African spiritual systems. Following the Azusa Street model, many early Pentecostal bodies gave women almost complete freedom to carry out a variety of ministries in the local congregations, in evangelistic work throughout their surrounding communities and on the mission field. COGIC's stratified structure of gender-related functions with a dual yet parallel political system that gave women a measure of power within ritual settings and church governance. Within both COGIC and the broader Pentecostal movement, older women enjoy a measure of reverence, afforded by the title church "Mother," and are vested with political status and (private) veto power as well as significant economic control.[74]

The Persistence of Africanisms in Pentecostal Worship

The Azusa Street Revival and COGIC are perhaps the most visible examples of African retentions within Pentecostal worship; however,

---

[73] Scandrett-Leatherman, "The African Roots and Multi-cultural Mission of Afro Pentecostalism: Bishop Charles Harrison Mason, Slave Religion in His Heart and Roots on His Desk," paper presented to the 35th Annual Meeting of the Society for Pentecostal Studies. Pasadena, CA: Fuller Theological Seminary, March 25, 2006.

[74] Ibid.

the influence of African spirituality continues throughout more than the movement's more than one-hundred-year history. The orality and communal essence of African spirituality resonate in the call and response communication of preaching and gospel singing. Tinney points to parallels between black Pentecostal or other expressive preaching and the African tradition of the griot. Characteristics of the black sermon, such as the antiphonal structure in which the preacher and audience form a joint choir with the preacher becoming the lead singer and the congregation the chorus, are more pronounced within Pentecostal worship. The longer and louder the preaching goes on, the more the audience talks back, and the rhythm of the preaching forms a cadence of its own.

African American Pentecostalism remains a communal affair. Testimony and tarrying services, congregational singing, the antiphonal call and response of preaching are all a part of that communal tapestry. Pentecostal testimony parallels the African practice of storytelling by the griot. No one testifies or sings alone. Though one person has the floor, the entire congregation is involved. Testimonies are not just my testimony, but *our* testimony. They don't just tell of what God has done for me, but of what God has done for *us*—in *our* family, *our* church, *our* community, and *our* history. They are the testimony of how God has, through the centuries, brought deliverance, as he did the children of Israel in Egypt and as he did in bringing a remnant through the Middle Passage, as he delivered us from slavery as well as the Jim Crow experience in America.

The biblical narrative is interwoven into the telling as if it were the story of the speaker. For, to claim that experience is to make it the experience of the entire congregation. That testimony or song is supported by "Amens" and "Hallelujahs," affirming that the story of deliverance is not singular, but corporate. It affirms both the universal experience of oppression as well as the universal hope for liberation.

Communal feasts are a regular part of the church year, not only reserved for special occasions or times. In keeping with the African sensitivities, there is a practical and spiritual element to shared meals. While inexpensive dinners served after Sunday worship service often provide necessary income for the congregation and respite for those who have toiled all week and still "pressed their way" to church on Sunday, they are a time for the saints to gather and fellowship. It is an opportunity to talk about "another day's journey" and to talk about struggles and victories.

A sense of community, ceremony, and celebration infuses even the most common act; and in each of these, color, as much as music, plays a significant role. This too has both sacred and practical implications, and has both ritual and social import, serving as a reminder of heritage and signaling who is truly part of the community.

The color, white, the symbol of holiness and purity, is employed on numerous occasions—communion, baptisms, women's day, and funerals. Other colors, such as purple denoting royalty or red denoting the blood of Christ, have their specific significance. These are not worn as the traditional vestments of black mainline churches, however, adopted from their white counterparts. Men, as well as women, adorn themselves for these occasions, sporting color to show their communal solidarity.

Even the shout takes on a communal aspect as brothers and sisters dance alongside the enrapture saint shouting in the Spirit, upholding him or her physically while affirming the spiritual reality of the experience. Sociologist, Harvey Cox takes note of the Africanicity of Pentecostal worship insisting that;

(t)here is an irony is all of this. The very features that Parham... anathematized at Azusa Street—the trance, the ecstasy of the "colored camp meeting," the interracial fellowship—were precisely what enabled Pentecostalism to speak with such power in the 20th century.[75]

The sense of the sacredness of all of life and everything in life allows Pentecostals to embrace, utilize, and enjoy rhythm in every arena, and incorporate that rhythm as part of the worship of the God through use of a variety of instruments that others may deem inappropriate. The assertion by Zora Neal Hurston that, "all black music is dance music" finds a parallel in the understanding that every instrument can be employed in worshipping God—the drum, the horn, the washboard, the tambourine.[76] Furthermore, all of one's body, including dancing feet, was a sacred vessel of praise.

With the dance, the tarrying ritual transports the ring shouts' communal structure and "dynamic pneumatology" into Pentecostal worship. Both correlate emotions with posture and employ a more primal mode of prayer.[77] These are not usually fully enacted within a congregation's most public venues. Instead, both the ring shout and tarrying have their fullest expression in more intimate settings. There they are hidden away from the eyes of the purely curious and reserved

---

[75]Harvey Cox, *Fire from Heaven: The Rise of Pentecostal Spirituality and the Reshaping of Religion in the Twenty-First Century* Reading. Boston, MA: Addison-Wesley, 1995, 100.

[76]Hurston, *Sanctified Church*, 103.

[77]David Daniels provides a discussion of the import of the tarrying ritual within COGIC in "Live So God Can Use Me" *Asian Journal of Pentecostal Studies* 3:2 (2000), 200-301.

for the initiated, true believers. Tinney vividly describes the tarrying process:

> The seeker prays, loud and long as hard and as fast as he can to get this power. He sweats and cries and screams and physically throws himself, demanding that God do what [he or she] wants. He [or she] commands the power of God as [his or her] own. It is a violent scene… carefully hidden from the casual visitor.[78]

In tarrying, the seeker approaches God through the repetition of particular words—"Jesus, Jesus, Jesus, Jesus," or phrases—"Thank you, Jesus; Thank you, Jesus; Thank you, Jesus; Thank you, Jesus" or "Hallelujah, Hallelujah, Hallelujah," in rapid succession, often to the point of exhaustion. This unifying experience was familiar to most black Pentecostals before the advent of the less formal structures of the Charismatic movement.[79]

Tarrying—actively seeking the experience of Pentecostal Holy Spirit baptism—is one of the most communal acts of the black expression of the tradition. Its goal is to elicit an exuberant demonstration of speaking in tongues, "as the Spirit gives utterance,"[80] as solid evidence that the seeker has, indeed, received the Pentecostal Holy Spirit Baptism. This experience is the rite of passage that signifies that she or he is a full member of the community.

---

[78] James S. Tinney, *A Theoretical and Historical Comparison of Black Political and Religious Movements.* Ph.D. Dissertation, Howard University, 1978, 239-40.

[79] Daniels, "Live so God Can Use Me," Asian Journal of Pentecostal Theology, 3:2 (2000), 299-301.

[80] Acts 2:4b.

Though adherents do not name it as such, Scandrett-Leatherman sees such a "foreign" element as ancestor veneration within Pentecostal worship as essential for connecting the traditions.[81] Founders of local congregations or entire denominations are honored; their claims of special revelation in dreams and visions hold a sacred place among present and future generations. Elaborate portraits or statuary of the long-deceased grace vestibules of the most modest sanctuaries like the portraits of saints in a Catholic chapel or artifacts of ancestors in African rituals.

Throughout the year, narrative exploits of these leaders are depicted in hagiographies. Their songs, no matter how esoteric, are given special reverence in congregational singing. Annual Founder's Day festivities celebrate their contributions. Parishioners listen intently to the retelling of how the Lord spoke to Bishop So-and-So, to tell him or her where, when, and how to start the church and give him or her promises of success. The sacrifices of these leaders, the persecution they endured, and the victories they won remind the congregation of their collective past and destiny. Recalling their exploits reengages these men and women in the ongoing life of the community as speakers recount, "I remember when I heard Bishop preach, and surrendered my heart to God," or "If Bishop were here, he would admonish us to…"

Practical elements of veneration emerge in the honorary designation "temple" that enshrines the memory of founders of so

---

[81] Scandrett-Leatherman, "The African Roots and Multi-Culturalism of Afro Pentecostalism: Charles H. Mason – Religion is his Heart and Roots on his Desk. Paper presented to the Society for Pentecostal Studies, 31st Annual Meeting, 2002.

many Pentecostal edifices and congregations.[82] Along with the names, the places that founders graced become important. A brochure from the 2007 COGIC convocation, for example, declares that,

> with exuberant praise and spirit-filled worship, the sounds of Pentecost will fill the air as saints stand on the sacred ground of their forefathers in witness to the faithfulness of God.[83]

Veneration is also shown to living elders through episcopal systems that allow pastors and bishops to remain in place long after they have passed the usual age of retirement and when they are, sometimes, unable to function at full intellectual or spiritual capacity. Congregants present monetary and other valuable gifts in tribute, and vie for the honor of making the largest contribution. In even more simple ways, elders speak first and are afforded higher authority and honor than younger community members. The special designation of older women as "mothers" and older men as "deacon" reflects the same African sensitivities. Such respect finds additional biblical warrant in instructions to "give honor to whom honor is due"[84] as well as wisdom literature that suggests that reverence is due to God's prophets and those elders who exhibit great wisdom.[85]

---

[82] While "Mason Temple" honors the name of the COGIC founder, several other congregations in major cities including Norfolk, Virginia, Kansas City, Kansas; Milwaukee, Tulsa Oklahoma and small towns such as Conway, South Carolina, Bartow, Georgia and Altheimer, Arkansas carry the same name.

[83] 2007 COGIC convocation, Memphis, TN: Church of God Publishing House, 2007.

[84] Romans 13:7.

[85] See for example, Leviticus 19:13 and Proverbs 23:22.

Distinctions from African Traditional Religion

Parallels and continuity between African Traditional Religion and black Pentecostalism should not obscure what Pentecostals claim as the biblical authenticity of what unfolds in their worship. Assuredly, black believers were attracted to certain practices because they resonated with familiar elements of traditional religion, but understood these as being part of the early Christian tradition and saw them as supported within Scripture.

The experience of spirit possession is an excellent example of such a distinction. The phenomenon runs through both traditions; the ideas of possession by the gods, the possession of spiritual power, and spirit baptism are older than Christianity itself and is a central theme in religious experience throughout the Diaspora.[86] The Pentecostal understanding of Holy Spirit baptism differs, however, from the understanding of spirit possession in African Traditional Religion. In traditional spirit possession, participants seek to return the disrupted community to a state of harmony. The goal is restoration to the past order of things.[87] This possession, then, denotes being controlled by another created being—an ancestor secondary spirit or lesser god. This is not possession by the high God, who is radically other, and ultimately transcendent and removed from mundane matters of life and inaccessible.[88]

---

[86] Archie Smith Jr., "Reaching Back and Pushing Forward: A Perspective on African American Spirituality." *Theology Today* 56:1 (1999), 44-58. In "African-American Worship in The Pentecostal And Holiness Movements" *Wesleyan Theological Journal*, 2:2(1997) 105-120, Cheryl Sanders points out that, "spirit possession is an important feature of virtually all the diasporic religions of New World Africans.

[87] Hurston, The Sanctified Church, 63.

[88] Ibid., 61-63.

Pentecostals contend, alternatively, that God's Spirit powerfully indwells personal and communal life. The intervention of the sacred is sought and expected—rather than cajoled—to create a new individual and community. The Spirit is made manifest, and its glory reveals something essentially other. What separates the African American Holiness and Pentecostal tradition from the purely African spirituality, however, is the belief that the possessing spirit bears the exclusive identity of the Holy Spirit—the third member of the Godhead. Possession by the Spirit is openness to God as the believer comes to share in the ultimate reality who is still essentially other, in a personal and intimate way.

Pentecostals insist on a qualitative difference between their experience of being "possessed by the Holy Spirit" and the traditional experience of being "spirit possessed." For them, a man or woman is possessed by the Holy Spirit with the ultimate goal of rebirth, regeneration, and renewal.[89] Yet, the sacred does not mount those affected, and distance is maintained between the subject and the object. In African Traditional Religion, to be possessed by the Spirit implies merger, infusion, oneness, if only temporarily of the sacred and the profane. In the Pentecostal experience of Holy Spirit baptism, the Spirit is always still the Spirit of God. The liminal state that results from such possession brings a sense of empowerment, but never results in a merging of the self with ultimate reality.[90]

---

[89] For a discussion of understandings of possession by the Spirit in African Pentecostalism, see Annette Beverly Collins, *African American Pentecostalism as an Ecstatic Movement.* D.Min. Thesis, University of Chicago, 1996.

[90] See for example, Bobby Alexander, "Correcting Misinterpretations of Turner's Theory, An African-American Pentecostal Illustration" *Journal for the Scientific Study of Religion 30:1 (March, 1991),* 26-44.

Early Pentecostals saw the Holy Spirit not just taking possession of individuals but of the entire community. No greater assessment could be made of a worship service than that the Holy Ghost "took control." Testimony after testimony of this phenomenon poured into the revival periodical, *The Apostolic Faith,* such as one telling of how "one afternoon the Holy Spirit took possession of the meeting and set aside the program, giving freedom to all who had received their personal Pentecost to witness and speak or pray in tongues."[91] Yet black Pentecostals understood intrinsically, as James Cone insists, that the "divine Spirit" who descends upon them "is not some metaphysical entity but rather the power of Jesus who breaks into the lives of the people giving them a new song to sing in confirmation of God's presence with them in their historical struggle."[92]

Most importantly, for Pentecostal believers, with possession comes power. They see Holy Spirit baptism as "a gift of power on the sanctified life," and empowerment for service. Either the Holy Ghost "came in mighty power" to a congregation, the power came upon a person, or they came under the power. In any case, those involved would testify that they were left powerless and unable to function under their own strength. This was the power to preach more effectively, thwart the plans of the devil, evangelize, and triumph over sinful habits.[93] The saints never equivocated about the source of that power. They were clear; this was no nebulous encounter with some ephemeral essence. "We only have power with God through Jesus. He

---

[91]"From Other Pentecostal Papers" *Apostolic Faith* 1:8, (May 1907), 3.

[92]James H. Cone, Sanctification, Liberation and Black Worship" *Theology Today* 35:2 (July 1978), 139-14.

[93]"Questions Answered" *Apostolic Faith* 1:11, (Oct 1907 – Jan 1908), 2.

puts the Spirit in us that He might recognize Himself... All we get from God—we get through Jesus."[94]

The Pentecostal attempt to tap into and harness spiritual power for the good of the individual and the community finds direct parallels in African traditional religion. The African worldview that lay at its roots provided openness to the supernatural. It also provided a strong critique of a heavily rational post-Enlightenment Christianity of the white church. Given that worldview, black Pentecostals found it problematic that the white church saw no contradiction in the biblical imperative to love one's neighbor as oneself and holding of an entire class of people first in chattel slavery, then in Jim Crow conditions that stripped their dignity and nullified their right to live as authentic, free human beings.

The experience of trance, closely tied to the experience of being possessed by the Spirit as a mechanism for communicating with and receiving from God, is another parallel with African Traditional Religion. One testimony in *The Apostolic Faith* declared,

> I wanted to pray, but the Lord tied my mouth. The power began to come in waves. The Lord took full possession. I fell over like a dead man. I was dead to the world. I tried to pray while lying on the floor, but when my tongue was loosened, it was in a different language... Jesus had come to me.[95]

Conclusion

The earliest Pentecostals stood only a generation and a half away from slavery with the psychic remembrance of slave religion lodged in

---

[94]"Prayer" *The Apostolic Faith* 1:12, (Jan 1908), 4.
[95]Untitled item, *The Apostolic Faith* 1:5, (Jan 1907), 1.

their souls. Despite Parham's protestations of animalisms, the tendency of both some white Pentecostals and mainline black religionists to dismiss suggestions of ties to African spirituality, and deliberate efforts of upper-class blacks to conform to black worship styles to that of "more dignified" white congregations they left, the spirituality of the African sacred cosmos has persisted over one hundred years of the movement's history. It can be found most openly in the lower-class, storefront congregations of inner cities and metropolitan suburbs, but it also exists within large congregations throughout the country. The very elements black church leaders had attempted to repress—the shout, possession by the Holy Spirit, emotive worship—rang true to the blacks who found their way to early Pentecostal meetings and attracted them to a way of being that allowed them to hold on to their ancestors' "old-time religion."

Hurston astutely saw the rise of the sanctified churches in America, not as the beginning of a new religious movement but as older forms of black religions reasserting themselves against the new modern realities.[96] She, ultimately, saw no direct link between African American Pentecostalism and African Traditional Religion. Yet, survivals from the slave's religious experience and their descendants through the centuries, that were played down by respectable black religionists rebounded as vital elements in black Holiness and Pentecostal worship. Conversion to Christianity did not force believers to shed their traditional religiosity and go naked into their new religion. Rather, it allowed them to incorporate that African worldview, culture, and spiritual identity into a new religious context. For them, as for their

---

[96]Hurston, *The Sanctified Church*, 103.

ancestors, the biblical world was not just a two-thousand-year-old historical reality, but a world of yesterday, today, and tomorrow.[97]

The same African spirituality that made a place for itself in slave worship and community, survived efforts by masters and "elite" black religionists to remove its vestiges from the slave psyche, was retained in news forms black Christians created—including Pentecostalism. The North American context did not provide a place for the fuller adoption of African spirituality found in the more welcoming Caribbean and South American context that bred quasi-Christian and new religious forms. It was precisely their African spirituality, however, that was open to such a phenomenon as tongues-speaking and Spirit possession, as well as more pragmatic areas as communal worship and more egalitarian structures that are the hallmark of African American Pentecostalism.

Finally, after all is said, Roswith Gerloff contends that these "non-white or African derived movements are closer to the New Testament and the pattern of thought within the Bible than are many European interpretations of doing theology after Christopher Columbus."[98] To support her contention, Gerloff emphatically asserts,

> I saw men and women who had… been whipped and beaten by the rigors of ghetto existence… politically, socially, and economically…, on the verge of pathology, and about to fall from the precipice of sanity and wholeness [who] would attend the spirited services licking

---

[97] John Mbiti, "God, Sin, and Salvation in African Religion" *Journal of the Interdenominational Theological Center* 16:1-2 (1988-1989), 60.
[98] Roswith Gerloff, "The Holy Spirit and the African Diaspora: Spiritual, Cultural and Social Roots of Black Pentecostal Churches, *EPTA Bulletin: Journal of the European Pentecostal Theological Association* 14 (1995), 85.

their oppressor- inflicted wounds and there encountering God's living presence. [They] would leave the services with the undeniable assurance that there had been given to them a reservoir of spiritual power with which they could face joyfully, the social ills of a hostile world.[99]

---

[99]Ibid.

Faith of Our Fathers: Recovering Black Theology in Early African-American Holiness-Pentecostal Thought

The insistence by liberation theologian, James Cone, that God is black[1] as well as the affirmation by womanist theologian, Jacqueline Grant, that the Jesus of black women (and by inference of the black community) is diametrically different than white women's Christ[2] are not, entirely, new concepts. In the 1960s and 1970s, black theologians such as Major Jones traced the development of the spiritual heritage that affirmed the ecumenical doctrines of the Trinity, Christology, soteriology, and pneumatology to African Americans from sub-Saharan Africa. In every instance, Jones insisted, one must ask, "What does this mean for Black people?"[3]

At first glance, much of this conversation seems strangely out of place in speaking of the African American Pentecostal community. The accusation that Pentecostalism is an, almost totally, otherworldly movement devoid of any relevant socio-political agenda has found a common script among contemporary religious scholars. Yet, the fact that a concept is often repeated, does not give it legitimacy, no matter who contributes to its promulgation. Despite what Amos Yong refers to as the "typical

---

[1] See James Cone, *God of the Oppressed*, Maryknoll, NY: Orbis Books, 1997 and *A Black Theology of Liberation,* New York: Orbis Books, 1886.

[2] Jacqueline Grant, *White Women's Christ and Black Women's Jesus: Feminist Christology and Womanist Response*. New York: Oxford University Press, 1989.

[3] Major J. Jones, *The Color of God: The Concept of God in Afro-American Thought*. Macon, GA: Mercer University Press, 1987, 84.

apolitical orientation of much of classical Pentecostalism"[4] and J. Deotis Roberts' contention that the movement is "notoriously short on social conscience and… sins" with "little concern for social transformation,"[5] if one looks closely, an Afrocentric, liberative ethos can be found in the various formulations of several early Holiness, Pentecostal, and quasi-Pentecostal sects and their leaders.

The contention that Pentecostalism is a chiefly oral expression, lacking the presence of those with either the intellectual acuity or ethical interest to craft systematic or constructive theological frameworks is also not entirely true. While the second contention is, on its surface, somewhat more valid, in that Pentecostal have developed no cogent body of systematic theology, it does not consider the substantial body of work Pentecostal thinkers have produced over the movement's life—not only in sermons and hymns, but in unpublished essays and monographs. These have been overlooked because they were not marketed as systematic tomes but developed in response to existential necessity. Though much of this work remains unpublished or published by small personal or denominational presses, critical examination of these resources allows us to mine from it a wealth of theology that provides a more rounded view of what early Pentecostalism has contributed to the discussion of social justice.

---

[4] Amos Yong, "Justice Deprived, Justice Demanded: Afropentecostalisms and the Task of World Pentecostal Theology Today," *Journal of Pentecostal Theology* 15:1 (2006), 130.

[5] J. Deotis Roberts, *Black Theology in Dialog*, Philadelphia: Westminster Press, 59.

It is easy to attempt to refute myths, without producing substantial evidence of a contrary reality. To escape the charge of being revisionist, however, argumentation for a distinct experience must expose not just isolated incidences that prove the exception, but, also, a sustained pattern of previously overlooked engagement. Such a pattern is evident when one takes the time to unearth the voice of protest inherent in Afro-Pentecostalism from the movement's inception.

Surely, the voices of Afro-Pentecostals were not as clearly communicated to the broader society as were those from other sectors of the black church—especially those considered more liberal. Much of Pentecostal rhetoric was addressed to its own constituents and focused on giving them a liminal lens through which to view themselves that refuted perceptions forced on them by the broader society, rather than engaging and challenging the society itself.

Four types of prophetic speech can be detected in early black Pentecostal rhetoric. Each has a different focus, but each redefines common theological concepts in a manner that addresses racial injustices and deficiencies of mainline white Christian theology. First, anthropological redefinition provided black Pentecostals with a sense of self-identity opposed to that suggested by the dominant society. This redefinition challenged false understandings of what it meant to be human while upholding an understanding of the full humanity and dignity of each person. Christological redefinitions posited a description of Jesus that aligned him with the suffering African American community and lifted themes of Christ as liberator. Soteriological redefinitions broadened the understanding of sin to encompass more than just failures of personal piety, but include the failure of individuals and institutions to live out, faithfully, the mandate for justice. Eschatological redefinitions posited a different future for African Americans than the present reality that held them hostage to injustice and deprivation. These formulations provided some sense that, in the end, true justice would prevail and would weigh in on their side.

Inheritance of Holiness Rhetoric

Black Pentecostals did not initiate their justice project without inspiration inherited from a tradition of religious protest by the antecedent Holiness Movement and depended on that tradition for much of its doctrinal and ethical foundations. The Wesleyan Holiness Movement was noted for its radical equality and openness to unprecedented racial inclusiveness. This inclusiveness, however, was not without limitation and black Holiness leaders responded by formulating theological positions that questioned the racial politics of even that movement, as well as the failure of white Holiness leaders to take a more active and visible role in attempts of their black brothers and sisters to gain full enfranchisement within American society.

Itinerant Holiness preachers such as Jarena Lee, Zilpha Elaw, Julia Foote, and Amanda Berry Smith used the language of sanctification as synonymous with liberation, insisting that "the blood of Jesus" freed them not only from personal sin but from less than adequate estimates of their divine worth as well. Smith's nearly six-hundred-page autobiography, for example, is laced with a social critique of both sexism and racism in the church and society. At one point, she insisted that "...some people would understand the quintessence of sanctifying grace if they could be black about twenty-four hours."[6] Significantly, her liberative legacy would later be picked up by two black Pentecostal matriarchs: Mary Magdalena Lewis Tate and Ida Bell Robinson.

William Christian intentionally set out to address racial inequality. From inception, his denomination, the Church of the Living God (Christian Workers for Fellowship), combated racist teachings, such as the claims of some late nineteenth-century Baptist preachers that blacks were not human, but the product of a human father and female beast.[7] To refute this teaching, Christian asserted that "the saints of the Bible belonged to the black race."[8] He grounded his anthropology in a reworking of Christology, teaching that since Jesus had no earthly father, he could be considered "colorless" and belonged to all people.[9]

The CWFF's statement of faith explicitly insists on "... the Fatherhood of God and the Brotherhood of man" and "... that all men are born free and equal."[10] At the same time, Christian insisted that, because of his lineage through Abraham and David, Jesus was black as, he also insisted, were many other Biblical saints. An excerpt from the CWFF catechism evidences the liberative

---

[6] Autobiography, 116-117.
[7] Hollenweger, "A Black Pentecostal Concept," 16-19.
[8] Ibid., 18-19.
[9] Ibid., 34.
[10] Statement of Faith, Church of the Living God (Christian Workers for Fellowship).

hermeneutic Christian employed to claim racial affinity with Jesus as well as other biblical persons:

Question: Was Jesus a member of the black race?

Answer: Yes. Matthew 1.

Question: How do you know?

Answer: Because He was in the line of Abraham and David the king

Questions: Is this assertion sufficient proof that Christ came of the black generation?

Answer: Yes...

Question: Should we make a difference in people because they are black?

Answer: No. (Jer. 13:23)

Question: Why?

Answer: Because it is as natural to be black as the leopard to be spotted. (Jer. 13:23)[11]

The last question must be understood, not as asking should people be treated differently because of their race. Rather, it is

---

[11] Catechism of the Church of the Living God (CWFF) at www.cotlgcwff.org/artilcles.htm.

asking whether black people should be discriminated against or denied dignity and respect because of their blackness.

Another Holiness leader, Charles Price Jones, founder of the Church of Christ (Holiness), was concerned with the social implications of the American race dilemma and sought to bring uplift to his black brothers and sisters. In his *Appeal to the Sons of Africa*, Jones was cognizant of the hardships caused by the social situation of black people and chose to employ what could be termed as a mixture of accommodationist and reform approaches to the issue. As such, he implored black people to refrain from responding to white oppression by engaging in immoral or unethical behavior. Instead, he called on them to do all they could to uplift themselves and trust God for their ultimate deliverance. Yet, even such accommodationism cannot be dismissed as totally otherworldly. For Jones was as concerned about the temporal welfare of the blacks he led as about their eternal state. He was intensely concerned that they respect and honor each other in the face of dishonor from the white community. In his poem, titled for the book, Jones declared that,

> I know we have a noble race
> Of curled hair and ebon face,
> And princes have from Egypt come;
> God has in Ethiop's breast a home
> Some of the noblest of men
> Have been of African descent[12]

---

[12] Charles Price Jones, *An Appeal to the Sons of Africa*, Chicago, IL: National Publishing Board, Church of Christ (Holiness) U.S.A., 2000, 17-18.

In this book, Jones spurred blacks to live out Christian convictions amid unchristian treatment. In another poem, "Little Black Boy" in the same volume, he envisioned a different future for which blacks should prepare themselves. And, in light of the recent political situation with the two-term election of a black man, President Barak Obama, Jones words can be considered prophetic, while those who received them at the time had no idea they could become a reality,

> As I looked in the depth of the little black eye
> And studied the soul that behind it did lie
>
> I wondered, "whatever on earth will he be?"
> No telling, no telling, the living will see
>
> He may be a governor, a president, or
> He may be a colonel or general in war
>
> He may be a minister, faithful to God
> He may be a doctor, or lawyer —or fraud.[13]

Early Pentecostals

The legacy begun by black Holiness and proto-Pentecostal leaders informed the radically egalitarian nature of the earliest Pentecostal meeting and its rhetoric, even while evidence of race prejudice was subtly or blatantly demonstrated by some early white Pentecostal leaders. Azusa Street Revival leader, William Seymour, was a proponent of racial unity among black, white, Latino, and

---

[13] Ibid., 47.

other believers. Within the popular imagination, the revival was noted for its ecstatic worship and its emphasis on Holy Spirit baptism with the initial evidence of speaking in tongues. But recent scholarship concerning the revival, that began in 1906 and lasted for more than seven years, highlights its unprecedented racial mixing, gender equality, and absence of class distinctions. Though many in attendance were poor and working-class, several participants were from the middle- and upper classes. Distinctions regarding who was allowed leadership in the meetings or clerical standing were dissolved as whoever the Spirit moved upon was allowed to exhort, preach, or pray.

Raised in post-reconstruction Louisiana, Seymour had witnessed first-hand, the racial atrocities perpetrated against blacks in that state. Escaping to the relative freedom of the North, he was, from time to time, subjected to discrimination at the hands of fellow religionists, as when he was forced to sit outside the classroom at Charles Parham's Bible school to listen to lectures instead of being seated in the room with white classmates. As pastor of his mission church, Seymour was as much concerned with racial unity and the liberation of his black brothers and sisters from unjust discrimination as he was for their eternal wellbeing. The phenomenon of Blacks and Whites worshipping together under a Black pastor seemed incredible to many observers. The ethos of the meeting was captured by Bartleman's declaration concerning the erasure of the "color line." People from all the ethnic minorities were represented at Azusa Street, so that Bartleman began to call Los Angeles, "the American Jerusalem."

Seymour came to believe that blacks and whites worshipping together was a surer sign of God's blessing and the Spirit's healing presence than speaking in tongues. He was genuinely concerned that his white brothers and sisters would be liberated from the sin of racism, and traveled throughout the United States, fervently preaching against racism. The interracial aspects of his meetings stood in striking contrast to the racism and segregation of the times. Yet Seymour's efforts were largely unsuccessful in staving off the seemingly inevitable division that occurred in the movement within a few years.

Seymour's project was not so much liberating the black race from the effects of racism within society as it was the liberation of all men and women from the demoralizing effects of racial prejudice within the Church. For, Seymour insisted that the lack of unity was as unfortunate for whites as for black, robbing them of the unity that Christ intended for his Church. In all of this, he never offered a sophisticated systematic theological argument for his position. At one point, however, he asserted, "Christ is neither black, nor white, He is neither Chinese, nor Hindu, nor Japanese–but God is a Spirit."[14]

Seymour simply attempted to live out a vision of Spirit-empowered mutuality, declaring, at one point, that:

> The colored brethren must love the white brethren and respect them in the truth so that the Word of God may have its free course, and our white brethren must

---

[14] William J. Seymour, *Doctrines and Disciplines of the Azusa Street Mission of Los Angeles*, edited by Larry Martin, Joplin MO: Christian Life Books, 2000, 13.

love our colored brethren and respect them in the truth so that the Holy Spirit will not be grieved.[15]

Part of Seymour's spiritual nurture came at the hands of the Evening Light Saints, the radically egalitarian Holiness group that was the forerunner to the Church of God (Anderson Indiana). It denounced all forms of racial, gender, and cultural discrimination as thoroughly unbiblical. During his tenure with them, Seymour gained an appreciation for the possibility of people of various cultures being in Christian fellowship and working together without regard for the restrictions that characterized the rest of society.

But Seymour was not oblivious to the racial realities of the culture in which he found himself, and ultimately, after several disastrously encounters with fellow white leaders, determined that the health of his local congregation could best be served by limiting its leadership to blacks, though not completely breaking fellowship with whites. Seymour's final exasperation with the race issue was evident in an item in the 1915 *Doctrines and Disciplines of the Apostolic Faith Mission,* fifty years after the Emancipation Proclamation declared slavery illegal, Seymour's parents had been slaves before his birth, but he had never been a slave. The memory of the deplorable conditions of slavery's aftermath must have been fresh on his mind in a seemingly anachronistic section entitled, "Concerning the Institution of Slavery," in which Seymour insisted,

---

[15] Ibid., 10.

We declare that we are as much as ever convinced of the great evil of slavery. We believe that the buying, selling, or holding of human beings, to be used as chattels, is contrary to the laws of God and nature, and inconsistent with the golden rule, and with that rule in our discipline which requires all who desire to continue among us to 'do no harm,' and to 'avoid evil of every kind.' We therefore affectionately admonish all our ministers and people to keep themselves pure from this great evil, and to seek its extirpation by all lawful and Christian means.[16]

Elias Dempsey Smith, the founder of Triumph the Church and Kingdom of God, made a distinction between the "church militant of whites and the peace-loving church of blacks."[17] He joined forces with Mason shortly after the former's Church of God in Christ was founded in 1904 but found Mason's openness to interracial cooperation and fellowship too conciliatory. After World War I, Smith became involved in the Back to Africa movement and Ethiopianism. In 1919, he hosted Marcus Garvey, head of the Universal Negro Improvement Association at the denomination's national convention. In 1920, he made a pilgrimage to Ethiopia, where he was given the reception of a king, including a lavish banquet. He died the next day.

---

[16] Ibid.
[17] "Triumph the Church and Kingdom of God" in Larry G. Murphy, J. Gordon Melton, et al., eds. *Encyclopedia of African American Religions*. New York: Routledge, 1993, 70.

Smith's foundation for establishing the denomination was based on what he saw as a God-given vision, in which an eagle, lion, and "brown skin damsel," dressed as a bride adorned for her husband. According to Smith, the vision symbolized that the truth given to him was higher than any existing understanding and that, through it, the strength God, as represented by the lion, would provide the black church and the entire black world with the ability to birth all its needs.[18]

The national anthem of the Triumph the Church declares its focus on Ethiopia as the center of civilization and God's redemptive plan for humanity.

Onward, onward Ethiopia (3x)
In this great triumphant church.

God is calling Ethiopia (3x)
To this great triumphant church.

Gather yourselves together Ethiopians (3x)
In this great triumphant church.[19]

Smith prodded his followers to stand against subtle prejudice and segregation in church and society,[20] and cautioned, "Don't be

---

[18]Constitution, 11.
[19] "Triumph National Anthem," viewed at http://triumphthechurchnatl.org/ Creed%20and%20Anthem.htm.
[20] George McKinney, "The Azusa Street Revival," A lecture presented at Beeson Divinity School, Sanford University in Birmingham, Alabama on October 3, 2001.

looking for a white Jesus coming down on a cloud..."[21] Today, Smith's denomination carries his convictions even further. It espouses an afro-centric ecclesiology, anthropology, and eschatology. Its catechism teaches, for example, that, "for God's everlasting kingdom, there is an original language that God gave man in the Garden of Eden when he created Adam and Eve.... for... the Holy Ghost will teach a language that the kingdoms of this world will not be able to learn unless they are filled with that Spirit." Further, it insists that,

> God will return every earthly kingdom to the people that came from beyond the rivers of Ethiopia. Many nations and kingdoms all over the world have been built by the blood, sweat, and slavery of Ethiopian descendants. The DNA of Ethiopia is everywhere on this earth.... God has (en)trusted the Jews with a dispensation, and... the Gentiles[22] with a dispensation, but God is now calling Ethiopia. God will turn every kingdom of this world over to us.[23]

Mason, Jones' one-time collaborator, took a different stance regarding issues of race. Mason, founded arguably the largest Pentecostal body in the United States, and certainly, the largest black US denomination, was dedicated to recovering the influence of Africa and preserving the cultural expression of slaves within

---

[21] Church Covenant, Triumph the Church and Kingdom of God in Christ. Sixth Episcopal District. http://:triumphthecnat'lorg/creed%20and%20anthem. htm#Creed/Anthem.
[22] (Or non-blacks).
[23] Ibid.

the black church.²⁴ Despite overtures toward racial inclusion, Mason unashamedly insisted that his organization incorporated elements of African spirituality. He incorporated Africanisms, including shouting (or dancing) and healing ritual, into the ministry of the Church of God in Christ and took pains to ensure that such expression was not only allowed but celebrated.

Though the majority of his rhetoric dealt with more eternal matters, Mason took a deliberate stand on two temporal issues: pacifism and lynching. His pacifist convictions and outspokenness on the issue kept him under surveillance by the FBI and led to his incarceration on at least two occasions.

Mason also drew attention from federal law enforcement officials because of alliances he maintained with white colleagues at a time when such overtures drew suspicion. Like Seymour, Mason viewed the dismantling of racial prejudice as a work of the Spirit. More importantly, he attempted to live out that conviction.

For him, lynchings were being carried out, "because the preachers are leading people away from the reproof of God and not to the glory of God. They are cowards until they are baptized with Jesus' baptism."²⁵

Ida Bell Robinson lodged a prophetic witness on two fronts. She moved out from a comfortable position as a celebrated pastor with her United Holy Church congregation to find a denomination in which women could freely pursue what they felt was their God-

---

[24] Ithiel Clemmons provides a detailed account of Mason contribution in *Charles Harrison Mason and the Church of God in Christ*, Los Angeles: Pneuma Life Publishers, 1996.

[25] This quote is from a sermon Mason preached on Sunday at Convocation, December 7, 1919. It raises a question of what cowardly preachers Mason was talking about—white or black, present or absent.

given call to preach the gospel. She founded the Mount Sinai Holy Church of America to liberate women from the dominance of hierarchical and exclusionary leadership structures in black Pentecostalism. Within her young organization, she deliberately set out to train and empower women to move into positions of leadership.

Robinson and her followers developed a newsletter, *The Latter Day Messenger*, to address social, ethical, and religious issues. Articles, sermon excerpts, testimonials, and praise reports and constituent letters showed the breadth of her congregation's concerns. Amid birth announcements or coverage of members' weddings, issues such as racial and economic discrimination, race relations, and women's role in the church stood alongside doctrinal discussions. Articles submitted by constituents included such as one from a young woman in Pensacola, Florida, entitled "What a Christian Teacher Can Do for the Negro."[26] It lauded Christian teachers' contribution to the secular education of African American children, testified to the writer's experiences as a teacher, and encouraged readers to consider the teaching profession.

As with the majority of black Pentecostals, Robinson was theologically conservative, socially progressive, and concerned as much with the material welfare and moral leadership of her congregations and the entire African American community. While she was interested in providing spiritual direction, Robinson was not afraid to take unpopular stands on controversial issues and was not without controversy within the circle of people who knew of her.

---

[26]M. E. Wood, "What a Christian Teacher Can do for Negro America" *Latter Day Messenger*, 2:2 (1934) 4.

In the 1930s and 40s, Robinson came under surveillance by the Federal Bureau of Investigation for several reasons. First, her congregation was racially mixed at a time when segregation, even in the North, was at its height. Among the whites who were a part of her congregation was her secretary, a German woman, married to an Italian man. During the war, the couple was suspected of sympathizing with the enemy—a situation that brought Robinson's congregation under suspicion of harboring enemy sympathizers.[27]

Like Mason and many other African American Pentecostals, Robinson was a pacifist. Members of Mount Sinai could serve in the armed forces, but only as conscientious objectors. She used her radio broadcast to expound on her moral convictions, including her stance against the war effort and twice, in 1942, she was on the FBI list of suspected agitators for remarks allegedly supporting Japanese victories.[28] Whether Robinson made the remarks is under contention; her name was later dropped from the list.

The proto-womanist's moral courage in tackling issues beyond the immediate spiritual needs of her constituency appears in an unsigned article, "The Economic Persecution." attributed to her in the periodical.[29] In it, she prominently attacked racial

---

[27] Interview with Harold Trulear, June 20, 2001.

[28] Federal Bureau of Investigation. Foreign Inspired Agitation among the American Negroes in Philadelphia Division. File No. 100-135-37-2, Section 39497 July, 1942 and File No. 100-135-37-9, September, 1942. In this document, available under the Freedom of Information Act, significant information is blocked, yet a list of those under surveillance is attached and Robinson's name clearly identified.

[29] Ida Robinson, "The Economic Persecution" *The Latter Day Messenger,* (May 23,1935), 2. Bettye Collier-Thomas cites this work as a sermon of Robinson's in *Daughters of Thunder: Black Women and Their Sermons: 1850-1979.* San Francisco, Jossey-Bass Publishers, 1998, 203-

discrimination in America and compared the lynching of Blacks in the Southern states with the persecution of Christians under pagan emperors.[30] She also attacked the hypocrisy of the Southern white church for not standing against the hideous occurrences she graphically depicted or against racism throughout American society:

> ... Our people in certain southern states are killed, their bodies dismembered and thrown to vultures. This... is a common occurrence, and unfortunately where "Christianity" is more prevalent... For... laws are made to uphold Christianity... and to prevent any teachings... that tend to distort, minimize, or otherwise change the principle... Christianity as taught in the Bible... anyone found guilty of teaching doctrine contrary to Christianity in any (state) supported school... shall be punished to the extent of the law... But these same people... will toss their own laws to the four winds and trample under feet the laws of Christianity and utterly ignore the words of the sacred "Book" they pretend to love so dearly, and esteem so highly...

> So let us Saints pray that the Constantine of our day... sends a letter to the modern pagans in the polluted southland in the form of "anti-lynching" legislation that is now pending in Congress. We can... and we

---

205.
[30] Robinson, "The Economic Persecution," 2.

will overcome... in this present world, the persecution we are made to suffer by our unjust brethren. It is written, the Ethiopians shall stretch forth their hands in righteousness to God, and by the help of God and the agencies He has so gloriously provided, we shall overcome. [31]

Liberative Themes in Black Oneness Pentecostal Thought

During the mid-twentieth century, black Oneness leaders generally paid homage to two men: Garfield T. Haywood and Robert C. Lawson as being progenitors. Haywood, the well-known leader and first presiding bishop of the interracial Pentecostal Assemblies of the World wrote hundreds of sermons and hymns and numerous books that have become standards among African American Pentecostals. His periodical, *Voice in the Wilderness*, dealt principally with doctrinal issues related to the dogmatic defense of oneness theology, yet he did not completely ignore the racial realities of his constituencies. From the beginning of Haywood's ministry, his Indianapolis congregation was interracial, even while the state of Indiana maintained a significant Ku Klux Klan presence. As long as he served as head, he struggled to maintain the interracial composition of PAW and its continued existence as an integrated body in the South as well as the North was a testimony to lived protest of twentieth-century American racial mores.

---

[31] Ibid.

As a young man, Haywood served as a writer and cartoonist for two secular African American newspapers in Indianapolis—the *Freedmen* and the *Recorder*. His caricatures depicted racial issues and both newspapers regularly commented on discrimination within the Indianapolis community and the nation. Since the majority of these periodicals' articles were unsigned, it is difficult to determine Haywood's contribution. And, though his writings on racial and social issues are not prolific, his commitment to maintaining an interracial body amid rampant racism in the surrounding society demonstrates a commitment never repeated in Pentecostalism.

Lawson, the founder of the Church of Our Lord Jesus Christ of the Apostolic Faith, was one of the most critical early black Pentecostal theological minds. The denomination that he founded became the parent—or grandparent of several major Oneness bodies. Lawson was a prolific songwriter, author, businessman and community leader, and pastor of one of the most influential congregations within the black Oneness movement. While like most other Pentecostals of his day, he espoused a strict personal moral code and a hopeful eschatological vision of ultimate justice. He also openly opposed segregation and represented an unrelenting Pentecostal challenge to the status quo of mid-twentieth-century American racial politics. Speaking to the church, in particular, he contended that it,

> should set the example of democracy and no man or woman should be denied the right to worship his God in any church in the country. There should be no

segregated episcopal districts [with] whites... set apart from Negroes when they are supposed to be worshipping the same God... It is the church's job not to foster, aid, or abet white supremacy through segregation but to eliminate it.[32]

Lawson shared with his predecessor, Seymour, the unrealized hope that the Pentecostal movement could redeem the Church from the "virus and plague of race prejudice and segregation."[33] He insisted that "a Christian's moral judgment should never represent the prejudice of the community." He further lamented, "(w)e have white Pentecostal churches and colored Pentecostal churches, white bishops, and colored bishops. We have Jim Crowed the Lord's table which is an effrontery to God.[34] Further, Lawson insisted that "racism within a Christian community is sin—a violation of the very gospel entrusted to it, and a 'spiritual monstrosity,' not just a question of one's preference or a spot on the garment of faith."[35]

Yet, Lawson wrote for a broader audience than the black church, challenging misguided conceptions of black inferiority by white Christians, and berating the abuse of the truth of the history of black people. He insisted that "the only thing to kill race

---

[32] Robert Clarence Lawson, *An Open Letter to a Southern White Gentleman on Racism*, New York: Privately Printed, s.d., 20.

[33] Robert Clarence Lawson, *The Greatest Evil In This World Is Race Prejudice*, s.l: s.n., 1957.

[34] Ibid.

[35] Roswith Gerloff, "Theology on Route of Migration: Inner Dynamics of the Pentecostal Oneness (Apostolic) Movement from North America to the Caribbean to Britain and Beyond," Paper delivered to the Annual Meeting of the Society for Pentecostal Studies, Fresno, California, 1992.

prejudice is to give truth, knowledge, and understanding to races…prejudiced against each other."[36] His critique, however, went beyond the church. Before the push for globalization, Lawson was cognizant of implications of the racist American pattern for global expansion of the Gospel, and insisted,

> The status of race relations is… affecting… the status of Christianity before the world… [B]ecause of color prejudice… the darker races have reached a point where they will not graciously accept a gospel of love and brotherhood when the denial of their essential manhood… negates the tenets that they are asked to accept.[37]

Nor did Lawson accept passivity toward the issue of race that simply waited for God to correct things in the Eschaton. Rather, he was an activist in a time when many Pentecostals eschewed activists' projects and he asserted, "it is time to protest."[38] Further, he cautioned with prophetic fervor,

> If the white brethren don't preach the fatherhood of God and brotherhood of man irrespective of color or nationality and exemplify the true spirit of brotherhood to all, their civilization is doomed.[39]

For Lawson, the prophetic intersection of Christology, soteriology, and anthropology is key to dismantling racial prejudice.

---

[36] Anthropology, 6-11.
[37] Ibid., 6.
[38] Ibid., 7.
[39] Ibid., 7.

In his essay, "Hamitic Contribution to the Anthropological Development of Jesus," he insisted that,

> it was necessary in the plan of God to develop the most perfect man of the human race, to mingle and inter-mingle the blood of the three branches (of the human race) to produce the best and most perfect man.[40]

Further, he declared that,

> God disrobed himself of his glory and overshadowed the Virgin Mary… in whose veins flowed the blood of Japheth, and of Shem, and of Ham. For so had been the purpose and work of God in mixing the blood of all three branches of the human race, that upon the basis of kinship, He might have the right to redeem all men.[41]

But, echoing a theme later heard in James Cone's theology, Lawson boldly made the audacious assertion that Jesus had "Negro blood" in his veins.[42] Though his assertion was more anthropological than philosophical, the similar implications of the assertion for the oppressed black community cannot be overlooked. For him,

> "[i]f any race has whereof to boast… relative to our Lord Jesus Christ, the colored race has more[,] for they gave the

---

[40] Ibid., 27.
[41] Ibid., 40.
[42] Ibid., 28.

two mothers of the tribe of Judah–out of which Christ came."[43]

Lawson attributed part of Jesus' blackness to two other women—Rahab the Jerichoian harlot (sic) who helped the advancing Israelites and Bathsheba, the wife of Uriah the Hittite, whom David seduced and married after murdering her husband. Solomon, the son of David and Bathsheba was of mixed parentage and it is out of this line, Lawson insists, that Jesus comes.

He also made the extraordinary proposal that "every other ill that afflicts humanity comes out of this evil [of racism] in the heart." [44] Further, he expressed disappointment that Pentecostals "had joined Baptists and Methodists in dividing their churches along racial lines," since according to him,

> the Lord, through mixing our human natures by the process of miscegenation… forever abolished the basis and principle of race prejudice and, [45]

> "God is a kinsman to all having their blood in his veins… [and] whatever race one chooses to hate,… our Lord is of that race—whether Semitic, Hamitic, or Japhetic.[46]

---

[43] Ibid., 29.
[44] Ibid., 34.
[45] Ibid., 33.
[46] Ibid., 47.

Lawson continued along this vein, by making the contention that,

> Although our savior isn't wholly any race... he is a relative of all... He is our savior. Not a Jewish savior, not a Negro savior, not an Anglo-Saxon savior. Jesus Christ is a human, universal savior [our kinsman] by virtue of the fact that the blood of Shem, Ham, and Japheth, who are representatives of the entire human race, flows through his veins.[47]

Smallwood E. Williams was perhaps, the closest rival to Lawson's sustained pattern of protest. Lawson's protégé, broke with him in 1957 to found Bible Way Church World-Wide, in Washington, DC. From this strategic vantage point, he became a local, and national, political force. He led the first sit-in as part of a legal assault on the city's segregated public schools, helped found Citizens Against Police Brutality, headed the local chapter of the NAACP, and served as vice-chair of the Democratic Central Committee.

Conclusion

The central focus of Pentecostal preaching is the offer of eternal life through the appropriation of the atoning work of Christ. Contrary to popular characterizations, for black Pentecostals, that offer is not rigidly couched in a pie-in-the-sky, white robe and golden slipper escapism. Instead, at times, it has been more broadly expressed in language that was socially, as well

---

[47] Ibid.

as spiritually, liberative. Some have taken the personal implications of Jesus' offer of abundant life that starts in the here and now seriously, and in more progressive understandings have extrapolated that abundance to refer to communal, as well as personal liberation.

It is problematic, therefore, to mistake black Pentecostals' religious conservativism for complete socio-political accommodation. Conversely, the conservatism that engages the Word of God as the authoritative warrant for principles for living out of life drives the prophetic impulse of African American Pentecostalism's socio-political agenda. While early rhetoric rarely employed the language of liberation, it implicitly communicated that what happened to in the Pentecostal experience had implications beyond ecstatic expression in emotive worship. Pentecostals knew that somehow, the God who had so powerfully visited and invested himself in them, was always concerned with their temporal reality and had a different assessment of their identity than espoused in the public arena. In their encounter with the Spirit, Pentecostals found what Ithiel Clemmons called a "spirituality of deliverance."[48]

Jones' questions continue to resonate: What does the experience of Pentecostalism mean for the present situation of black people? What does it mean that Jesus is the Christ? What does it mean that we are saved? What does it mean that we claim a supernatural measure of God's empowerment? How does that empowerment enable us to negotiate the oppressive terrain that does not grant us complete dignity as being fully created in the

---

[48] Clemmons, "C. H. Mason," 68.

same image of God as those within the dominant culture? How does Pentecostal empowerment enable believers to reject the white racist God that capriciously discriminates against one branch of his Creation?

Despite the inability of Black Pentecostals to effectively communicate answers to these questions, J. Deotis Roberts' broad critique of the general social conscience of Pentecostalism concedes that,

> Black Pentecostals have been formulating a black theology for a long time. They have relied on oral traditions, African cultural retentions, and the like. Blacks join African, Latin American, and Asian tongues groups in rejection of the definition of whites.

Roberts critique should be taken seriously, as he continues,

> In essence…black Pentecostals have called attention to the racism that has splintered the Pentecostal ranks… [they have] provided a very perceptive critique of the authenticity of the fellowship, theology, and practice of white Pentecostalism. The fruit of the Spirit are absent in regard to humanity of blacks and the poor… This critique of this movement by black theologians may be a service to the entire church after all.[49]

---

[49] Roberts, 62.

Ecumenism of the Spirit: An Alternative Interpretation of Glossolalia[1]

> *And they were all filled with the Holy Ghost, and began to speak with other tongues, as the Spirit gave them utterance. And there were dwelling at Jerusalem Jews, devout men, out of every nation under heaven. Now when this was noised abroad, the multitude came together, and were confounded, because that every man heard them speak in his own language. And they were all amazed and marveled, saying one to another, Behold, are not all these which speak Galileans? And how hear we every man in our own tongue, wherein we were born?... we do hear them speak in our tongues the wonderful works of God. Acts 2:4-8, 11b (KJV)*

> *The believers... who came with Peter were amazed because the gift of the Holy Spirit had been poured out even on the Gentiles. For they heard them speaking in tongues and extolling God. Acts 10:45-46. (KJV)*

Before the 1960s, the Christian experience of speaking in tongues was limited primarily to Pentecostal congregations comprised mostly of lower- and working-class constituents who understood the phenomenon of glossolalia solely as the initial evidence of the baptism of the Holy Spirit. These Pentecostals derived their name from the belief that the biblical account, in the second chapter of Acts, of the outpouring of the Holy Spirit with speaking in tongues on the Jewish feast of Pentecost[2] is the model for contemporary spirituality and worship. They were often chided with derogatory names such as "holy

---

[1] This chapter was first presented at the 32nd annual meeting of the Society for Pentecostal Studies held at Asbury Theological Seminary, Wilmore, KY., March 20-22, 2003.
[2] Act 2:4 refers to this moment as, "[w]hen the day of Pentecost was fully come..."

rollers" and derided by other Christians, as well as non-Christians, as being ignorant or mentally limited. Much of this derision came precisely because of the practice of speaking in tongues, or glossolalia, coupled with other emotive modes of expressive worship.[3]

The early 1960s Charismatic Renewal moved the experience of glossolalia closer to the mainstream of Christianity. The first effects of this renewal unfolded among young adults on college campuses within Roman Catholic and Episcopalian denominations. This movement has since grown to engulf almost every segment of the Christian Church so that hardly a denomination remains untouched. Millions of contemporary Christians have shared the experience of speaking in tongues. While many of these are found in "classical Pentecostal"[4] churches, the proportion of those who are not is steadily growing.[5] Yet,

---

[3] For a good overview of this type of characterization of early 20th century Pentecostalism, see Anderson, *Vision of the Disinherited:* or Luther P. Gerlach and Virginia H. Hines, *People, Power, Change; Movements of Social Transformation.* Indianapolis: Bobbs-Merrills, 1970.

[4] Classical Pentecostals are those historically Pentecostal denominations that came out of the Wesleyan Holiness and related movements around the turn of the century. "Charismatic" most often relates to non-denominational churches or smaller groups within existing congregations (especially Catholic parishes) who experience tongues and who place emphasis on the use of spiritual gifts (or charismata) but have fewer social restrictions than classical Pentecostals. Neo-Pentecostal (or third-wave) includes individuals who report having the Pentecostal experience who remain in mainline congregations and who prefer to maintain their denominational affiliation but who are essentially Pentecostal or charismatic in their beliefs and style of worship.

[5] Evidence of a growing trend of incorporating glossolalia into worship of other than classical Pentecostal churches can be seen, for example, in the founding of the Full Gospel Baptist denomination that openly embraces tongues as well as other charismatic gifts and the Aldersgate Renewal Ministries affiliated with the General Board of Discipleship of the United Methodist Church.

for many, within and outside the Christian community, glossolalia remains an experience shrouded in mystery and confusion.

The term comes from the Greek words *glossa* meaning tongue (in both the anatomical and linguistic senses) and *lalia* meaning to speak. The phenomenon is not unique either to twentieth-century Pentecostalism or to Christianity. Several pre- and non-Christian sects employed glossolalia in corporate worship or personal spirituality. Within the Christian context, however, it describes prayer or praise of God involving speaking in syllables, words, or phrases using language(s) distinctively different from that which practitioners naturally use for regular communication and that they have not learned.

Glossolalia has variously been characterized by those who stand outside the Pentecostal traditions as, at best, having no relevance for the modern Church or, at worst, a decidedly un-Christian practice bordering on the psychotic, neurotic or demonic. These differing views have contributed to misunderstandings about what Pentecostalism is and to, often, making ecumenical efforts between Pentecostals and other Christian groups less than successful.

The spread of the Charismatic Renewal to the Catholic Church and mainline Protestant denominations has opened opportunities for new dialog among the various groups. Within this new openness, interpreting glossolalia through an ecumenical lens can, potentially, help facilitate unity in the body of Christ by removing theological stumbling blocks between Pentecostals and other Christians.

When parochial agendas take second place to ecumenical concerns, those involved in the dialog can begin to do two things. First, together, they can develop a broader appreciation of implications for the continued existence of glossolalia within a segment of the Church. Second, they can develop more ecumenical ways of interpreting what the recent spread of the phenomenon means within the broader Church.

Such understandings cannot be developed in isolation. They must consider the experiences, presuppositions, and the biases of dialog partners. Since these cannot be, entirely, suspended, participants must take pains to ensure that they are honestly and thoroughly examined. In this way, we can come to new understandings that further, rather than hinder, discussion.

Attempts to understand glossolalia in various segments of the Church suggest that the difficulty of reconciling conflicting understandings is a hermeneutical problem. Each interpretation has some validity for the respective audiences who adopt it.[6] But, some divide rather than unify, the body of Christ, either by restricting conversation to those partners who hold the same understandings or by failing to take seriously the contribution of those holding differing views.

For successful ecumenical dialog, neither the strict interpretation as *the* initial evidence of Holy Spirit baptism nor that of lack of validity for the modern Church bears useful fruit. Rather, an understanding of the experience as unifying disparate Christian traditions through an ecumenical, non-reductionist hermeneutic, and an attestation to a common spirituality bears theologically exploration. Any attempt to develop such an interpretation brings up several questions that cannot be answered here. Yet, this discussion attempts to answer two concerns germane to any effort to place glossolalia in an ecumenical framework:

---

[6]See Paul Ricoeur, *Conflict of Interpretation: Essays in Hermeneutics.* Evanston, IL: Northwestern University Press, 1974, 31.

- How can ecumenical dialog be aided by enlarged understandings of glossolalia?

- What are the salient issues relating to the development of such a hermeneutic?

Understanding the current thinking on the subject necessitates engaging prior conceptions as well as ongoing scholarly and denominational discussions. It also requires classifying interpretations to identify their most salient features. Historical interpretations of the experience trace its initial appearance in the New Testament Church, then look at its demise within the patristic Church, various episodes of re-emergence throughout Church history, and its explosion into the early twentieth-century Pentecostal revival and modern Charismatic renewal. Constructing general topologies allows for a theological and hermeneutical critique of various interpretive schemes. Finally, a hermeneutical critique of existing understandings might allow the development of a potentially more fruitful interpretative scheme for advancing ecumenical dialog.

Proponents and critics of tongues in Christian worship employ a range of explanatory schemes in the fields of psychology, history, sociology/anthropology, linguistics, as well as disciplines of religious and biblical studies, theology, or spirituality. Built into their critique are biases and presuppositions based on their particular religious heritage.

Numerous works whose central themes more generally relate to pneumatology or ecclesiology reserve substantial discussion for the topic of glossolalia.[7] This is also true of numerous works that attempt

---

[7] Steven Land, *Pentecostal Spirituality*; George Montague; *The Spirit and His Gifts: The Biblical Background of Spirit-Baptism, Tongues-Speaking, and Prophecy*. New York: Paulist Press, 1974 and Guy Duffield and Nathaniel

a systematic theology—especially from a Pentecostal/Charismatic perspective.[8] These works attempt to link speaking in tongues and the overall work of the Holy Spirit in the individual, the local congregation, the Church, and the world. In any case, a closer examination of the subject through these explanatory lenses will prove helpful.

Psychological Explanations

Psychological assessments assume that glossolalia can be explained in cognitive—or rational—rather than spiritual terms. These explanations carry the strongest weight among those critics who characterize glossolalics as having a form of psychological dysfunction. They see glossolalia as a mild hypnotic trance, most often self-induced through some type of mass hysteria or suggestion.[9] Another psychological argument assumes that glossolalia involves cryptomnesia, or exalted memory, in which persons have been previously exposed to a foreign language that they have not learned but stored in their subconscious, and later recall it in moments of stress.[10]

VanCleave, *Foundations of Pentecostal Theology,* Los Angeles: L.I.F.E. Bible College, 1983.

[8]See J. Rodman Williams, *Renewal Theology Vol 2 - Salvation, the Holy Spirit and Christian Living.* Grand Rapids, MI: Zondervan Publishing House, 1990; John Higgins et al., *An Introduction to Theology: A Classical Pentecostal Perspective*, Dubuque, IA: Kendall/Hunt Pub., 1993, and Stanley Burgess and Gary McGee, *Dictionary of Pentecostal and Charismatic Movements.* Grand Rapids MI: Zondervan Publishers, 1987.

[9]George Marston in *Tongues Then and Now,* Phillipsburg, TN: Presbyterian and Reformed Publishing Co, 1983, and Felicitas Goodman in *Speaking in Tongues: A Cross-Cultural Study of Glossolalia*, Chicago: University of Chicago Press, 1972, support this position. George Cutten attributes this state to group excitement in *Speaking in Tongues: Historically and Psychologically Considered.* New Haven: Yale University Press, 1927, 127.

[10]See Neil Babcock *A Search for Charismatic Reality: One Man's*

The third type of psychological argument asserts that speaking in tongues is an attempt by immature individuals to regress. These explanations, identified by Babcock as "ad hominem," attack persons who hold that speaking in tongues is viable, rather than the viability of the phenomenon itself.[11] They view glossolalics as, at best, fanatics, divisive, unbalanced, immature and exclusivist, and, at worst, pathological and having exhibitionist tendencies.[12]

Psychological interpretations include the view that glossolalics receive cognitive benefits that manifest themselves in the increased ability to cope. They hold that the experience is useful to those forced to exist in conditions of stress such as poverty, lack of social standing, or some form of oppression.[13]

Proponents, however, stress that glossolalics are of no precise psychological or personality type that predisposes them to speak in tongues.[14] Roman Catholic Charismatic theologian, Kilian McDonnell, asserts that it is not necessary to construe psychological interpretations as reductionist because a "phenomenon has a psychological explanation does not exclude it from being a gift of the (Holy) Spirit."[15]

Pilgrimage, Portland, OR: Multnomah Press, 1985, 34-35 for a discussion of this phenomenon.

[11]Ibid., *32.*

[12]Babcock provides a catalog of these dysfunctional characterizations attributed to Christian glossolalics in his work.

[13]This description fits Robert Mapes Anderson's characterization in *Vision of the Disinherited.*

[14]William J. Samarin, *Tongues of Men and Angels: the Religious Language of Pentecostalism,* New York: McMillan, 1972, 228.

[15]Kilian McDonnell, *Charismatic Renewal and the Churches.* New York: Seabury Press, 1976, 154.

Historical Explanations

Historical arguments against tongues in modern worship posit that there are no substantial recurrences of tongues speaking from the time of the first century Church until contemporary times. These arguments allege that evidence supporting the widespread practice of glossolalia throughout church history cannot be substantiated. They contend that from the New Testament period on, the only evidence of glossolalia has been from "fringe heretic groups" such as the Gnostics and the Montanists.[16]

Those who support glossolalia historically assert that the church fathers, such as Origen and Irenaeus, acknowledged awareness of the experience in their writings and appeared to equate it with a foreign language.[17] They insist that Augustine valued glossolalia as a mark of the birth of the Church in earlier centuries.[18] John Chrysostom also referred to glossolalia in his "Homily 29 on Corinthians."[19] And, Francis Xavier, missionary to India, claimed the gift of xenolalia[20] and asserted that he was able to speak to the people of that country in their native tongue without having learned the language.

---

[16]Merrill Unger, *New Testament Teachings on Tongues*, Grand Rapids, MI: Kregel Publications, 1971, 14.

[17]Josephine Massyngberde Ford, "Toward of Theology of Speaking in Tongues" in Watson E. Mills, *Speaking in Tongues: A Guide to Research on Glossolalia,* Grand Rapids, MI: Wm. B Eerdmans Publishing Co., 1986, 264.

[18]Russell Spittler, "Glossolalia" in Gary McGee, et al., *Dictionary of Pentecostal and Charismatic Movements*, 339. Interestingly, however, it was Augustine's argument that all of the charismata (including speaking in tongues) ended with the age of the Apostles that continues to make tongues problematic for some segments of the modern church.

[19]Ford, "Toward a Theology of Speaking in Tongues," 275.

[20]The speaking in a *known* tongue which one has not naturally learned.

These proponents point out that no period of history is completely devoid of at least sporadic outbursts of speaking in tongues in a given segment of the Christian Church. They insist that when tongue-speaking has been incorporated into any arena of Christian worship, practitioners have been persecuted and the phenomenon has been prohibited by leaders; they identify this as the reason it did not spread to the wider Church.

The catalog of later episodes of the phenomenon begins in the 12th century with the Albigensians (or Cathari) in southern France.[21] In the 13th century Italy, the Waldenses—the followers of Peter Waldo who were heavily persecuted by the Catholic Church—made use of speaking in tongues in their worship. The 16th Century, Jansenists, an evangelical group in the Catholic Church, were persecuted by the Jesuits for a variety of reasons including speaking in tongues, prophesying, "discerning of spirits" and praying for the sick. In the 17th Century, the Camisards or Huguenots were French Protestants who experienced an outbreak of speaking in tongues within their worship during a time of intense prayer brought about by Catholic persecution. They also experienced prophecy and divine healing. In the 19th London, a Pentecostal revival, complete with tongues, took place in Edward Irving's congregation that included some of that city's most prominent citizens, including physicians, scientists, artists, and politicians. In the 20th century, two years before the Azusa Street Revival that catapulted the modern Pentecostal movement into prominence, attendees of the Welsh Revival spoke in Old Welsh, a dialect they had not heard or learned.[22]

---

[21] A group that held heretical views concerning the humanity of Christ.

[22] For a good historical overview of occurrences of glossolalia See Samarin, *Tongues of Men and Angels*.

Historical proponents argue that it took the American climate of religious freedom that allowed people to worship as they saw fit without the threat of persecution from a mother Church or from church-controlled governments for the experience to flourish. Even in the American context, however, unofficial persecution of such practitioners as the Mormons in the 1840s, the early 19th century Shakers,[23] the Quakers, and to some degree, Pentecostal themselves, limited the early spread of the experience.[24]

Historical critics note that the Reformers did not give much credence to the experience and dismissed it as inconsequential.[25] Proponents contend, however, that tongues have played a part in almost every modern western revival movement since the Reformation, including the Great Awakening and the nineteenth-century Holiness Movement, to name specifically American examples.[26] Additionally, they contend that John Wesley, the founder

---

[23] These two former groups, though they consider themselves Christians did not see speaking in tongues as an exercise of the influence of the Holy Spirit, but rather according to Bach they saw it as coming from an undifferentiated "spirit force." See Marcus Bach, *The Inner Ecstasy*, New York: The World Publishing Co., 1969, 112.

[24] These groups were not only persecuted because of speaking in tongues, but for a variety of ideologies and practices considered heretical. However, this persecution kept their numbers small and limited their influence on the broader Church, thereby limiting exposure of other Christians to glossolalia.

[25] Ernest Best, "Interpretation of Tongue" in *Speaking in Tongues: A Guide to Research on Glossolalia*. Grand Rapids, MI: Wm. B. Eerdmans Publishing Co., 1986. 298.

[26] Interestingly, glossolalia cannot be tied solely to emotionalism or emotionally charged religious movements. The most emotionally charged modern American movement, the Cane Ridge Revival in Kentucky in the early 1800's, had evidence of many phenomena–shaking, quaking, barking, falling and fainting. However, no tongues were evident. In contrast, the 1960s Charismatic renewal movement brought about tongues among many otherwise quiet and controlled mainline Christians.

of Methodism, endorsed tongues as well as other charismatic gifts and lamented their cessation.[27] They further suggest that the diminution of tongues signifies the Church's increasing departure from the faith and purity of the New Testament Church.[28]

Anthropological Explanations

One stream of anthropological critique regards tongue speaking as a "heathen" (sic) experience or a syncretistic merger of Christianity with paganism. These critics argue that this phenomenon is common among "savages" (sic) and "pagans" (sic) considered of lower culture[29]—those without modern language or communication skills. Another stream of anthropological critique sees tongues as "play-acting" induced by euphoric expression in worship. For those holding this view, Christian glossolalia is motivated by an uneducated religious zeal that is not necessarily Christian.[30]

Proponents supporting an anthropological explanation of glossolalia suggest that the broader existence of tongues within non-Christian contexts does not detract from its special significance for Christian believers. They assert that this significance comes from the unique interpretation Christian believers hold of what they are doing when they speak in tongues. Unlike non-Christian practitioners, who

---

[27]It is significant that Wesley's Methodism is the movement that is the precursor of the Holiness movement out of which came modern Pentecostalism. See Donald Barnett and Jeffrey McGregor, *Speaking in Tongues: A Scholarly Defense*, Seattle, WA: Community Chapel Publications, 1986, 241.

[28]Ibid., 229.

[29]Unger, *New Testament Teaching on Tongues,* 165 and Margaret Poloma, *The Charismatic Movement: Is There a New Pentecost?* Boston: Twayne Publications, 1982, 53.

[30]George Marston, *Tongues Then and Now,* Phillipsburg, TN: Presbyterian and Reformed Publishing Co, 1983, 62.

see themselves as tapping into the spirit world that includes both good and evil forces and manipulating it for their benefit, Christian adherents see themselves as communicating directly with God and participating in an exercise in which evil forces have no place.[31] They see the phenomenon as manifesting a common consciousness of God among believers.

Linguistic Explanations

Linguistic arguments against speaking in tongues refer to it as the babbling of non-sense syllables and insist that it is, in no way, a true language.[32] These critics assert that the comparison of sounds made by tongues speakers to those of known languages indicates no relation with authentic linguistic patterns. They insist that the tongues spoken of in the New Testament were forms of known languages while the modern tongues are not and assert that claims for their validity, then, must be false.[33]

Proponents claim that glossolalia is a linguistic "symbol of the sacred."[34] Some of these proponents see it as pre-conceptual, non-discursive language.[35] For them, it is comparable to other religious discourse such as liturgy, prayer, psalms, and hymns[36] and such artistic expression as music, poetry, and dance.[37] Richard Baer, for example,

---

[31] For a discussion of the self-authenticating aspects of glossolalia for the Christian believer see Cyril G. Williams, "Strange Gifts" in Mills *Speaking in Tongues,* 72-83.

[32] Unger calls it "gibberish," 166.

[33] Babcock, *Search for Charismatic Reality*, 38.

[34] In *Tongues of Men and Angels,* Samarin repeatedly makes this assertion.

[35] Rene Laurentin, *Catholic Pentecostalism*, Trans. By Matthew J. O'Connell, Garden City, New York, Doubleday, 1972, 93.

[36] Samarin, 229-231.

[37] Ibid., 232.

contends that it is useful for praying in situations so devastating or splendid that they render the individual with "no other appropriate words."[38]

Biblical Explanations

Biblical critics cite such passages as I Corinthians 13:8 as suggesting that glossolalia would cease after fulfilling its temporary function of providing ongoing revelation to the New Testament believers.[39] One argument supporting this train of thought is that references to tongues were only included in Paul's earlier writings[40] on the charismata and in his later lists of gifts,[41] such references are completely absent. Further, critics suggest that Paul deprecated the operation of the gift of tongues in deference to the gift of prophecy.

Critics also contend that there is no biblical evidence that Jesus ever spoke in tongues. For many, this is reason enough to deny the legitimacy of the experience since much of the liturgy and ritual of the modern Church has a perceived link to Jesus' actions or discourses. Jesus was baptized and so faithful believers undergo that rite. He initiated the Eucharistic supper when he dined with his disciples before the crucifixion and his command to "do this in remembrance of me." Though he was never married, his presence at the wedding in Cana

---

[38] Richard Baer, "Quaker Silence, Catholic Liturgy and Glossolalia." in Watson E. Mills, *Speaking in Tongues: A Guide to Research on Glossolalia*, Grand Rapids, MI: Wm. B. Eerdmans Publishing Co., 1986, 315.

[39] "Where there are tongues, they shall cease..." The typical argument espoused by scholars such as Unger is that after the New Testament scripture was given, "the need for direct inspirational prophecy, knowledge, and interpreted tongues passes away."

[40] For example, I Cor 12 and 14.

[41] See. Rom 2:6-8 and Eph 4:7-11.

signifies the sacramental nature of marriage. The calling of the twelve disciples establishes a precedent for some kind of special rite for validating individuals for ministry. He prayed publicly and so we pray.

But the Bible never mentions Jesus engaging in anything remotely resembling speaking in tongues. The Holy Spirit's descent at his baptism is interpreted, by some, as the indwelling of his human nature by the Spirit. In that depiction, however, there were no tongues—no ecstatic expression. Even in the temple, when he made his prophetic proclamation concerning his fulfillment of the Isaiah 61 passage, Scripture does not report an ecstatic outburst. Jesus was known to speak in simple Aramaic, the language of his fellow Galileans. Critics also point out that tongues were not an essential element of Jesus' proclamation of the coming kingdom of God. The only passage in which Jesus is purported to have spoken *about* tongues is in the disputed ending of Mark's gospel.[42]

Biblical proponents of the modern tongues movement begin with the contention that there are over thirty references to speaking in tongues in the New Testament and suggest that glossolalia accompanied most biblical accounts of the "outpouring" of the Holy Spirit. As such, they see it as the fulfillment of the Joel 2:28 passage that speaks of a "last days" outpouring and as the *initial* evidence of the baptism of the Holy Spirit and one of the biblical gifts Paul describes in I Cor 12:8-10, as available to all believers.

---

[42]Liberal scholars point out that most "knowledgeable" persons reject the Mark 16:17 passage ("... and these signs shall follow them that believe, In my name they shall cast out devils, they shall speak with other tongues") as authentic. They hold that it comes from a later source than the earliest manuscripts and is annotated in several translations including the NIV and RSV to show this. Conservative and Evangelical scholars reject this assertion.

Theological Explanations

Theological critics dismiss glossolalia on several grounds. Fundamentalists—extreme theological conservatives—exclude any variation from their limited assessment of the Christian faith and quickly denounce speaking in tongues as heresy born out of misguided religious zeal. Liberal critics dismiss it on the grounds of its being a throwback to the mythical or superstitious interpretation of Scripture. Both groups claim, however, that no physical sign is necessary today as evidence of Holy Spirit baptism. Conservatives suggest that this is because Holy Spirit baptism is an empowerment every believer receives when he or she is "born again." Liberals, on the other hand, suggest that such a baptism is more broadly symbolic of self-actualization.

Merrill Unger provides a concise, fundamentalist argument against glossolalia.[43] For him, there are three major problems with glossolalia in the modern Church. First, he sees the phenomenon as usually manifested in an atmosphere of unsound doctrine.[44] Secondly, he contends that the "tongues movement" promotes the experiences of those who participate in it, based on emotional excitement that "attempts to be a substitute for accurate teaching and clear exposition of [S]cripture."[45] And, thirdly, for him, glossolalia is a major source of division and misunderstanding in the Church because it is a "distortion and perversion of Scripture that leads to error..."[46] For conservatives such as Unger, Pentecost was a once-for-all and unrepeatable occasion, so there can be no such thing as a "modern Pentecostal experience"

---

[43] Unger, *New Testament Teaching on Tongues,* 149-155.
[44] Ibid., 149.
[45] Ibid., 150.
[46] Ibid., 155.

and any referral to it should be considered a "misunderstanding or fraud."⁴⁷

Theological support for the validity of the experience comes, primarily, from practitioners who, again, see it as either the initial evidence of the baptism of the Holy Spirit or a gift of the Spirit available to all believers for personal and corporate spiritual edification. This support assumes dispensational and eschatological understandings of the in-breaking of the Holy Spirit in the Church Age, in which the Spirit is free to work among believers in new ways. They contend that with this in-breaking, the Spirit provides the Church and its members with supernatural giftings or abilities to accomplish God's mission on earth. Within this framework, tongues are one of these giftings that signal God being with believers in an intimate and personal way.

Spiritual Explanations

Spiritual arguments opposed to glossolalia cast tongues speakers as demonically deluded and see the contemporary phenomenon as a demonic counterfeit of the biblical experience.⁴⁸ Unger states emphatically that, "Satanic power must be regarded as… a source of the modern tongues phenomenon."⁴⁹ Marston asserts that " (t)hose who speak in tongues today have permitted Satan to delude them…"⁵⁰ With these claims, opponents refute claims of any spiritual authenticity. They insist that practitioners suffer from "relative ignorance of sound

---

⁴⁷ Ibid.

⁴⁸Unger and Gromacki are among several scholars that take this stand. See Unger, 149-154; Gromacki, 46-47.

⁴⁹Unger, 154.

⁵⁰Marston, 51.

doctrine regarding the authority and sufficiency of Scripture and the nature of the Christian life itself."[51]

On the other hand, proponent, Russell Spittler, counters that the reason for this strong refutation of the validity of speaking in tongues is that the first glossolalics to be studied by scholars were spiritualists and mediums.[52] Unfortunately, these early studies have often served as the foundation for further investigation and have colored any findings concerning the operation of the phenomenon among Christian groups.

Like Spittler, other proponents see the experience as a miraculous occurrence and a form of spontaneous prayer. For them, this supernatural gift of the Holy Spirit cannot be explained in natural terms, and can only be understood by those who experience it by faith as a "pre-conceptual, nonobjective way of praying,"[53] and encountering the presence of God.

Limitations of Existing Explanations

In exploring the varying explanations, Werner G. Jeanrond's assertion regarding hermeneutics makes an important statement relative to current scholarship:

> Since there is no purely objective interpretation of any texts or phenomenon, the experience of tongues, as with every complex phenomenon demands a plurality of interpretations... Proponents and critics alike are limited by their horizon and... in need of the support of the entire

---

[51] Ibid., 61.
[52] Spittler, "Glossolalia," 336.
[53] Poloma, 52.

ecumenical community for a critical assessment of their particular interpretation... ideological distortions.[54]

Paul Ricoeur sheds further light on the problem of the various explanations with his notion of the inadequacy of any approach that attempts to provide a definitive explanation of any religious experience.

> The first characteristic of the phenomenology of religion is that its aim is descriptive, not explanatory. Its intent is to relate the phenomenon and its object as is it intended and given in faith, ritual, cult, and myth rather than to its causes, origins, and functions.[55]

According to Ricoeur, each argument regarding glossolalia is legitimate within its limited context.[56] However, each has at least two elements that limit its utility for ecumenical dialog–whether it supports or condemns speaking in tongues. First, those using any argument tend to look at one aspect as if it were *the* definitive characteristic and attempt to interpret the overall experience in light of that single aspect. Second, proponents and critics alike seek not so much to understand or describe the phenomenon, but to explain it, or explain it away, and be done with it.

In either case, each camp makes the erroneous assumption that their particular argument(s) is sufficient to accomplish what they set out to do. While each may succeed in proving or refuting a specific point to their satisfaction, they go only a small way in interpreting an experience that over the last century has grown to be increasingly

---

[54]Werner G. Jeanrond, "Hermeneutics" in Joseph Komanchak, ed., *The New Dictionary of Theology*, Wilmington, DE: Michael Glacier, 1986, 464.
[55]Ricoeur, *Conflict of Interpretations*. 318.
[56]Ibid., 323.

evident in the worship and devotional life of congregations across an increasing number of Christian traditions.

To say, for example, that the experience of speaking in tongues is not uniquely Christian does not disprove its viability for Christian worship. Several practices within Christian worship are also present within non-Christian, occult, or even non-religious settings. Yet, their appearance within these other contexts has not historically been seen as sufficient foundation or dismissing their applicability to the Church, their meaningfulness to the Christian community, or their appropriateness for communicating religious meaning.

Healing ritual, for example, occurs in many non-Christian contexts and is carried out in a variety of settings. The argument has not been made, however, that God does not heal today in a variety of ways, including the miraculous. Neither is exorcism confined to the Christian milieu and occurs within several non-Christian contexts. Still, many modern church leaders and theologians continue to attest to exorcism as a legitimate practice of the Church. Similarly, initiation rites are practiced both within and outside the Christian faith, but that, in no way, diminishes their legitimacy or efficacy for Christians. Each of these—healing, exorcism, and initiation rites—has a distinctly Christian character when practiced by the Church. They are symbolically focused on the person of Jesus Christ and transmitting the Christian understanding of redemption through His atoning work on Calvary. Each has special significance for Christian believers, no matter what they mean in another context.

The same is true of the symbolic nature of tongues within Christian worship and personal devotion. Christian believers who practice speaking in tongues have a decidedly Christian understanding of the experience devoid of any non-Christian milieu association. They do not see themselves in communion with all people who practice glossolalia. Instead, they perceive themselves as, specifically, in communion with other Charismatic Christians everywhere throughout the church age who share or have a shared appreciation of the presence of the + in worship and personal spirituality.

Given a purely Christian understanding of glossolalia as a starting point, there remain several stumbling blocks to an ecumenical understanding of the experience among Christians. To begin, the limited classical Pentecostal *insistence* that the Bible portrays speaking in tongues as *the* initial evidence of Holy Spirit baptism stifles ecumenical dialog. In any case, Pentecostals fail to make a convincing case on this point, for three reasons.

First, Scripture never explicitly identifies speaking tongues as *the* initial evidence of Holy Spirit baptism. Jesus promised his disciples that the outpouring of the Spirit would come with an infusion of supernatural power to accomplish the work of witnessing to the efficacy of his life and ministry. According to his prophetic words, speaking in tongues was among several signs that would follow Spirit-filled believers along with the abilities to withstand physical attack, cast out demons, and work miracles.[57]

Second, inferences from New Testament depictions of Holy Spirit baptism do not exhaust the entire history of the outpouring of the Holy Spirit during the earliest period of the Church. Presumably, only the five most spectacular episodes were reported in the text of Scripture,

---

[57]Mark 16:17. This proclamation of Jesus is problematic from an ecumenical stand point, however, in that while most within Evangelical Christianity, including Pentecostals, take these as genuine words of Jesus, they are found in a portion of Scripture which many Christians who utilize historical-critical method contest as not being from the original manuscript documents, but as a later addition to Mark's gospel.

and only in three of these is a direct reference made to speaking in tongues.[58]

Third, other evidence of Holy Spirit baptism, such as increased love for God, the Church and for the people of God, increased efficacy in ministry and evangelism, increased piety and religious devotion, and an increase in the exercising of the other spiritual gifts, have been recorded throughout history. Lacking evidence of at least one of these other signs, speaking in tongues, in and of itself, may be spiritually superficial, and of limited benefit to the Christian community.[59] Seymour insisted, for example, that a surer sign of Holy Spirit baptism than tongues is love.[60]

Even within Pentecostalism, the debate over whether speaking in tongues is *the* or *an* initial evidence of Holy Spirit baptism remains; as does ambiguity about just what is meant by *initial* evidence. Those within the tradition, who support the term "the" are quick to point out by this that they do not mean that it is the *only* initial evidence or even the most important evidence. [61] This is certainly true among the growing number of Charismatic and Neo-Pentecostal adherents whose backgrounds have been outside traditional, classical Pentecostalism. These discussions point out the failings in attempting to read the Acts passage regarding Pentecost with too narrow a lens.

---

[58] The three passages are Acts 2; 10:45-46 and 19:6. Two other passages (Acts 4:31 and 8:14-24) only insinuate that glossolalia was present.

[59] Which is explicitly Paul's point in the I Corinthians 13 passage.

[60] William J. Seymour, "To the Baptized Saints," Apostolic Faith (Los Angeles), 1:9, June-September 1907, 2.

[61] In *Church of God Distinctives*, Ray H. Hughes speaks of tongues as the initial, *outward, physical* evidence of the Baptism of the Holy Spirit, suggesting that there are other initial *internal, non-physical* evidences. 21.

Another stumbling block is the belief held by many Christian detractors that glossolalia only occurs in highly ecstatic, emotionally charged, out-of-control circumstances. Margaret Poloma refutes this contention by reminding us, "supernatural does not necessarily mean out of control."[62] Samarin declares that glossolalia is not abnormal; it is only anomalous or uncommon, departing from run-of-the-mill speech.[63] And, Ervin further refutes the tie of glossolalia to excessive emotionalism by noting that what generally distinguishes the Christian experience of glossolalia from similar phenomena in the non-Christian or non-religious context is the "very aspect of rational and voluntary control."[64]

In any case, an insistence on reading the phenomenon of glossolalia as a hysterical, over emotive response to some stressor is a major impediment to its use within the wider Christian community. However, exposure of those within the broader Charismatic circles has gone a long way in laying to rest the stereotypic reading of the phenomenon as the only possible context in which is it operable.

Applying an Ecumenical Hermeneutic

In applying ecumenical principles to glossolalia, both proponents and critics must lay bare their ideological suppositions. Barriers to dialog stem from the limitations of applying any one of the existing dogmatic positions (especially those held by denominational hierarchies) regarding the validity of tongues, their appropriateness for

---

[62]Poloma, 72.
[63]Samarin, 228.
[64]Howard M. Ervin, *Spirit Baptism: A Biblical Investigation*, Peabody, MA: Hendrickson Publishers, 1987, 135.

Christian worship, and their relevancy for Christian unity as if they were the entire essence of the experience of glossolalia.

The first temptation that could table the development of an ecumenical understanding of glossolalia is stressing implications of the experience for the individual. Such singular focus on its importance—or problem—for the individual believer, local congregation, denomination, or at the most, for Pentecostal, Neo-Pentecostal, and Charismatic Christians is inimical to an ecumenical dialog for at least two reasons. First, while the individual is presumably the conduit through which any manifestation of the Spirit's presence is made, such manifestation happens within a socio-spiritual context that is facilitated by the openness its members have to these experiences.[65] Secondly, while certain psychological or socio-cultural dispositions influence whether an individual will be open to glossolalia, they are more likely to engage in glossolalia or accept it as valid if they have been exposed to the experience through involvement with groups that practice it.

Individualistic, parochial interpretations of glossolalia significantly inhibit exploration of its potentially broader implications and leave its potentially unifying force largely untapped. Through such lenses, those who stand outside of a specific psychological/socio-spiritual mold, or who have limited exposure to glossolalics, may consider the chasm too wide to mine for its ecumenical implications. For its such potential to be realized, then, we must acknowledge both its possible individual and corporate meanings. More importantly, we must acknowledge and be willing to explore the multiple meanings—historical, socio-cultural, and socio-political—that a spiritual phenomenon can have.

---

[65] See Margaret Kelleher, "Liturgy: An Ecclesial Act of Meaning" in *Worship* 59 (1985) 482-497, for an understanding of the interaction between individual and corporate action in signifying meaning in worship.

To unleash the potential power of glossolalia as a force for ecumenism, the phenomenon, and its scriptural referents, must be approached with a hermeneutic that releases the experience from these limited, parochial interpretations—or "conflict of interpretations"[66]—that posits it as either/or and rather than both/and. Opening the experience to multiple interpretations can shape new points of engagement for the contemporary church, rather than limiting it as the symbol of a specific Christian community or as an interpretation of a scriptural narrative with a single possible meaning.

Moreover, narrow individualistic interpretations are problematic even in classical Pentecostalism, since not all adherents experience speaking in tongues. Only a fraction of those who believe that the experience is legitimate regularly engage in it.[67] Even as speaking in tongues is regularly evident in Charismatic worship, individualistic interpretations of the phenomenon can have negative consequences. When such understandings prevail, the social or spiritual status of glossolalics may be elevated above others within the group, placing attention on the individuals rather than on the Holy Spirit's work. Tongues speakers can be seen as more pious and deserving of the "gift" of the Holy Spirit, though God distributes this gift as God wills.

Broader understandings do not in any way undermine important benefits that accrue to the individual engaged in glossolalia. Even though Cutten declares that "(i)t would be difficult to find a more

---

[66]Ricoeur deals explicitly with this type of hermeneutical problem in *The Conflict of Interpretations.*

[67]According to Poloma in *New Pentecost,* one estimate from the Church of God (Cleveland, TN) a major Pentecostal denomination, indicated that only 60% of its adult adherents claimed to have the baptism of the Holy Spirit with the initial evidence of speaking in tongues.

useless gift" (and)... "at no time has it been of practical value,"[68] proponents are quick to point to specific individual benefits. Among them are reminding the individual of the nearness of God[69] and intensifying the sense of the presence of God.[70] As a vehicle for personal communication with God in prayer and praise,[71] it opens the believer to a deeper experience of the other gifts of the Spirit by signaling a point when the believer's faculties are fully yielded to God and God's power.[72] Further, glossolalia allows the Christian believer to pray in situations where, for even the most intellectual or articulate among us, words fail to communicate the depth of feelings either of joy and exaltation or loss and grief.[73]

Kilian McDonnell points out that speaking in tongues has often been experienced as a "catalyst or trigger" that "opens the soul to a new dimension of life in Christ."[74] As Lutheran Charismatic leader, Larry Christenson expresses it,

> ... the essence of a number of testimonies from charismatic Christians... is that the experience of speaking in tongues has intensified the sense of the presence of God (so) that the word of God has become more

---

[68]Cutten, *Speaking in Tongues*, 237.

[69]Samarin, 11.

[70]Larry Christenson, *Speaking in Tongues and Its Significance for the Church*. Minneapolis: Bethany Fellowship, 1968, 14.

[71] Josephine Massyngeberde Ford, Cyril Williams, and Dorothy and Kevin Ranaghan also see this as an integral element of glossolalia. See Ford, "Toward a Theology of Speaking in Tongues," 274; Ranaghan and Ranaghan, *Catholic Pentecostals*. New York: Paulist Press, 1969, 206; Williams, "Strange Gifts" in Mills *Speaking in Tongues*, 73.

[72]Poloma, 72

[73]Idem.

[74]Kilian McDonnell, *Toward a New Pentecost for a New Evangelism*, New York: Seabury Press, 1976, 50.

contemporary, believable: Christ the Lord has become more real—in a word, faith has been strengthened.[75]

Nevertheless, except for its use for private devotions, personal benefits could have implications for the public worship of the community. When a communal interpretation is employed, the experience takes on a more powerful meaning. For when the Spirit speaks through an individual, the Spirit is perceived as speaking to the entire gathered community. No one is left untouched by the encounter. Even the skeptics who hear it must acknowledge that something has happened, that somehow God has been present.

Proponents contend that within the congregation, glossolalia adds a new dimension to corporate worship as an audible reminder of the activity of the Holy Spirit and God's presence and power.[76] For them, it is an arresting sign to the unbeliever, hopefully attracting attention to the gospel message to be preached in the vernacular.[77] For some, it marks the demarcation point between the sacred and profane in corporate worship and signals a shift of attention from the individual to God.[78]

What is neglected in these discussions, however, is an understanding of the genuinely communal importance of glossolalia as a foundation for developing an ecumenical hermeneutic of the

---

[75]Larry Christenson, *Speaking in Tongues and Its Significance for the Church*. Minneapolis, Dimension Books, 1972, 14.

[76]Poloma, 72.

[77]See Donald Gee, 201. It is important to note here that it does not take the place of the preaching of the gospel message in the vernacular, just as the Latin Mass made room for a homily in the vernacular, since as the Apostle Paul clearly points out, praying in tongues (in the Spirit) does nothing for my intellectual, cognitive understanding.

[78]Samarin provides insight into the dual aspects of the spiritual import of the tongues in corporate worship. See *Tongues of Men and Angels*, 10-11.

experience. All the benefits ascribed to the individual or congregation could stand within an ecumenical gathering of believers who were open to a new interpretation of the phenomenon and who were willing to approach it within an ecumenical hermeneutic. In signaling or intensifying that sense of God's presence, whether the utterance comes through one person or a few individuals, all within that setting who were open to such an interpretation could share in the wonder of the nearness of God to each of those gathered.

If there were an area where words fail, it is in attempting to pray adequately for unity in the church. So much is at stake, the tasks seem so large, the barriers appear overwhelming, and the possible places of agreement seem so few. We bring our agendas to the ecumenical table; our demands and prejudices are with us. We pray within the confines of those demands that God would somehow change the people with whom we interact. We pray that God would help them see our side and understand us. And, we pray that God would straighten out what is wrong in their doctrine—that we might be one. But what if the Spirit were allowed to provide a different agenda—to pray through us about what is necessary for ecumenism?

Josephine Massyngberde Ford understands that the communal dimension of tongues is as important as the personal dimension.[79] She sees the importance of Peter's speech to the gathered crowd in the Pentecost passage with its reference to the pronouncement of the prophet Joel as indicative of these communal aspects of the outpouring of the Spirit.

Ford, contends that the Apostle, Paul, sought to correct this lack of understanding of the communal aspect of tongues in the Corinthian

---

[79] See Josephine Massyngberde Ford, "Toward a Theology of Speaking in Tongues," *Theological Studies* (January 1, 1971), 25-26.

episode.[80] There, each person saw the possession of the gift of tongues as an opportunity to outshine others within the community, rather than to contribute to the building of community. They had missed a critical point about what the use of all the gifts brings to the community. They failed to understand that what the Spirit expressed through the individual was, explicitly, meant to increase Christian unity. For as Paul states in his letter to the Ephesian church, the gifts of the Holy Spirit, including tongues, are for,

> *... equip(ping) the saints for the work of ministry, for building up the body of Christ, until we all attain to the unity of the faith and of the knowledge of the Son of God, to mature manhood, to the measure of the stature of the fullness of Christ...[81]*

The ministry of reconciliation that Paul addresses in II Corinthians 5:18-19[82] gives a further basis for our modern understanding of the Christian community or ecumenism. In that passage, he declares that the ministry of reconciliation is incumbent upon all believers and is a part of our identity as Christians—"God was in Christ reconciling the world to Godself."[83] So we should be engaged not only in reconciling the world to God, but reconciling the divergent members of the Church—the Body of Christ—to each other through whatever means the Spirit makes available. And, these means may be different in different ages, because they are as the Spirit wills at any given time.

---

[80] I Corinthians 14.
[81] Ephesians 4:12-13
[82] In Corinthians, he specifically addresses abuses of the spiritual gift of speaking in tongues within public worship of the local congregation.
[83] II Corinthians 5:19.

Tongues may have been an inappropriate or unnecessary ecumenical tool during the first sixteen centuries when there was essentially one Church and everyone spoke the same liturgical language.[84] Further, immediately after the Reformation, there was a general understanding of what constituted the Church and worship since there were only three or four major divisions. But must that necessarily mean, as some suggest, that this gift is hereafter to be forever silent? In our age, with its proliferation of Christian denominations and the modern bent toward individualism, intellectualism, and disbelief, renewed interest in spirituality can serve as an equalizer and a medium for reconciliation.

Jürgen Moltmann appreciates this aspect of Charismatic renewal, arguing that "the gifts [or] charismata (including tongues) are seen by Paul as connected with the building of the community of Christ's people."[85] He further argues that any individualistic carries the danger of disengagement from the problems of social justice in the world that God so loved and the possible collapse into a world of "religious dreams."[86]

Surely, any process of conciliation requires speaking a common language or at least speaking about what is common in our faith experience. It demands, therefore, a language that transcends constricting denominational structures or doctrinal stances to promote a collective understanding of what is essential to Christian faith and

---

[84]Some scholars, including Laurentin and Baer, have suggested that the Latin language used in the mass served the same function as tongues during this period, signifying the distinction between the sacred and the profane as well as the presence of God.

[85]Jürgen Moltmann, *The Spirit of Life: A Universal Affirmation*, Minneapolis, MN: Fortress Press, 1992, 183.

[86]Ibid., 186.

what is needed to bring about Christian unity. The language must be devoid of special interest and open to bringing fresh insight into long-standing problems within the ecumenical movement.

Existing interpretations of the Acts 2 passage exemplify what is at the heart of what is divisive about existing interpretations of glossolalia. Pentecostals have historically reduced the passage to the affirmation of their practice of seeking the initial evidence of speaking in tongues as a sign of Spirit baptism. They viewed it as and vindication for speaking in tongues in public worship and private devotions. Their critics, as we have seen earlier, have dismissed these singular interpretations on numerous counts.

Either approach looks to the passage for answers to specific questions: "What is the initial, biblical evidence of the baptism of the Holy Spirit? How will one know when he or she has been filled with the Spirit of God?" If Pentecostals go to the passage with only this question in mind, they can take from it only one possible answer. If they do not nuance the question, for them, there can be no nuancing of the answer. If we see no other implications because we approach the passage with a hermeneutic of validation, we see any other interpretation as missing the point. So as we enter ecumenical dialog, if we fail to grasp the possibility of a broader interpretation and chafe at the idea of it being more than the sign of Holy Spirit baptism, the rich implications of our encounter with the divine as a reconciling encounter are left untapped.

But, what if the passage is approached for all it can say about speaking in tongues within the Christian experience? And, what if (realizing the limitations imposed by a singular reading) the value of the experience is laid open to alternative interpretations? Might there be more present in the scene that unfolds in Jerusalem on that day and regularly within Pentecostal/Charismatic spirituality and worship, than a cursory reading provides? Might there be, as Ricoeur suggests, other meanings and a "plentitude of symbols"[87] within the passage? Might the phenomenon of glossolalia be seen beyond the one-sided symbolism of initial evidence of Spirit baptism? Yet, in the variety of interpretations—and misinterpretations, we must seek meanings that add to, rather than take away from, the move toward ecumenical dialog.

What is called for, in the words of Elizabeth Schussler-Fiorenza, is a deliberate "re-reading" of the passage and the phenomenon[88] through the eyes of Christian unity. The focus must be on what the Spirit was attempting within the disparate communities that made up the fertile ground for the first Christian evangelism campaign and is attempting in those that make up the dis-unified institution that is the contemporary church. We cannot find elements of unity where there are none. But, we must be intentionally open to inferences pointing in that direction wherever they may be found.

Suenens concurs that rereading Acts within the ecumenical contexts allows us to discern the intersection of the Charismatic and ecumenical movements. He says specifically,

> ... We have to reread Acts—together—... to steep ourselves in the faith of the first Christians for whom the Holy Spirit was a primordial and personal reality... By

---

[87] See, for example, Paul Ricoeur, *The Symbolism of Evil,* translated by Emerson Buchanan. Boston, MA: Beacon Press, 1986 or *The Conflict of Interpretations: Essays in Hermeneutics.* Evanston, IL: Northwestern University Press, 1974.

[88] See Elizabeth Schussler-Fiorenza, *In Memory of Her: A Feminist Theological Reconstruction of Christian Origins.* New York: Crossroad Publishing Company, 1990.

> looking at the experience of the Spirit from this vantage point... we will be... restored to our native land, to our common virgin birthplace, where it is easier to rediscover the meaning of Christian brotherhood and of the fellowship of the Holy Spirit that was once its very soul.[89]

Multivalent readings of the text and phenomenon suggest two important points for the ecumenical project. First, glossolalia is a sign of God's presence among his people directing them towards unity. Secondly, it is a metaphor for the Church's empowerment by the Spirit to bring about the essential unity of the kingdom of God. Both require further exploration.

What exactly does Acts 2 suggest about the sign of God's presence? What was the strange occurrence that is described by Luke in such detail? Prophetic utterances were not completely foreign in the historical perspective of these religious Jews who gathered at Jerusalem from all over the Empire to keep the Feast of Tabernacles.[90] There had been a long history of ecstatic prophets proclaiming the majesty and judgment of God throughout Israel's history.[91] But there had not been many tongue talkers—at least not recorded in Scripture or their secular history—so this occurrence was strange. It arrested the attention of everyone (both Jew and Gentile) assembled in the proximity of the

---

[89] Leo Joseph Cardinal Suenens, in *Ecumenism and Charismatic Renewal: Theological and Pastoral Orientation*, Ann Arbor, MI: Servant Books, 1978, 28.

[90] The Jews who came to Jerusalem, came to observe this Old Testament Feast. The term "Pentecost" was not used by them. It only took on significance after the account of the Upper Room episode gained wide acceptance within the New Testament community.

[91] For example, King Saul had been given to ecstatic outbursts so much so that the saying was coined among his subjects "is Saul among the prophets?" More recently, John the Baptist had made an appearance in the Judean Wilderness.

motley group and allowed them to hear a clear message of the awesomeness of God.

God was in their presence, speaking their language. God was speaking not past them or above them, but *to* them. Whether it was a miracle of speaking or hearing,[92] they all heard in their tongue, "the wonderful works of God." Everyone in the vicinity, everyone in earshot, no matter what language they spoke, no matter what culture they represented, could discern a clear message of the sovereignty and providence of God. The passage is clear that there were people there from almost every part of the then-known world—devout men—representing different regional interpretations of the Jewish faith. The passage also is clear that they were there to celebrate a common heritage, though it may have looked different within the various diasporic communities. They had different ideas about what it truly meant to worship the one true God, based on their regional Jewish traditions. Yet they all, somehow, heard those in the Upper Room speak of the awesome works of God. And this common experience reminded them that, somehow they were all—despite differing traditions—Jews. And, further, it situated them in a place together to be open to the message that followed. The arresting noising of God's presence among them provides a starting point for engaging in dialog about God's new project. For they shared at least one thing—the experience of that presence among them.

And it is this shared spiritual experience that—at least for the moment—puts contemporary believers on an equal spiritual footing and provided a starting place for the dialog. For together they can say, "Yes, we do worship in diverse ways, and we do come from diverse

---

[92]Simon Tugwell, *Did You Receive the Spirit?* New York: Paulist Press, 1972, 73.

places, but didn't we all just hear and experience God in our presence, telling us of his marvelous works. What should our shared response be?" And thus each one is drawn into the discussion. The possibility of a united community opened up.

The metaphor of empowerment of the church to bring about unity comes from the reading of the Pentecost passage as antidotal to the Tower of Babel paradigm.[93] Whether taken literally or allegorically, the Tower of Babel is the place where language is viewed as a disunifying force and a means of separating nations. The paradigm exemplifies misunderstanding generated by disparate interpretations of the meaning of tongues and an understanding of the importance of language for building or destroying community. Babel represents language used to divide people into separate communities, just as the various attempts to explain the phenomenon of glossolalia has kept the church divided for centuries. It represents communities unable to communicate with and understand each other because of their loss of a common language. Further, it represents the disruption of a project that required people to be in constant communication with each other

The spiritual implications of the Babel project—a challenge to God's sovereignty and authority, as well as communal implications—the prospect of community building are evident. Because the common language was destroyed the project was disrupted, and with it, the endeavor of community building based on rational rather than spiritual strategies was discredited. In the years between Babel and Pentecost, no medium for rebuilding that community and re-establishing that communication had been completely adequate to bridge the gulf between the Jews and Gentiles. Elements were evident—in the Torah,

---

[93] See Genesis 11:1-9. Rene Laurentin is one scholar who sees this as a viable interpretation of glossolalia. See *Catholic Pentecostals, 59.*

in the ceremonial Law, in the prophets' messages of the universal concern of God for all nations.[94] But these had proven inadequate to break down barriers of otherness built partly through the misuse of language.[95]

The Pentecost passage stands as a reversal of this Babel scenario and the basis for an ecumenical understanding of tongues. In this second instance, language has the potential for becoming a unifying, community-building force since, again, all who were there from the variety of nations heard them speak the same thing. They all heard them speak "the wonderful works of God." As the mystical experience unfolded, each group, despite their linguistic or cultural differences, experienced the mediation of the divine. In this encounter, God's presence was so powerfully felt that diversity found a second place to the shared experience. At that moment, no one sensed their difference as alienating them from the other.

In this event, language was not used to challenge God's authority, but to acknowledge God's majesty. This time, they heard and understood, not incoherent jabber, but attestation of the mighty works of God. They shared in the common experience as either a speaker or hearer without barriers of nationality, culture, language, or allegiance to any Jewish sect limiting their potential for hearing about God's great works.[96] Within this interpretive scheme, what was important is what

---

[94] The theme of God's universal love in prominent in such prophets as Amos, Joel, Jonah and Zephaniah, for example.

[95] The episode in Judges 12 between the men of Ephraim and Gilead over the pronouncement of "Shibboleth" or "Sibboleth" exemplifies how language was used among the various Hebrew tribes to establish rather than break down barriers.

[96] Various scholars estimate that those present spoke at between twelve and fifteen different languages or dialects.

glossolalia tells us about God. It speaks of God's project of reversing the Tower of Babel paradigm through the experience of Pentecost. The words of God that each heard the Spirit speak in his language were words of reconciliation.

Even here, however, the miracle of glossolalia brought with it only the potential for building community. The decision about whether to participate in the experience either as speaker or hearer was an individual one. Some hearers perceived its ecumenical potential—discerning the presence of God and its unifying power. But others heard it as pure gibberish, supposing the speakers to be drunk. They chose to view the entire episode as a drunken, ecstatic, orgy.

Historically, much of the exegesis of this passage focuses on the ecstatic experience of the worshipers rather than on what was being accomplished. So, again, we can miss what the passage and phenomenon have to say to the modern church. Sympathetic readers, who use narrow lenses, take from their encounter with the passage a picture of some fantastic, one of a kind, never to be repeated, encounter with God. In a spectacular occurrence, reminiscent of one of Hollywood's most ambitious epic depictions, the wind blows, fire descends from heaven and alights on each worshiper's head. Since no modern, enlightened person has had such an encounter, many dismiss this as mythical (in the Biblical sense); not completely untrue but with only limited direct relevance to the Church today. Along with this dismissal, the ecumenical potential is dismissed.

Beginning with the Charismatic movement and the entrance of glossolalia into Neo-Pentecostal churches, a theology of glossolalia began to broaden the lens of interpretation of the passage and phenomenon and make evident the ecumenical potential of glossolalia. This Charismatic movement itself has been characterized by some as a major ecumenical force.[97] And within it, genuine rapprochement began between divergent camps when large numbers of Pentecostals and Neo-Pentecostal/Charismatics shared a similar experience of what the Holy Spirit was already effecting within their separate traditions.[98] That the movement has touched every major denomination in the Christian community speaks of its potential to foster a new ecumenical spirit. As Charles Colson, president of Prison Fellowship International characterized it:

> When historians examine and record this era in church history, they will doubtless note the singular contribution of the Pentecostal/ Charismatic movement toward unity in the Body.[99]

Hints of the ecumenical potential of glossolalia are evident when believers from many Christian traditions share the common experience that regularly brings them together to bear witness to what the Holy Spirit is affecting in their sister churches. Another evidence is that entirely new parachurch organizations have sprung up in which participation has little to do with denominational distinctions, but whose sole unifying element is an appreciation for charismatic worship including glossolalia and the other gifts of the spirit[100]

---

[97]For a concise, excellent synopsis of the Charismatic movement's contribution to ecumenical dialog see Suenens, *Ecumenism and Charismatic Renewal*.
[98]Kilian McDonnell, *Toward a New Pentecost.* Collegeville, MN: The Liturgical Press, 1974, 50.
[99]Charles Colson and Evelyn Vaughn, *The Body: Being Light in Darkness.* Dallas, TX: Word Publishing Co., 1992, 111.
[100]Among these are organizations such as the Society for Pentecostal Studies founded in 1971. Its members include (with a large number of classical

The classical Pentecostal camp has not always been appreciative of the impact of the Charismatic Renewal. The fact that Charismatic believers were the first to begin to formulate a theology of Holy Spirit baptism and speaking in tongues drew sharp criticism from some segments of the former community who felt that the newcomers lacked the historical astuteness to make a meaningful contribution to the discussion. But, Pentecostals have begun to concede to their Charismatic brethren and sisters that there are additional individual and corporate benefits of the experience itself. Encounters with Charismatic believers have led to small refinements or dramatic changes in Pentecostal worship including the incorporation of written liturgies, wider use of vestments, and more openness to scholarly training of clergy and lay leaders. These refinements point to even more appreciation for what Charismatic and Pentecostal groups have in common, and have cracked the ecumenical door a little wider.

There is also evidence of movement from the other side. In early Catholicism, the ability to speak in a strange tongue or to understand it when spoken by another was seen as one of the symptoms of demonic possession. However, today Catholic Charismatics see their movement as a part of the fulfillment of Pope John XXIII's prayer that "the Holy Spirit's wonders might be renewed in our time in all of Christendom."[101] Evidence of greater Catholic openness to the Charismatic Renewal can be summarized in a statement by Suenens:

Pentecostals) scholars from mainline denominations who are themselves Neo-Pentecostal or Charismatic or have invested themselves heavily in the study of Pentecostal culture. Additionally the Full Gospel Businessmen's Association and its sister organization, Women Aglow, provide a venue for adherents from every denomination to come together for charismatic worship including prayer and praise in tongues, praying for divine healing and exuberant singing.

[101]Samarin, 13.

... at its own level it can help to bring Christians of various confessions closer together by offering them, a privileged ecumenical meeting point: 'communion in the Holy Spirit,' a communion which opens them to God and to their brothers.[102]

Conclusion

Formulating an ecumenical interpretation of speaking in tongues requires glossolalics and non-glossolalics determine what the phenomenon has in common with elements of Christian worship and spirituality outside the Charismatic stream. These points of convergence can be used as a starting point for dialog in the broader arena. Ford points out, for example, that glossolalia has much in common with early Catholic mystical experiences such as those reported by St. Teresa of Avila, Bernard of Clairvaux, and Alphonso Liguori.[103] It also has much in common with the modern contemplative prayer movement. Baer contends that glossolalia, like Quaker silence and Catholic and Episcopalian liturgy,

> ... permits the analytical mind, the focused, objectifying dimension of (a person's) intellect to rest, thus freeing up other dimensions of the person, what we might loosely refer to as (the) Spirit for a deeper openness to divine reality.[104]

Like Baer, Samarin sees the compatibility of tongues with other religious symbols, and, especially, with other religious languages,

---

[102] Suenens, *Ecumenism and Charismatic Renewal,* viii.
[103] Ford, "Toward a Theology of Speaking in Tongues," 11.
[104] Baer, 314.

because he says that religious discourse is by nature uncommon. He further contends that glossolalia (like any other religious behavior) can be acquired by any believer and is easier to learn than other "religious language." Just as in liturgy, the Eucharist and the pre-Vatican II, Latin masses, a person is not necessarily saying something intelligible in tongues, he contends, but rather the person is saying something about what he or she is involved in.[105] And sociologist, Margaret Poloma, points out that even the ascetic methods employed by many classical Pentecostals to invoke the baptism of the Holy Spirit and the evidence of tongues is not decidedly different from other ascetic movements willingly embraced by the historic Catholic Church.[106] Efforts at finding and exploiting these places of commonality are well worth the potential ecumenical return they might yield.

Likewise, those outside the Pentecostal/Charismatic stream must allow their Pentecostal/Charismatic brothers and sisters freedom to exercise their charismatic gifts within the context of mixed gatherings. Within these encounters, openness to applying an ecumenical hermeneutic to a shared experience of worship and spirituality and willingness to hear what the Spirit is saying to the Church, about the Church, and about Church unity can only further ecumenical dialog. McDonnell's assertion that what hinders engagement in tongues is a lack of its social acceptability makes it clear that all must come to the table ready to hear from God in new venues. All must be ready to experience the announcing of the mighty works of God through a

---

[105]Samarin, 229-231.

[106]For a comparison of Pentecostal/Charismatic ritual with ritual in the larger church see chapter 8 of Margaret Poloma's, *"You Shall be my Witnesses": Strategies of Recruitment and Initiation,* 157-170.

different avenue, in a different voice and a different language than what is easily comfortable.

Frank Macchia speaks of the ecumenical opportunity to be delivered from the "tyranny of words,"[107] since existing religious language is not only difficult for many to learn, but loaded with potential theological hot spots and booby traps that could potentially sidetrack any attempt at dialog before it begins. Whether this deliverance is entirely possible remains to be seen. However, one is again struck by the pattern set by the Charismatic movement. Within the framework of interfaith Charismatic meetings, people from divergent denominations and traditions come together for worship focused not on what distinguishes them, but what they hold in common—an experience of the Spirit in which individual traditions take second place to a shared experience of the sacred–what they name and interpret as an experience of the presence of God.

Within this shared experience, people coming together to dialog about spiritual matters, believers representing different traditions civilly talk about God, the Church, and its role in the world in a way that formerly would have not been possible. These mutual experiences mark the beginning of grassroots ecumenism between people who previously held parochial views of the Church and who had, therefore, remained within whatever enclave they had been born or reborn into.

After these shared encounters, people go back to their existing congregations, taking with them an appreciation for a Church that is broader than anything they had previously believed and experienced it to be. As they share this appreciation (not only of the Charismatic

---

[107]Frank Macchia, "The Tongues of Pentecost: The Promise and Challenge of Pentecostal/Roman Catholic Dialogue" Paper delivered to 25th Annual Meeting of the Society for Pentecostal Studies, March 1996, Toronto, CN.

experience but also of their encounter with other believers outside their fold) with others in their congregations, this appreciation for the experience—and for other Christians—grows. Out of this exposure, cooperative efforts and cross-pollination of liturgical styles begin to be evident within the church.[108]

As individuals and congregations come to a grassroots understanding of the experience and what needs to be understood at the theological level is not an either/or topology, but a both/and understanding. Glossolalia has the potential for edifying the individual and building up the congregation for the ecumenical task.[109] It is both prompted by the divine and freely initiated by the individual. It is both an evidence of Holy Spirit baptism and a vehicle for prayer and praise, and Christian unity. It is both a miracle of speaking and of hearing–or at least being open to hearing–the awesome works of God in moving His Church toward unity.

Though embracing components of existing ecumenical dialog, an ecumenism of the Spirit engendered by an ecumenical hermeneutic of Glossolalia and supported by openness to tongues as a vehicle for Christian unity could broaden the conversation. First, it would fully incorporate grassroots Christians as well as the theologically and/or scholarly elite in the discussions. Doing so would eliminate much of the elitism of ecumenical dialog based on intellectual, spiritual, or other self-interest. For it is among these grassroots communities that such interaction has already begun, and those within this segment of the community have much to add. Further, without their participation,

---

[108]Cross pollination involves such elements as gospel music and more free form choirs in Catholic and Episcopal masses, while Pentecostal congregations embrace more liturgical forms and vestments.
[109]See Ricoeur, 318.

ecumenism remains a largely intellectual undertaking with little import for the local church.

Secondly, such ecumenical dialog would involve the entire body of Christ, not just specific already engaged segments. All Christian traditions that accept the deity and centrality of Christ must be invited to the table. Evidence of its potential breadth can be attested to by the unbounded reach of the Charismatic renewal in which no segment of the church remains untouched. While fundamentalist traditions that deny the validity of modern glossolalia would, almost by definition, exclude themselves from such dialog, even this arena has not remained totally outside the spreading Charismatic Renewal.[110]

The Neo-Pentecostal movement has been embraced by many denominations in which ever-larger proportions of congregations are open, if not encouraged to embrace the glossolalia in public worship and personal devotions. Many church leaders who previously rejected the experience as either un-Christian or not viable for the contemporary Church have a new openness to it.

Suenens correctly points out that the Charismatic renewal is different from most post Reformation renewals. Earlier renewals

---

[110] The latest group touched by the phenomenon are Southern Baptists whose fundamentalist stance made them most resistant to such renewal. The appearance of Charismatic phenomenon (including tongues) in some Southern Baptist congregations has led to a crisis in which churches have been asked to leave the convention. A rigidly fundamentalist stance is found in the Statement of Faith of Washington Bible College that, "We believe the sign gifts of the Holy Spirit, such as speaking in tongues and... healing, were temporary and speaking in tongues was never the common or necessary sign of the baptism... of the Holy Spirit.." Perspective applicants must sign this statement or are ineligible to graduate, though allowed to matriculate. However, such a Southern Baptist stalwart as Jerry Falwell has made public concessions to the Charismatic movement by involving their speakers in television broadcasts and making alliances with these leaders on projects of common interest.

(included the early Pentecostal movement on the issue of tongues) tended to carry with them, a confessional exclusiveness that isolated them from other segments of the church. However, in the Charismatic Renewal, a substantially similar event occurring in most Christian churches and denominations provides the common ground for dialog.[111]

He is, again, correct that it is not coincidental that the impulses for the ecumenical movement and the beginning of the modern Pentecostal came to fruition during the same decade.[112] However, it took the openness of the Charismatic Renewal to set the stage for an ecumenical hermeneutic of what had been held as a Pentecostal experience.

---

[111]Suenens, 21.
[112]Ibid., 22.

Limited Liberty: The Myth of Women's Freedom in Ministry in the Early Pentecostalism

How lovely on the mountains are the feet of him who brings good news, who announces peace and brings good news of happiness, who announces salvation[1]

Some observers have characterized Pentecostalism as essentially "women's religion" because of the greater proportion of women than men who have historically been perceived as participating in the movement.[2] However, the story of the role of women within Pentecostalism has been one of mixed experiences. From the beginning, women were attracted in larger numbers than men and took on roles from bench members and worshippers to Bible teachers, evangelists, and pastors. Further, a cursory examination provides examples of women's leadership from the beginning of the movement. In those earliest years, there appeared to be almost absolute freedom for women to pursue whatever course they felt God was leading them to follow. In keeping with the sect-type pattern identified by Max Weber, women ministers within early Pentecostalism enjoyed a greater degree of freedom than their contemporaries in most other branches of the Christian church–except their Holiness forerunners.

According to Weber, new religious movements in the formative, sect, stage depend for leadership on charismatic, rather than hierarchical or institutional, structures. These groups, therefore, allow room for women—and others who are often overlooked—to take on leadership roles. As these groups grow more formalized, however,

---
[1] Isa 52:7.
[2] Lawless, *God's Peculiar People: Women's Voices and Folk Tradition in a Pentecostal Church*, 6.

structures come into place in which charismatic leadership is "routinized" into more traditional patterns that marginalize women's leadership.[3]

Before World War I, while many sociologists of religion still classified the Pentecostal movement as a sect,[4] women were given "limited" liberty to pastor churches, serve as missionaries, preach, teach, exhort and carry out other areas of ministry as was needed and as they desired. With some restrictions, they were given not only autonomy in carrying out their ministries as they saw fit, but they also had a role in denominational governance and leadership. Though even this initial freedom was more perceived than real, that historian, David G. Roebuck asserts that women were so prominent in early Pentecostalism… that even some Pentecostals lamented "the effeminacy of our present ministry."[5] Due in part to attitudes such as this, this apparent degree of freedom lasted only a few years and quickly gave way to numerous formal and informal restrictions on women's leadership in most Pentecostal bodies.

As the movement neared the end of World War II, it attempted to gain a sense of respectability and take on more of the characteristics of middle-class denominations—whether mainline or Evangelical—including greater curtailment of the role of women. Though women were still free to preach and exhort, leadership and governing roles

---

[3] Max Weber, *Sociology of Religion*, translated by. E. Fischoff. Boston: Peabody Press, 1963, 103-105.

[4] Some classified Pentecostalism among the cults. See for example, Fauset, *Black God's of the Metropolis*: *Negro Religious Cults of the Urban North.* Philadelphia: University of Pennsylvania Press, 1944 and Miles M. Fisher, "Organized Religion and the Cults," *Crisis* 47:1 (January 1937), 8-10.

[5] David Roebuck, "Loose the Women" *Christian History* Issue 58, 17:2 (1998), 39.

became more limited and women's ministry and leadership within these bodies grew to look more like the hierarchical patterns they once denounced in mainline bodies.[6]

As Pentecostalism passed the mid-century point, the degree of women's freedom and access to leadership began to lag behind that offered in more liberal denominations that had begun to respond to the changing social climate. In part in reaction to this modernist trend, restrictions became more pronounced and leadership roles grew even more limited.

Today women clergy within classical Pentecostalism find themselves in a precarious situation in which they lag began women in most other denominations—whether liberal or conservative—except fundamentalist Evangelicals. However, the current situation represents a continuum—not a break with an earlier pattern of limited freedom. For the correction to this pattern, therefore, we must return to the roots of the problem. These roots were built into the fabric and foundation—the woof and the weave of the movement. So let us turn back and identify the unfortunate trends that land us Pentecostals where they are today.

Women in Parham's Faith Healing Movement

Charles Parham organized his Bible school in Topeka Kansas to "fit (both) men and women to go to the ends of the earth to preach."[7] He ordained women, as well as men, and commissioned them to ministry. Many of these women and men assisted Parham in his evangelistic campaigns throughout the country. Under his leadership,

---

[6] See Charles H. Barfoot and Gerald T. Sheppard. "Priestly vs. Prophetic Religion: The Changing Roles of Women Clergy in Classical Pentecostal Churches" *Review of Religious Resources* 22:1 (1980) 2-17.

[7] Roebuck. "Loose the Women," 38.

a woman is credited with ushering in the entire modern Pentecostal movement when shortly after midnight on January 1, 1901, Agnes Ozman became the first person to speak in tongues publicly with the understanding that it was the initial evidence of Holy Spirit baptism.[8] Ozman had attended T. C. Horton's Bible School at St. Paul, Minnesota, and A.B. Simpson's Bible School at New York City and for some time had been attending Parham's school,[9] while she was doing home mission work. But after her solo, historical contribution to the early movement, she moved into obscurity as it grew and spread, even as she continued her work as a peaching evangelist.

One significant woman to emerge from Parham's ministry was Anna Hall who played a significant role in the connection of Parham to the Azusa Street Revival. By 1904, Hall was conducting successful meetings for Parham throughout the Midwest in such cities as Joplin, Missouri, and Lowell and Lawrence, Kansas, and sometimes shared the revival duties with him. In August 1906 she reported that she was one of the persons Parham sent to Azusa Street in response to a telegram he received from Seymour telling of the power falling in Los Angeles and asking for additional help and she was shortly involved in arranging his visit. She became an active participant in the early evangelistic outreach from the revival.

Mabel Witter Smith Hall was another woman who was close to Parham. In 1905, the young widow taught school during the day, but in the evenings, she worked on his team from the first few weeks of his

---

[8] "When The Latter Rain First Fell: The First One to Speak in Tongues." In *The Latter Rain Evangel*, (January 1909), 2.

[9] Agnes Ozman, "Personal Testimony of being the first person to Receive the Holy Ghost at "Stones Folly" in Topeka, Kansas. (January 1, 1901), Printed in *The Apostolic Faith* (April 1951.) https://www.apostolicarchives.com/articles/article/8801925/173171.htm.

revival meetings. That year, the evangelist brought Smith, as part of his group, to Zion City, Illinois, to hold a revival. Though he was certainly the leader in these meetings, he allowed Smith and others to preach. Yet, even after visiting Azusa Street, Smith's loyalties remained with Parham and by 1907, Smith had migrated to Massachusetts and was attempting to arrange for him to hold a revival meeting.

Parham operated on a hierarchical, individualistic model that precluded anyone but himself from having too much of the spotlight. Neither men nor women were given too much liberty within his ministry.

The immediate results of Parham's work were rather sparse. It fell to one of his disciples, William J. Seymour, the largely self-educated former slave to head the revival that began relatively insignificantly among "disinherited" washerwomen and maids but grew to encompass a worldwide outpouring of the Holy Spirit that now touches the lives of millions. At his side were several women who became significant for the growth of Pentecostalism.

The Azusa Street Mission–Establishing a Pattern of Women's Limited Involvement

The 1906 Azusa Street Revival–one of the main beginning points of the modern Pentecostal movement is both an excellent example of the limited liberty afforded women throughout the movement and the foundation for this pattern of limitation on women's leadership and ministry. Women played a prominent role in Seymour's ministry and the Apostolic Faith Mission that grew out of it.[10] It was a woman who

---

[10]For a detailed account of the role women played in the Azusa Street Revival see, Douglas, *For Such a Time as This* and James S. Tinney, "William J. Seymour: Father of Modern Day Pentecostalism," *Journal of the*

introduced Seymour to the distinctively Pentecostal doctrine of tongues as initial evidence of Holy Spirit baptism. A woman was the catalyst for the move of Seymour's ministry to Los Angeles. Women were prominently evident in every aspect of the leadership of the Azusa revival and the local church that grew out of it. And, finally, women were important in moving the Pentecostal message from Azusa Street across the United States and around the world.[11] An overview of women's involvement with the revival leads one to conclude that the impact of the Azusa Street meeting would have been greatly reduced had women not been involved.

Women's roles in bringing the revival to pass began to unfold several months before the meetings got underway. Several of these women did not come to Azusa Street as novices, but had experience in ministry as pastors and evangelists throughout the country. Not only Lucy Farrow but Neely Terry had been acquainted with Charles Parham's ministry in Houston, where Farrow had already received the experience of speaking in tongues.[12] As pastor of the church Seymour attended in Houston before he began attending Parham's Bible School in 1905, Farrow holds an important, yet often overlooked, place within Pentecostalism.

It was Farrow who introduced Seymour to the doctrine and experience of the baptism of the Holy Spirit with tongues as initial evidence. Farrow asked Seymour to serve as interim pastor while she traveled to Topeka, Kansas to serve as governess for the Parham

---

Interdenominational Theological Center 4 (Fall, 1976), 213 - 225.

[11] *Like as of Fire* provides a running account of the exploits of these women as they traveled throughout the country and around the globe and filed reports back to the mission in their personal letters and testimonials.

[12] Valdez, A. C. *Fire on Azusa Street,* Costa Mesa, CA: Gift Publications, 1980, *18.*

family. As such, she had been allowed to listen to his lectures on the baptism of the Holy Spirit at his Healing Home and Bible School. On later returning to Houston (probably when Parham relocated his ministry there), she resumed the pastorate of her church. It is here that Seymour heard her speak in tongues in a worship service. When he asked Farrow about her experience, she explained what she had learned from Parham about the doctrine of initial evidence and subsequently introduced Seymour to him.[13]

After Seymour went to Los Angeles, Farrow followed him to assist in teaching at the Bonnie Brae Bible study and stayed on to work beside him as a teacher at the Azusa Street Revival. She regularly spoke of her Spirit baptism experience at Holiness conventions, and after leaving Azusa Street, she established a church in Norfolk, Virginia, then traveled as a missionary to Africa.[14]

Neely Terry was a Los Angeles resident who belonged to Julia Hutchins' small Holiness Church. Terry had met Seymour while visiting Farrow's church in Houston. On returning to Los Angeles, she convinced her pastor and congregation to invite Seymour to Los Angeles to serve as associate pastor. Though he only preached one sermon in that church before being locked out, it was this invitation orchestrated by Terry that brought Seymour to that city.[15]

---

[13] Farrow's and Seymour's early relationship is detailed in Susan Hyatt, "Spirit Filled Women" in Vinson Synan, *The Century of the Holy Spirit: 100 Years of Pentecostal and Charismatic Renewal.* Nashville, TN: Thomas Nelson Publishers, 2001, 245-246.

[14] Untitled articles, *The Apostolic Faith*, 1:1 (Sept, 1906), 1; 1: 2 (Oct, 1906), 3 (7); 1:11 (Oct, 1907-Jan, 1908), 1 (4-5) in Fred T. Corum and Rachel A Hayes Sizemore, ed., *Like As of Fire: Newspages from the Azusa Street World Wide Revival.* Washington, DC, Mid Atlantic Regional Press, 1991) 1.

[15] Tinney, "William J. Seymour: Father of Modern-Day Pentecostalism," 218.

Of the twelve elders initially appointed to handle the finances, correspondences, and examination of persons for ordination at the Azusa Street Mission, six were female. Five of these six—Lucy Farrow, Ophelia Wiley, May Evans, Clara Lum, and Florence Crawford—were to play important roles in the upstart movement. Little is known of the extent of Phoebe Sargent's—the other woman member—involvement in the mission though she probably worked as a street evangelist

Within the revival, white women from various walks of life joined black washerwomen and household servants with no formal education or theological training. Both were allowed to exercise their ministry gifts in speaking in tongues, interpreting glossolalic messages, prophesy, intercession, and leading worship. They could also be found at the altar praying with new converts and seekers for the baptism of the Holy Spirit or healing. Indeed, one element that drew public attention, and secular press derision, was the regular sight of white men, many of them somewhat prominent clergy or community members, kneeling before praying black women to receive Holy Spirit baptism.

Howard Goss, a later Assemblies of God leaders who was a key figure in expanding the Pentecostal movement into the lower Midwest had previously rejected the idea of initial evidence but progressively accepted Pentecostal doctrines. He heard Farrow speak at the Azusa Street revival, and, according to his diary, as he witnessed fellow mourners lining up to have her pray for them, being touched by the Holy Spirit, and speaking in tongues,

> his heart became hungry again for another manifestation of God... So I went forward that she might place her hands upon me. When she did, the Spirit of God again struck me like a bolt of lightning; the Power of God

surged through my body, and I again began speaking in tongues[16]

Further evidence of the inclusion of women in the leadership of the Mission comes from an interesting sidelight. Disenchanted by the racial attitudes of some entrusted whites, Seymour later incorporated into the formal structure of the Mission's governing documents directions that his successor should be a person of color. He did not specify a *man* of color, leaving room for the possibility that the person could be a woman. Perhaps the greatest evidence of Seymour's prophetic understanding women's role in the revival and movement it helped birth is reflected in a statement in *The Apostolic Faith* in which he said,

> [b]efore Jesus ascended to heaven, holy anointing oil had never been poured on a woman's head; but before He organized His church. He called them all into the upper room, both men and women, and anointed them with the oil of the Holy Ghost, thus qualifying them all to minister in this Gospel. On the day of Pentecost, they all preached through the power of the Holy Ghost. In Christ Jesus there is neither male nor female, all are one.[17]

Florence Crawford[18] received the baptism of the Holy Spirit at the revival. At the same time, she reportedly was instantaneously healed

---

[16] Ethel Goss. *The Winds of God: The Story of the Early Pentecostal Movement (1901-1914) in the Life of Howard A. Goss*. Hazelwood, MO: Word Aflame Press, 1977, 56.

[17] Apostolic Faith 1:10, (1907), 4.

[18] "Florence Crawford" in Stanley M. Burgess, Gary Magee and Patrick H. Alexander. *Dictionary of Pentecostal and Charismatic Movements*. Grand Rapids, MI: Zondervan Publishing House, 1988, 229. See also, Apostolic Faith Mission, *An Historical Account of the Apostolic Faith, a Trinitarian-*

from a variety of serious ailments. Some credit her as being the first of all the Azusa Street converts to take the Pentecostal message on the revival circuit. Beginning in Los Angeles, she moved on to principal cities of the Northwest including Portland, Oregon and Seattle, Washington. Then she went east to Minnesota and Canada.

Crawford was instrumental in distributing *The Apostolic Faith*, the weekly newspaper that chronicled the events of the revival to Seymour's supporters. Eventually, she and Seymour disagreed regarding his decision to marry and Crawford took the newsletter mailing list and moved to Portland, where she set up her Apostolic Faith Church.

Besides serving on the governing board of the Mission, Clara Lum served as its secretary and co-editor (along with Seymour) of *The Apostolic Faith* from 1906 to 1908. She, like Crawford, objected to Seymour's marriage to Jennie Evans Moore, left the mission, and moved to Oregon. She corroborated with Crawford in taking the national and international mailing lists to Oregon, leaving Seymour with only the Los Angeles list. She later joined up with Crawford and the two began republishing the newsletter, at first without acknowledging that Seymour was no longer affiliated with the newsletter.[19]

Ophelia Wiley preached, from time to time, in the Azusa Street meetings and authored articles for *The Apostolic Faith* newspaper. She

---

Fundamental Evangelistic Organization: Its Origin, Functions, Doctrinal Heritage, and Departmental Activities of Evangelism. Portland, OR: Apostolic Faith Pub. House, 1965.

[19] "Clara Lum" in *Dictionary of Pentecostal and Charismatic Movements*, 561.

also went out as part of evangelistic teams to spread the news of the revival in various cities throughout the northwestern United States.[20]

Though not initially an elder at the Azusa Street Mission, Jennie Moore was one of the women present at the Bonnie Brae prayer meetings. Moore was one of Seymour's earliest adherents[21] to experience the baptism of the Holy Spirit with tongues and reportedly "played the piano in the Spirit" without prior training.[22] She went with Seymour to Azusa Street and was an active participant in the revival and the leadership of the church. She and Seymour later married and during his lifetime, she worked alongside him in leading the mission. Upon his death, she served as pastor of the then dwindling mission.[23]

Several women were among the many evangelists and missionaries who took the Pentecostal message around the globe. Ivey Campbell preached revivals throughout Ohio and Pennsylvania and won many to the Pentecostal experience.[24] Louisa Condit went first to Oakland, California, and then to Jerusalem.[25] Lucy Leatherman first went to Oakland, California, then to Colorado Springs and Denver, Colorado, and New York before embarking as a missionary to Israel, Egypt, and

---

[20] See, for example, Ophelia Wiley. "Sermon on a Dress," *Apostolic Faith* 1:2 (Oct, 1906), 2; "Spreading the Gospel," *Apostolic Faith* 1:3: (Nov, 1906) 1.

[21] Some report her to be the first person to speak in tongues in the Bonnie Brae Street prayer meeting, before the group moved to Azusa Street. See "Jennie Evans Moore" in *Dictionary of Pentecostal and Charismatic Movements*, 628.

[22] Ted Olsen. "American Pentecost: The Story Behind the Azusa Street Revival, the Most Phenomenal Event of Twentieth Century Christianity," *Christian History,* Issue 58, Vol 17 No 2, (1998), 14.

[23] Ibid.

[24] "Report from Ohio and Pennsylvania," *The Apostolic Faith* 1:6: (Feb.-Mar., 1907), 5 (29) and "Pentecostal Meetings," *The Apostolic Faith*, 1: 8 (May, 1907), 1 (33).

[25] "Missionaries to Jerusalem" in *The Apostolic Faith* 1:1 (Sept 1906), 2 and "Missionaries' Farewell" in *The Apostolic Faith* 1:2 (Oct 1906), 4.

Palestine,[26] and later to Chile and Argentina. By the time she visited Argentina, she had joined with the Church of God and is credited with helping to establish the denomination in that country.[27] She reportedly received the gifts of xenolalia[28] and was able to speak Arabic.[29]

Julia Hutchins took the message to Africa. Hutchins had been the pastor whose church originally objected to Seymour's identification of tongues with the baptism of the Holy Spirit and locked him out of the church. She was later won to his point of view and participated in the Azusa Street Revival. After affiliating with Seymour's mission for a while, she traveled as a missionary, preaching in several U. S. cities before taking the Pentecostal message to Liberia.[30]

Often missionary couples were sent out from Azusa Street both as revivalists within the United States and as missionaries to other countries. The women in these couples not only accompanied their husbands to play the expected role of a supportive minister's wife. They were also actively involved in every aspect of ministry, including preaching, teaching, and praying for the sick and converts. Among those couples listed as moving out from Azusa Street were a Hispanic couple, Abundio and Rosa Lopez who worked the altars at the Azusa Street revivals and held street worship services in the Hispanic sections of Los Angeles.[31] G.W. and Daisy Batman went as missionaries to

---

[26] "Missionaries to Jerusalem" in *The Apostolic Faith*, 1:1 (Sept, 1906), 4.

[27] Mickey Crews, *The Church of God: A Social History*. Knoxville, Tennessee: University of Tennessee Press, 1990, 96.

[28] Xenolalia is believed to be an actual existing language or dialect rather than an unknown or "heavenly" tongue.

[29] "Missionaries to Jerusalem" in *The Apostolic Faith*, 1:1 (Sept., 1906), 4.

[30] "Testimonies of Outgoing Missionaries" in *The Apostolic Faith 1:2* (Oct., 1906), 1 and "Speeding to Foreign Lands" in *The Apostolic Faith*, 1:5 (Jan., 1907), 3.

[31] "Spanish Receive Pentecost" in The Apostolic Faith 1:2:4 (8) and

Liberia.³² Samuel and Ardell Mead had been Holiness missionaries to Liberia for twenty years before they came to Azusa Street. After attending services there for a while and testifying to having had the Pentecostal experience of Holy Spirit baptism, they returned to the mission field in that country and helped spread the Pentecostal message.³³

But, again, this picture of complete disregard for the traditional boundaries of gender is not the complete picture. Within the freedom that appeared to be available to women as Azusa Street, limitations on leadership were encoded into the structure of the revival and the mission church that housed it. These increased as the work took on more structure. Though Seymour was indebted to several women for making him aware of the Pentecostal experience, getting him to Los Angeles, and supporting his ministry, his reluctance in granting them complete equality in leadership was evident in two moves in the developing structure of the Azusa Street Mission.

First, in developing its doctrinal statement, Seymour clearly distinguished the roles that men and women were to play in worship and ministry leadership. According to the *Doctrines and Disciplines of the Azusa Street Mission of Los Angeles California*, he insisted that "all ordination must be done by men... Women may be ministers but not to baptize or ordain in this work."³⁴ The liturgy he developed for the ordination service indicates that all laying on of hands and prayer within such service were to be done by "elders." This might suggest

---

"Preaching to the Spanish" in *The Apostolic Faith* 1:3 (Nov. 1906), 4 (12).

³² *The Apostolic Faith,* 1:4 (Dec. 1906), 4.

³³ The Meads sent several short testimonials back to the Azusa Street Mission and these were published in *The Apostolic Faith* Vols 1-5.

³⁴ Seymour *Doctrines and Disciplines of the Azusa Street Mission of Los Angeles California,* 91.

that already the levels of ministry to which women might aspire were somewhat restricted. Might it have been that later, the rank of elder, and then bishop, was restricted to men, with women relegated to lower ranks with less ministerial authority?

Secondly, though there were women members of the loosely organized administrative board that operated in the earliest days of the missions, for the most part, the increasingly tighter structure during the latter years excluded women in other positions of authority. Four of the five people who served on the board of trustees that finally had legal responsibility for the governance of the mission were men. The only woman on that board was Seymour's wife. So while one eyewitness applauded the dissolution of racial division,[35] evidently the gender line may have been strongly bent but, clearly, was never broken.

Later Developments

The Azusa Street Revival lasted eight years. By its end, in 1914, there were more than twenty denominations and several hundred congregations in the United States that identified themselves as Pentecostal and held to the doctrine of tongues as the initial evidence of Holy Spirit baptism. In the twenty years following the close of the revival, several more denominations and several thousand congregations had been established in the United States and several hundred existing congregations had jumped into the Pentecostal camp. The Pentecostal message had circled the world with women, as well as men, communicating that message, building up congregations, and establishing denominations.

---

[35] Frank Bartleman, *How Pentecost Came to Los Angeles*. Los Angeles: F. Bartleman, 1925, 54.

As the movement formed into denominations, the degree of freedom granted women varied widely, but generally was less than was experienced at Azusa Street. A small number of Pentecostal denominations granted women what Mark Chavez defines as full clergy rights—ordination, and all the rights and privileges inherent with it—from their inception.[36] According to Chavez, denominations that grant full clergy rights are those in which there is "... formally open access (for women) to all religious positions within a denomination."[37] He distinguishes that from denominations that grant women ordination or license them for ministry but bar them from holding institutional leadership.[38]

The bodies founded by women—Mary Magdalena Tate's Church of the Living God the Pillar and Ground of the Truth, "Mother" Florence Crawford's Apostolic Faith Mission, Bishop Ida Robinson's Mount Sinai Holy Church of America and "Sister" Aimee Semple McPherson's International Church of the Foursquare Gospel, Eva Lambert's Saint Marks Holiness Church, Carrie Gurry's King's Apostles Holiness Church[39] appeared to make a way for women's freedom. Yet, even within these groups, the liberty of all women to

---

[36] In *Ordaining Women: Culture and Conflict in Religious Organizations* (Cambridge: Harvard University Press, 1997), 2-3.
[37] Ibid., 3.
[38] Ibid.
[39] Other denominations founded by women include Eva Lambert's Saint Marks Holiness Church, Carrie Gurry's King's Apostles Holiness Church Beulah Count's Greater Mt. Zion Pentecostal Church, Mozella Cook's Sought Out Church of God, Magdalene Mabe Phillips' Alpha and Omega Pentecostal Church of God of America, Helen Smith's Cainhoy Miracle Revival Center, Florine Reeds' Temple of God and Lulu Phillips' Glorious Church of God in Christ. In many of these cases, the second and subsequent generations reverted to predominantly male leadership.

fulfill their God-given call was problematic. Tate's group was rife with nepotism so that almost all of the women she promoted to positions of leadership were in some way related to her (either by blood or marriage).

McPherson exercised a great deal of freedom in building what is probably the fourth largest Pentecostal body in the Western hemisphere. She involved women in numerous ministries in her church. Yet she had convoluted relationships with most of the women in her life and never allowed a woman to preach in her coveted pulpit when she was present at the 5,000 seat Angeles Temple. Further, except for Mt Sanai, and some denominations that evolved from Tate's original group, the leadership of these groups fairly reverted to men.[40]

The Pentecostal Holiness Church, begun as a Holiness body in 1895 and later incorporated Pentecostal doctrinal statements into its polity, was among the first of the Pentecostal bodies to grant women full ordination.[41] As late as 1935, the Open Standard Bible Churches, founded as an offshoot of McPherson's denomination, also accorded women this privilege as part of its founding polity.[42]

Many Pentecostal denominations granted women "limited ordination" or credentialing, without giving them governing authority. For example, in the United Holy Church, out of which Ida Robinson

---

[40] Within Mount Sinai, women prevailed as Presiding Bishop through six tenures. However, since 2001, leadership of that denomination has been male. In Tate's case, one of the three bodies that succeeded the parent denomination was headed by her daughter-in-law, Mary Frances Lewis Keith–The House of God, Which is the Church of the Living God, the Pillar and Ground of the Truth Without Controversy, Inc., and the current presider is a woman. Within the other two bodies, leadership immediately was succeeded to a male. However, subsequently women served as presiders at various times.

[41] Chavez., 16.

[42] Ibid., 17.

came, women were licensed or ordained to the ministry but received little material or spiritual support from male colleagues who only tolerated them. Robinson left the United Holy Church to form her denomination specifically because of limitations put on women's ministry and the decision of the United Holy Church to cease publicly ordaining women.[43]

Even where the official dogma concerning women clergy was egalitarian, the unofficial tradition concerning "male-only" leadership was often not different from other traditions. While the official doctrine or polity opened all levels of ministry to all called and qualified men and women, this unofficial tradition held that only men could hope to hold top positions, such as presiding elder, district overseer or superintendent, bishop or other denominational head.[44] As the Pentecostal historian, Edith Blumhofer, succinctly states:

> (P)entecostals have always had reservations about women who departed from their 'proper sphere.' Like their other evangelical contemporaries, (P)entecostals authenticated the witness of 'prophesying daughters.' They also usually denied women any institutional presence. Pentecostal women flourished as evangelists and missionaries, but not as pastors or denominational leaders. They enjoyed cultural authority but not institutional voice.[45]

---

[43] See Estrelda Alexander, *Limited Liberty: The Legacy of Four Pentecostal Women Pioneers*. Cleveland, OH: Pilgrim Press, 2008.

[44] McKenzie, Vashti M. *Not without a Struggle: Leadership Development for African American Women in Ministry* (Cleveland, OH: United Church Press, 1996), 35.

[45] Edith Blumhofer, "Women in Evangelicalism and Pentecostalism" in Melanie May, ed. *Women and Church: The Challenge of Ecumenical Solidarity in an Age of Alienation*. New York, Wm. B. Eerdmans Publishing Co., 1991, 4.

The unofficial tradition also held that women, generally, could not hope to be appointed as pastor of congregations of any substantial size or with any real degree of financial stability.

The original freedom women held—even when limited—resulted from several factors. First, Pentecostal eschatology supported the premillennial understanding popular in this period. Early Pentecostals saw their revival as a fulfillment of the biblical prophecy of Joel 2:28:

In the last days, saith the Lord, I will pour out of My Spirit on all flesh, and your sons and your daughters shall prophesy.

With this understanding, the Pentecost scenario, in the second chapter of Acts, constituted the "former rain" and the contemporary Pentecostal revival constituted the "latter rain"—the culmination of the "age of the Spirit." Early Pentecostals understood themselves, therefore, as living in the last days, before the return of Christ, when he would establish his millennial kingdom of peace on earth. They held the belief that anyone who was not a born-again Christian (not "saved") at Christ's return would be doomed to eternal hell and, therefore, They felt an urgent need to enlist everyone in the business of winning as many souls for God's kingdom as possible. Therefore, women, as well as men, were enlisted to preach the gospel and win souls in whatever venue they found themselves.[46]

Second, Pentecostals saw individuals as empowered through baptism in the Holy Spirit to do ministry as the Spirit willed.[47] They felt that God would supernaturally anoint both men and women, without regard to social class, education, or other formal preparation, to do this ministry. For them, proof of one's called lay in their testimony to such

---

[46] Barfoot and Sheppard. "Priestly vs. Prophetic Religion", 9.
[47] Ibid., 4.

a call and the perceived fruit of a Spirit-empowered ministry, rather than in any formal ecclesiastical system of selection or promotion. Those who demonstrated preaching skill and the ability to convey a convincing gospel message, and who displayed charismatic ministry gifts such as divine healing, exorcisms, or the ability to win others to salvation were enlisted into action. So, it did not matter whether they were women or men.[48] Bartleman, an early Azusa Street participate and one of the first historians of the movement, originally seemed sympathetic to women's voices reporting that,

> ... we had no pope or hierarchy... we had no human program; the Lord Himself was leading... The Lord was liable to burst through anyone... All seemed to recognize this and gave way. It might be a child, a woman, or a man. It might be from the back seat or from the front. It made no difference.[49]

Third, in the early days of the movement, this understanding of ministry was coupled with a general disdain for hierarchical church structures and denominationalism, at least at first. Such disdain resulted in what appeared to be radical egalitarianism.[50] Summarizing the effects of the egalitarian understanding fostered in the ministry of women within Pentecostalism, an early Pentecostal periodical editor wrote:

> Obscure men and women, boys and girls, have received from God definite calls... A marked feature of this "latter day" outpouring is the Apostolate of women... They did

---

[48] Ibid., 7-8.
[49] "Pentecost: 'Women's Emancipation Day?'"
[50] Barfoot and Sheppard contend that "to many mainline denominations, (Pentecostalism) was scandalous because of its shift away from traditional patriarchalism, 3.

not push themselves to the front, God pulled them. They did not take this ministry on themselves, God put it on them.[51]

Yet competing theologies complicated the picture for women ministers in the early movement. Preaching women modeled themselves after their Holiness predecessors, who also took their authority from the Joel 2:28 passage and held to a radical concept of the equality of the sexes in ministry. However, restorationist elements within Pentecostalism sought to return the church to "New Testament simplicity and purity." For some, an essential rudiment of this restoration was the felt need to follow Pauline restrictions on the ministry of women within the church.[52] Scriptural prescriptions such as "let the women keep silent in the church" or "I suffer not a woman to usurp authority over a man," or "the bishop must be the husband of one wife" were used as literal justification for limiting the ministry of women.

These few apparent strictures on the involvement of women in congregational leadership seemingly provide the needed biblical warrant for the imposition of second-class status on the ministry of women. They also serve to mask the patriarchal and androcentric motivations that penetrate every level of Pentecostalism. Unfortunately, the adoption of stances based on this rigid eisegesis

---

[51] *The Weekly Evangel*, 131 (March 18, 1916), 6.

[52] Pauline proscriptions include I Corinthians 14:34-35, "Let your women keep silence in the churches: for it is not permitted unto them to speak; but they are commanded to be under obedience as also saith the law. And if they will learn anything, let them ask their husbands at home: for it is a shame for women to speak in the church." They also include 1 Timothy 2:11-12, "Let the woman learn in silence with all subjection. But I suffer not a woman to teach, nor to usurp authority over the man, but to be in silence."

provided an effective weapon for silencing the challenge that generations of gifted and anointed women might pose to the status quo. Many Pentecostal women took, and in many cases still take, their cues for acquiescing to their second-class status from skewed understandings of these passages.

Pentecostals also sought to distance themselves from any association with modernity and "worldliness." These included any ideas about the "new woman" that were coming into fashion just as the movement took off. Pentecostals sought by outward appearance exhibited in dress codes, social constraints, as well as rhetoric, to ensure that there was a recognizable distinction between the modern, "unsaved" world and themselves. They saw the women's movement as threatening the God-ordained social order prescribed in Scripture that represented rebellion against God.

Bartleman's earlier seeming support for the role of women in the movement is betrayed by a later apparent change of heart about the contribution of women. In 1920, fourteen years after the movement began, he asserted that,

> ... men are supporting an effeminate ministry, following women. A female ministry is naturally a weak ministry [w]ith doubtless a very few noticeable exceptions. The character seen in the faces of men of a generation ago is gone. And now we have Flapper Evangelism.[53]

From the movement's inception, Pentecostal women, as well as men, held conservative understandings of women's role within the family and society in tension with an understanding of the freedom and

---

[53] Frank Bartleman, "Flapper Evangelism, Fashion's Fools Headed for Hell," Privately published Assemblies of God Archives.

empowerment imparted to all believers through Holy Spirit baptism. This tension only deepened when the movement sought to align itself more closely with the broader Evangelical community. Like other segments of that community and many segments of the broader society, early Pentecostals believed that the proper place for women was in the home. Married women were expected to uphold the role of submission to their husbands and with the expectation that they would support their husband's ministry. Nonetheless, like other Evangelicals, it made a place for those few, exceptional women who God might choose to use in an extraordinary way.

In some Pentecostal denominations, women desiring to be in pastoral ministry face an unofficial limitation. Leaders generally gave them the freedom to "dig out" or plant new congregations and nurture them to the point of viability. But, they were also encouraged to take on congregations that were at the point of failure and use their gifts of preaching, evangelism, and administration to rebuild them to the point that it became self-sustaining.[54]

Once these newly planted or rebuilt congregations grew to sizeable memberships capable of economically sustaining a full-time pastor— as well as other local church financial obligations—leaders would replace the woman with a male pastor. Leaders then sent the woman to another community to dig out another new work or repair another failing congregation. Over several decades, a woman might start or renew several congregations in this manner, but would never be allowed to take them past this point.

---

[54] David Roebuck alludes to this pattern of deployment in the Church of God (Cleveland, Tennessee) in *Limiting Liberty: The Church of God and Women Ministers, 1886-1996,* Doctoral Dissertation for Vanderbilt University, Nashville, TN, 1999, 125.

Leaders also sent male ministers to plant new churches or bring failing congregations back to a point of viability. They often replaced these men with a new pastor once the planter brought a congregation to a viable point. However, for men who were successful in this endeavor, replacement often meant promotion to a larger congregation—rather than starting all over in similarly dire circumstances.

Two rationales undergirded this limiting thinking. First, some Pentecostal denominations prohibited women from carrying out the ordinances of the church and from conducting the business of the local congregation.[55] These leaders felt that women would not regularly have to do either so long as the congregations were small and struggling. When an occasion arose for carrying out ordinances or conducting meetings, leaders expected and encouraged women to call a male colleague from a neighboring congregation within the denomination.

Secondly, many leaders felt that women could depend on their husband's income or that of some other male relative to provide for their material needs. Therefore, they felt that women did not require the same level of financial support as their male colleagues. Since this was believed to be the case, when a congregation became financially viable, these leaders felt it necessary to give the leadership of the congregation to a male minister who would have to depend on the finances to support his family. They would then send the woman to a new, or smaller, congregation that could not provide adequate support for a full-time pastor.[56]

---

[55] Both the Assemblies of God and the Church of God (Cleveland, TN) took this stance for several years.

[56] Margaret Poloma, *The Assemblies of God at the Crossroads,* Knoxville, TN: University of Tennessee Press, 1989, 110-112.

Women who wished to remain in ministry within existing denominations were faced with accepting these limitations. Those who felt called to pastoral ministry accepted the inequitable life of a perpetual church planter. Others took to the evangelistic circuit, preaching wherever they were asked and supporting themselves on whatever "love offering" they might be offered.

As the movement moved from infancy to adolescence, examples of the stance of various loosely organized bodies and more structured denominations illustrate the mixed situation for women. From Parham's Bible School and Healing Home, Seymour's Azusa Street Revival, and the Apostolic Faith Mission, to the flowering of the earliest denominations, apparent full freedom quickly gave way to limited freedom, then to gradually increasing, formal restrictions on women's ministry and leadership.

The Church of God in Christ

The Church of God in Christ (COGIC) reconstituted itself as a Pentecostal body less than one year after the start of the Azusa Street Revival. Within that body, among the largest Pentecostal denominations in the United States, and the largest African American Pentecostal body in the country, the ministry of women was restricted from the outset. Drawing on his Baptist roots,[57] COGIC founder,

---

[57] The historic Baptist attitude toward women in leadership is similar to that put forth by Southern Baptists today. Women were expected to serve in support positions, not ministerial or pastoral leadership. For an excellent discussion of this context, see Evelyn Brooks Higginbotham, *Righteous Discontent: The Women's Movement in the Black Baptist Church*, 1880-1920. Cambridge: Harvard University Press, 1993.

Charles Harrison Mason, saw women playing a "vital" but distinctive role from men. Within it, Mason,

> ... restricted (women's) influence by preserving the office of pastor and title of preacher for men. Women expounding on Scripture were said to be teaching–not preaching–and they were allowed to speak only from a secondary lectern, not from the pulpit.[58]

According to Ithiel Clemmons, late COGIC bishop, church historian, and Mason biographer,

> By forming a unique church structure (for women)... the denomination harnessed the spiritual fervor, mental acumen, physical energy, and economic potential of its female members while maintaining male authority. As a result, the church cultivated female leadership without alienating the men, took advantage of women's abilities to "plant" new congregations without authorizing them to preach or pastor, and established an auxiliary structure that sustained basic [P]entecostal-[H]oliness church doctrine through periods of strife among the church's male leaders.[59]

As Clemmons euphemistically interprets these limitations, women within COGIC:

Function[ed] in the ambivalent position of shared, but *secondary* authority... preserv[ing] the male dominance that

---

[58] Clemmons. *Bishop C.H. Mason,* 109.
[59] Ibid., 101-102.

conformed the denomination to biblical (sic) imperatives...[60]

Within this formally instituted structure, women could not be ordained but could be licensed as "evangelists" or "missionaries"[61] to preach and teach primarily other women and work in what the COGIC leadership termed these "vital" roles. Women could raise funds for local congregations and the national denomination, direct local, regional, and national women's programs and provide material support for the pastor and his family. During the century-long history of the denomination, this dual structure remains in place, and restrictions on the ministry of women have continued. The exception is that women can be ordained as chaplains to work in military, prison, hospital, and similar institutions.

The Assemblies of God

Within the Assemblies of God, the second-largest Pentecostal body in the United States, women played a significant, but distinctive, role from men from the beginning. When the first General Council of the Assemblies of God met in 1914, in Hot Springs, Arkansas to organize itself into a body, almost one-third of the delegates were women ministers. Though such a large number were present, the body authorized the ordination of women only as evangelists and missionaries, explicitly denying them the right to serve in pastoral

---

[60] Ibid., 109. Emphasis my own.
[61] These terms do not carry the usual connotation of one who goes out to win others to Christ. These women worked inside a local church to support its ministry and that of its pastor.

ministry or any position involving holding authority over men.[62] Later that year, women missionaries serving outside the United States were granted the right to perform funerals, marriages, baptisms, and the Lord's Supper, in case of an emergency and when a man was not available.[63]

In 1917, the General Council dropped distinctions of ordination) and voted that all ordination be "to the full gospel ministry." However, they did not lift the practical restrictions on women's ministry so that (except for missionaries) they still were unable to perform the ordinances (or sacraments).[64] In 1919, that same body restricted the vote to male ministers only,[65] but in 1920, the Council had an apparent change of heart and granted women the right to vote.[66] Women clergy[67] in the United States were given the right to perform the sacraments on an emergency basis in 1922.[68] It was not until 1935, that women were granted full ordination—full clergy rights—without restriction on serving or voting.[69] Even this concession did not materially improve the most women's ministry or reduce the predominance of male leadership at congregational and administrative levels.

---

[62] Minutes of the General Council of the Assembly of God, 1914, 13-16.

[63] Executive Presbytery Minutes of the General Council of the Assembly of God, November 23, 1914, 1.

[64] Minutes of the General Council, 1917, 6.

[65] Minutes of the General Council, 1919, 7.

[66] Minutes of the General Council, 1920, 48.

[67] These women were still considered clergy. They were pastors, missionaries and evangelists. They were ordained, as the men, to the "full gospel ministry." What was withheld from them was the right to perform sacraments, the vote or governance, and the right to participate at any level of institutional leadership.

[68] General Council Special Rule, 1922, 1.

[69] Minutes of the General Council, 1935, 111.

Church of God (Cleveland, Tennessee)

One of the most often quoted statements related to women's early involvement of women in the Church of God (Cleveland, Tennessee)[70] is that "five of the seven founding fathers... were actually founding mothers."[71] This characterization highlights the fact that at the 1898 meeting that saw the creation of the Christian Union (the organization that eventually became the Church of God), the majority of those who form the organization were women. Yet, women have played a decreasing role in the denomination since its beginning. Initially, they were encouraged to serve as evangelists and pastors and to preach and teach the word of God wherever they could. However, again, the leadership of women incurred some limitation from the outset. The story of the Church of God is an example of how such limitations quickly grew and spread.

By the end of its second General Assembly in 1907, reports from individual congregations indicated that the group had more women adherents than men.[72] Though women were frequent speakers and had full voting rights in the early General Assemblies, increasingly more restrictive measures were put in place with every succeeding session. Within a few years, the rights of women to serve in leadership roles within the body were almost entirely reduced to a few highly prescribed functions.

---

[70] The designation, "(Cleveland Tennessee)," distinguishes this body from several other smaller Holiness and Pentecostal bodies that carry the name Church of God – some that have additional identifiers and several that do not.

[71] David Roebuck, Limiting Liberty: The Church of God and Women Ministers – 1886 -1996. PhD Dissertation, Graduate School of Vanderbilt University, 1997, 152-153.

[72] 2nd General Assembly Minutes, 1907 in General Assembly Minutes, 21.

The third General Assembly in 1908 declared that "women who are qualified and feel the call to work should be appointed by the churches" (as pastors).[73] These women were given the title deacon and, appeared to have the same rights and privileges as their male counterparts. Just one year later, in 1909, the fourth General Assembly determined that women should not be ordained since there was a "lack of precept and example in the New Testament" for women's ordination.[74] Further, it was determined, that, at least for the short term, wives of deacons would be considered deaconesses "by virtue of the position and ordination of their husbands."[75] With this move, a woman—no matter what her gifts, talents, or calling—could not become a deaconess unless she was married to a deacon. In 1912, the Assembly decided that women should have no part in the business meetings of the sessions.[76]

The 1913 Assembly precluded women ministers from performing marriages and put forth as official church polity that women could have no part in the business and government of the local congregations.[77] During the 1916 meeting, the Body of Elders was formed. This body was made up of ordained ministers only. It had the responsibility for conducting the business of the denomination

---

[73] 3rd General Assembly Minutes, 1908, 49.

[74] 4th General Assembly Minutes, 1909, 63. This is the same argument maintained by the denomination until 2000, when it finally granted women limited ordination–without full clergy rights. It denied women access to the bishopric–its highest rank of ministry as well as denying them the opportunity to serve in most institutional leadership positions at either the local, regional or national level based on the same argument of lack of precept or example in the New Testament.

[75] Ibid.

[76] 7th General Assembly Minutes 1912, 133.

[77] 8th General Assembly Minutes, 1913, 228.

through the General Assembly. Since only ordained ministers could be a part of this body and vote, this solidified the 1913 motion concerning women not being involved in the business of the denomination, as well as taking the vote away from laymen.[78]

By 1926, the General Assembly decided that there should be different licenses for male and female evangelists. The male license specifically granted men the authority to "establish churches, baptize converts, administer the Lord's Supper, and the washing of saints' feet;" the female license simply authorized a woman to "do all the work that may devolve on her as a prophetess or FEMALE MINISTER of the gospel."[79]

Conclusion

Barfoot and Sheppard's work on the ministry of women in early Pentecostalism places the beginning of the decline of women's leadership after World War I.[80] They rightly attribute the decline, in part, to the move from a prophetic to a priestly movement. As a prophetic movement, anticipating Christ's imminent return, adherents enlisted everyone possible to preach the gospel to a world that might otherwise be doomed. Eager to reach all who were lost, they did not adopt the institutional trappings of gender stratification and denominational hierarchy.

The authors contend that later, as part of a priestly movement, living with the realization that Christ's return may be delayed, Pentecostal leaders sought to bring order to a church that might have

---

[78] 12th General Assembly Minutes, 1916, 242.
[79] 20th General Assembly Minutes, 1926, 109. No explanation of what that work would be was provided.
[80] Barfoot and Sheppard, 9-10.

to endure for several more years.[81] Yet, as demonstrated above, the leadership of women within was in a tenuous state from the beginning and some degree of restriction existed on their ministry and leadership almost from its outset. That degree of restriction varied, depending on the Pentecostal sects or denominations with which they were affiliated.

Scanzoni and Setta rightly identify the beginning of the decline as occurring much earlier than Barfoot and Sheppard suggest. They, like I, see the motions for decline being in place at the movement's inception with the incorporation of "limited restrictions" that resulted in only "limited equality"[82] or limited liberty. They also identify the ambivalence regarding the issue of the public ministry of women that was part of the movement's ethos. Many Pentecostals understood, for example, a woman as being able to be a "spiritual leader" at church but under her husband's leadership at home. Another ambivalent understanding held that women were God's second choice, employed only when a man was not available for a specific ministry.[83]

Many Pentecostal women accepted these understandings and the restrictions to their ministries that came with them. For one reason, as Scanzoni and Setta point out, women who acquiesced to these tenets fared better among their male colleagues than those who were outspoken.[84] Even such women leaders as McPherson and Tate took no public stand on the position of their sisters in the church or society

---

[81] Ibid., 10.

[82] Letha Scanzoni and Susan Setta. "Women in Evangelical, Holiness and Pentecostal Traditions" in Rosemary Ruether and Rosemary Keller, eds., *Women in Religion in America, Vol 3, 1900-1968*. Cambridge, MA: Harper and Row Publishers, 1981, 229.

[83] Ibid.

[84] Ibid.

unless they were pushed to do so. They only responded when their ministry was directly questioned on grounds of gender.

What had started as limited restrictions on the ministry of women grew to be increasingly severe restrictions. Just as women's original limited freedom resulted from several factors, several factors contributed to the gradual decline of women's leadership roles. First, the eschatological, premillennial hope of Christ's imminent return faded with the realization that several years had passed and Jesus had not returned. Secondly, the sectarian, anti-denominational, anti-structural bias of the Pentecostal movement gave way to the realization that some sort of organization was needed if the movement were going to last until Christ did return. Loosely tied sects began to form denominations with written polity and doctrine.

Along with the more pronounced structure came, what Blumhofer describes as, growing "professionalization." One sign of this, according to her, was differing criteria for credentialing men and women for ministry, exemplified in hierarchical ranks of ministry with dual tracks for women and men. Another was the move of ministry from a primarily voluntary vocation to a paid occupation—at least for men.[85] Barfoot and Sheppard characterize it as Pentecostal bodies seeking to pattern themselves after major Protestant denominations.[86]

In 1908, five years after Tate planted her first congregation, and two years into the life of the Azusa Street Revival, Pentecostal women were playing a vibrant, though somewhat restricted, role in the movement. By 1923, two years before McPherson started building

---

[85] Edith Blumhofer, *The Assemblies of God: A Chapter in the Story of American Pentecostalism, Volume I – To 1941*. Springfield, MO: Gospel Publishing House, 1989, 357.
[86] Barfoot and Sheppard, 16.

Angeles Temple, within the Assemblies of God where she had held credentials for five years, the restrictions on women's ministry had begun in earnest. The larger denominations had begun to exclude women from a variety of areas and relegate them to the lower levels of ministry. In 1925, when Ida Robinson's Mount Sinai Holy Church was holding its first convocation and electing her as its first presiding bishop, the Church of God, in which she had previously served as a pastor, had stripped women of most of their ministerial rights.

Though Pentecostal women have persisted in entering the ministry, Barfoot and Sheppard showed that increased restrictions have led to the steady decline in the actual numbers of women who answer the call to pursue public ministry and leadership or has held them from attempting to move beyond the limited roles prescribed for them. In many Pentecostal denominations, that decline, though somewhat abated, continues today.

From Azusa Street to Cleveland, Tennessee: The Shared Legacy of William Joseph Seymour and Ambrose Jessup Tomlinson

Introduction

Within a decade around the turn of the twentieth century, two separate yet powerful movements began unfolding as a foundation for a fresh outpouring of the Holy Spirit and the renewal of the contemporary Christian Church. Both began with eruptions of spiritual enthusiasm in a manner that was exceedingly and abundantly above anything that could have been imagined by their participants. Though separated by ten years and 2200 miles and taking shape in communities as conspicuously different as the congregations they represented, these events paralleled and related to each other in ways that, to the casual observer, might not be obvious. Still, their common heritage and witness have significant import for contemporary Pentecostals.

Both movements involved a defining event that moved them, almost immediately, from near obscurity to having at least some notoriety, and each has reached legendary status within their respective communities. Further, with renewed interest in Pentecostal studies, the contribution of each has been rediscovered and work precedes on numerous fronts to decode their significance for a new generation.

At the forefront of these movements stood two men—one an early heir to leadership, the other the progenitor—who, while not intimately known to one another, shared a vision of a unified body of Christ that contested the racial politics governing the American society of their time. Both worked arduously and advocated continuously to bring their vision to pass. Yet, for one the vision would lay dormant and virtually unfulfilled for most of the twentieth century. For others, the partial fulfillment of that vision would require a change of venue.

Looking closer at the early period of these two movements – the Church of God movement[1] and the contemporary Pentecostal movement, these two events—the 1896 Shearer Schoolhouse Revival and the 1906 Azusa Street Revival, and the two men who stood at their forefront—William Joseph Seymour and Ambrose Jessup (A.J.) Tomlinson—sheds light on Pentecostalism's spiritual heritage of justice speaking and pushes adherents to reflect on what their legacy might mean for the contemporary racial climate within Pentecostalism as well as for the future of the movement. Recovering that heritage could help focus the attention of contemporary Pentecostals on a dynamic center that often seems to get lost among the din of the pursuit of every new spiritual experience that has developed.

The Shearer Schoolhouse Revival

The first of these events, the Shearer Schoolhouse Revival, unfolded in the summer of 1896 in Cherokee County, North Carolina, a part of the Appalachian region of the United States that lies in the westernmost county in the state. The revival was a primarily localized event among white, predominantly Baptist, Methodist, and other Holiness farmers. These believers were joined by others who would become Church of God pioneers.[2] Holiness camp meeting style

---

[1] This includes the parent body, the Church of God (Cleveland, TN), and the Church of God of Prophecy.

[2] See Charles Conn. *Like a Mighty Army: A History of the Church of God.* Cleveland, TN: Pathway Press, 1977, 5-69 for a discussion of the work of these early pioneers.

services were characterized by expressions of ecstatic worship including prayer for divine healing and excited outbursts that participants believed to be an experience of "supernatural joy" that had biblical warrant—a desired, but not requisite, experience. Leaders, therefore, did not promote the experience of tongues-speaking as essential for salvation or a godly life, but rather as a significant blessing poured out on the earnest, sanctified believer.

The relatively short-lived revival experienced its most intense period for approximately ten days with the spiritual afterglow lasting approximately four years. It was hosted in rigorous mountain terrain, difficult to reach for all but the most committed. Consequently, not many outside the members of a small number of local congregations in surrounding counties took part.

During those following years, the intensified desire for personal revival saw a slow, steady increase in the spread of the experience of Pentecostal Holy Spirit baptism within the region—a phenomenon that most did not understand, and many feared as extremism. It also saw increased episodes of fanatical teaching, rigid asceticism, and seeking after ever more emotionally exhilarating, spiritual experiences, to an extent that eventually leaders backed off from its promotion.

Yet, while they did not promote it, these leaders did not renounce their experience of glossolalia and that experience continued to abide within them as they went about their lives and ministries. Significantly, while that revival made little impact beyond the immediate region, the intense personal commitment it engendered spurred several to renew or intensify their evangelistic efforts and to keep its embers burning hotly for another decade before it would again flare into full flames within these same communities. The outgrowth of this renewed enthusiasm was the formation of what would become two denominations– the Church of God (Cleveland, TN) and the Church of God of Prophecy.

The Azusa Street Revival

A little more than half a decade after the turn of the century, in Los Angles, California, people of every race and culture came together for what has been categorized one hundred years later as one of the most significant religious events in modern history.[3] The most intense period of the revival occurred during the first three years. From 1906 to 1909, people came from across the nation and the globe to partake of its spiritual vitality. That revival was characterized by much of the same phenomena evident earlier in North Carolina, except this time the experience of glossolalia—speaking in tongues was understood and welcomed as the unique biblical evidence of Holy Spirit baptism. Those who took part saw themselves as ushering in a new age of the Spirit in which tongues-speaking was one among other "signs and wonders" such as divine healing and prophetic utterances that would become common occurrences. They saw tongues-speaking as biblical evidence that they had been empowered by the Spirit to live a sanctified life and accomplish supernatural ministry for the kingdom of God.

Considerably easier to get to than the mountains of North Carolina, the revival was located in, what has been described by some as, a seedy neighborhood in what was becoming a bustling city. With its population of around 200,000, it was considered one of the most important centers on the country's West Coast. It drew the type of

---

[3] Roger G. Robins Roger G. Robins "Pentecostal Movement," in Daniel G. Reid, ed.; *The Dictionary of Christianity in America*. Downers Grove, IL: InterVarsity Press, 1990, 885.

racial, ethnic, and cultural diversity that would be the diluted hallmark of this dynamic movement for decades to come.

Many of the revival's participants would become prominent leaders in the global Pentecostal movement. Among them would be Charles Harrison Mason, founder of the Church of God in Christ, one of the largest black denominations in the nation; Florence Crawford, a woman who would establish her denomination, the Apostolic Faith Mission; and renown missionary and faith healer, Alfred Garrison (A. G.) Garr. Alexander Boddy, who visited the mission after Seymour's death, would become a leader of the movement in Great Britain.

Gaston Barnabas (G. B.) Cashwell would play a significant role in bringing several Holiness bodies into the new movement. Glenn Cook, who would become a leader among Oneness Pentecostals, at one time had assisted with the publication of *The Apostolic Faith*, the mission's newspaper, answered correspondences, and handled the mission's finances.

Many who did not find their way to Azusa Street were touched directly by someone who had. Others vicariously partook of the heady atmosphere through *The Apostolic Faith*, correspondences with revival leaders, and regular attendees.

With few exceptions, contemporary Pentecostal denominations—whether white, African American, Latino or other race—can either trace their theological roots directly or indirectly to that revival, or pay obeisance to its influence in the development of their theological understanding of speaking in tongues as the initial evidence of Holy Spirit baptism.

The Two Events

Despite apparent differences in the two events, a cursory examination indicates several points of convergence. Both were deeply rooted in the Wesleyan Holiness tradition, and drew on its doctrine of sanctification—going on to perfection and the pure love of God. Both exhibited exuberant worship with ecstatic phenomena, trances, prayer for divine healing, dancing in the Spirit, as well as speaking in tongues. Participants of both groups suffered persecution from their former congregations as well as from other religious leaders and members of the surrounding communities. Further, in diverse ways, participants in both events understood the experience of speaking in tongues as a key element of an empowered Christian life.

There were also points of divergence between the two events. For example, the Shearer Schoolhouse Revival was a localized, Holiness meeting, mostly drawing people from the surrounding mountain communities and remained largely unheralded outside of this small group of committed believers. While exact numbers were not kept of either event, at its height, the Shearer Schoolhouse Revival only reached hundreds. The leadership of this revival was largely white and made up of the white people who populated the surrounding rural countryside. Tomlinson, himself, may have never visited that meeting, but was influenced by its fruit at the Holiness Church at Camp Creek—the beginning of the Church of God movement.

Further, the Church of God (Cleveland, Tennessee), the original progeny of that revival retained its racial homogeneity during its earliest years. Yet, efforts by Tomlinson to introduce more racial inclusive was, reportedly, in part, responsible for his departure from the parent organization to found what would become the Church of God of Prophecy.

The Azusa Street Revival became global fairly quickly. Almost immediately after it was underway, news of the goings-on in Los Angeles spread across the country and globally within a few months. It drew the attention of notable Holiness leaders, many of whom made their way to its doors. That revival lasted approximately eight years. More than one hundred Pentecostal denominations can trace their roots to this singular event that catapulted the movement into national and world prominence. Though Seymour was African American as were prominent figures like Lucy Farrow and Jennie Evans Moore—the woman who would later become Seymour's wife, the revival's leadership not restricted by race or gender.

For both groups, the phenomenon of speaking in tongues was significant, but in different ways. Those at the Shearer Schoolhouse viewed ecstatic worship as the experience of "supernatural joy" that simply sprung up out of religious enthusiasm equal with many phenomena Biblically substantiated, tongues stood at the peripheral of the greater work that God was doing in their midst. Conversely, after its Holiness leaders searched the Scripture for several months, Seymour's mentor, Charles Parham, and his Topeka Bible School students concluded that glossolalia was the initial "Bible evidence" of Holy Spirit baptism. This understanding was adopted by the Azusa Revival participants, and speaking in tongues stood as a central experience of the revival. There the experience was not simply seen as supported by Scripture; it was believed to be biblically prescribed. Seymour, as leader of the revival, would later offer a more nuanced understanding of the phenomenon, seeing tongues as standing alongside the ethical mandate of unity within the body of Christ and love among Christians of all races and more genuinely scriptural evidence.

The Two Men

Importantly, the role of each man within their respective venues evolved differently. Though Seymour stood at the head of Azusa Street Revival, as the movement engendered by that revival grew, his influence waned. So, near its end, he was largely overlooked by those who would ascend to positions of leadership.[4] On the other hand, Tomlinson, who would come into the Church of God nearly a decade after the beginning of this seminal event, would rise in stature to become its first general overseer. After being ousted from the denomination would go on to establish the organization that would become the Church of God of Prophecy.

Both men had been part of the Holiness Movement before embracing Pentecostalism. While neither had had the experience of glossolalia as their ministries began. Both, however, had embraced and experience of sanctification as an essential element of their spiritual development. Seymour had had the experience while with the Evening Light Saints and Tomlinson after coming into the Church of God.

William Joseph Seymour

William Joseph Seymour, the black son of freed slaves, was born in 1870 in Centerville, Louisiana, a community whose pre-Civil War farm economy had been depleted by the war and Emancipation, reducing it to a shadow of its former self and impacting freed slaves as

---

[4] See Estrelda Alexander, "The Color Line was Washed Away in the Blood: William Seymour and the Azusa Street Revival" in *Black Fire: One Hundred Years of African American Pentecostalism*. Downers Grove, IL: InterVarsity Press, 2011, 110-158.

much as former owners. Seymour was born in abject poverty in a social context that circumscribed every aspect of his existence.

Though scholars supposed him to have been either illiterate or completely self-taught, no one is sure how much education he completed. Yet later, the myth of Seymour's illiteracy was put to rest by his detailed sermons and articles in *The Apostolic Faith* newspaper and the doctrinal statements he developed for the Apostolic Faith Mission.

Seymour was probably raised as a Baptist in heavily Catholic and heavily segregated Louisiana. As a young man, he left that area, traveling to the Midwest where he worked a variety of manual labor jobs and embarked on a religious journey that would take him through Methodism to the Holiness Movement where he would find his identity as a preacher. Shortly before coming to Los Angeles, he traveled to Houston, Texas where he encountered Lucy Farrow and, through her, Charles Parham. Through the two of them, he was introduced to the doctrine of initial evidence and the practice of speaking in tongues—two elements that would color his life

Earlier, Seymour's encounter with Daniel Warner's, Evening Light Saints also introduced him to a rigid standard of personal piety. They did not drink stimulants such as tea and coffee. Men did not wear neckties. Women did not wear lace or ruffles. Neither men nor women wore gold jewelry. With the Saints, Seymour claimed the experience of sanctification and was exposed to a level of racial inclusiveness unlike any he had witnessed. The Saints saw interracial worship as a sign of the true church, and black and white races worshipped and ministered regularly in their services. More importantly, they gave racial prejudice a theological critique. Instead of testifying that they were saved, sanctified, and filled with the Holy Ghost, Saints asserted that they were "saved, sanctified, and prejudice removed," and their radical criticism of racism extended beyond the church to the American society.

Ambrose Jessup Tomlinson

A.J. Tomlinson was born in 1865 in Westfield, Indiana. At the age of twelve, Tomlinson had a religious experience in which he heard his name called. When he graduated from grammar school at seventeen, he immediately enrolled in the local Quaker academy, Union High School, in his hometown—a community known for its religious and racial diversity. Notably, Tomlinson grew up in the heart of Evening Light Saints territory The Saints who were influential in God's Bible School that he purportedly attended in Cincinnati, were also influential in Seymour's formation.

His grandparents were Quaker abolitionists who resigned from one meeting to join an anti-slavery meeting of the Society of Friends. His family, like many Indiana residents, were active in the Underground Railroad and boycotted products produced by slave labor. Tomlinson's grounding within the Evangelical wing of the Friends tradition played a significant role in his life as he was raised in an interracial Quaker community and attended camp meeting worship services put on by black congregations.

As a teenager, Tomlinson engaged in Republican party politics. Later, he ran unsuccessfully as county auditor under the banner of the Populist Party (a political movement closely tied to Holiness ideals). After that, he quit politics altogether.

He experienced salvation after a bolt of lightning struck his home during a severe thunderstorm and became active in the local Quaker church founded by his grandfather. Even before he became a minister or joined with the Church of God movement, Charles Conn describes Tomlinson as, a deeply spiritual, educated man who was able in Scripture.[5]

As one of the earliest and most influential leaders in the nascent movement, Tomlinson became acquainted with this body as a young man when it was the Holiness Church. Interestingly, though whether or not he may have irregularly attended those services is uncertain, he did not formally join himself to the growing movement until 1903[6] Even then, he initially showed no urgency in seeking the experience of Holy Spirit baptism with speaking in tongues. Further, while Church of God lay historian, Charles Conn, asserts that several people who would go on to become members and leaders within the Church of God had visited the Azusa Street Revival, Tomlinson did not.

Yet, as his involvement within the budding organization grew, so did his appetite for a deeper spiritual experience. At the end of 1907, Tomlinson invited Azusa Street emissary, Gaston B. Cashwell, the "Pentecostal Apostle to the South" to come to Cleveland to attend the General Assembly.[7] When Cashwell arrived in early 1908, he preached for the Saturday night session and stayed over to visit Tomlinson's local congregation the next Sunday where he preached to him and

---

[5] Conn, *Like a Mighty Army*, 49-53.
[6] Conn, *Like A Mighty Army*, 25.
[7] Vinson Synan, *The Holiness-Pentecostal Tradition: Charismatic Movements in the Twentieth Century*, Grand Rapid, MI: Wm. B. Eerdmans, 1997, 116.

several others. During that visit, Tomlinson received the Pentecostal Holy Spirit baptism.

In 1903, Tomlinson was ordained as a minister in the Holiness Church at Camp Creek, North Carolina.[8] Within a year, he was chosen pastor of the Camp Creek congregation, as well as pastor of three of the four related local groups. The next year, he moved to Cleveland, Tennessee. By 1906, he was acting as the Ruling Elder. He was selected as the general moderator in 1909. This title was changed to General Overseer in 1910. In 1914, he was selected as the general overseer and an agreement was made by the General Assembly that he would continue in that position until God removed him.]

During his tenure, he was an early advocate of racial equity within the movement and his attitude toward race differed markedly from many of his contemporary colleagues in the denomination. As the general overseer, he attempted, to introduce racially progressive measures into its polity and integrate African Americans more fully into the life of the church. Later, as leader of the Church of God of Prophecy, he would insist that the true Church,

> [is] not... made up of white people only, or of colored people only, or of any one race exclusive of all others. But... requires the union of whites, the colored, the browns, the Indians, called the red men, the yellow races—and all under one government, one rule, one faith or doctrine...[9]

---

[8] The early name for the Church of God.

[9] A.J. Tomlinson, The Annual Address to the Twenty-Seventh Annual Assembly—September 7-13, Cleveland, TN, in the *General Assembly Annual Addresses, 1928-1943.* Cleveland, TN: The White Wing Publishing House, 2012, 142.

Tomlinson, was among the earliest white Pentecostals to acknowledge the man he called "Dr. Seamore" (sic) and give priority to the Azusa Street revival as an authentic progenitor of the Pentecostal movement. [10] He would later articulate that a genuine sign of the outpouring [of the Holy Spirit] on the church was its interracial and multicultural appearance.

In his position, Tomlinson often promoted black men and women in the ministry of the church. Before Tomlinson's ouster and the subsequent denominational split in 1923 (a year after Seymour's death), he, several credentialed black men and women as evangelists and black men as bishops (or overseers) within the Church of God.[11]

The Two Movements

Seymour's Pentecostal Movement

Notwithstanding contentions from some contemporary scholars that the modern Pentecostal movement resulted as a direct work of the Holy Spirit, and no one person can be credited as the catalyst for its beginning, the contribution of William Seymour and the early twentieth-century Los Angeles revival he led is so important to Pentecostalism's spread that Charismatic scholar, Peter Hocken asserted,

> ... if the developments associated with Charles Parham had not been followed by the outbreak at Azusa Street, the former would have probably only have been another

---

[10] Ambrose J. Tomlinson. *Last Great Conflict*. Cleveland, TN: Press of Walter E. Rodgers, 1913, 136.

[11] For a discussion of these appointments see, David Michel, *Telling the Story: Black Pentecostals in the Church of God (Cleveland, Tennessee)*. Cleveland, TN: Pathway Press, 2000.

variation on the baptism of the Holy Spirit as a personal experience... hav[ing] no greater claim to validity than many interpretations of individual experiences in Holiness circles.[12]

When news of the outbreak of tongues traveled through the Los Angeles Holiness community, and the committed and curious flocked to see, The saints gathered daily, day and night, for three intense years for worship. These services were radically egalitarian during the height of the Jim Crow era when such meetings were frowned on by society and, in many cases, illegal. Though most worshipers were from the lower and working classes, there was no stratification either by social status, race, gender, or age in involvement or leadership in the services. People of different races and cultures came together to experience this "new religion" and worshiped side-by-side without the constraint of segregated seating evident, even in mixed-race meetings of the period. Men and Women, adults and children, black, white, yellow, and red freely worshiped God and admonished each other to holiness of life through speaking in tongues and interpretation, prophesy, testimony, song, prayer, miraculous signs, and preaching. This degree of racial harmony led Frank Bartleman to make his famous declaration. Another characterization put it more explicitly:

> It was something very extraordinary...white pastors from the South were eagerly prepared to go to Los Angeles to Negroes (sic), to fellowship with them and to receive through their prayers and intercessions the blessings of the Spirit. And it was still more wonderful that these white

---

[12] Peter J. Hocken, *The Glory and the Shame The Glory and the Shame: Reflections on the 20th-Century Outpouring of the Holy Spirit*. Gildford, UK: Eagle, 1994, 53.

pastors went back to the South and reported that they had been together with Negroes (sic), that they had prayed in one Spirit and received the same blessing...[13]

Clearly, Seymour was instrumental in bringing the mission into being and, for sixteen years until his death in 1922, served as its pastor. Though he kept a low profile, he displayed inner strength when needed to handle the myriad of demanding situations arising within the congregation. Frequently, he was challenged to defend not only his position as pastor, but his authority as head of the fledgling movement. As time passed, it became evident that he was, indeed, the leader of the little mission, if not of the revival itself.

As the congregation increased, he introduced more structure, appointing a committee to oversee the congregation's administrative needs, and selecting, credentialing, and appointing people to lead within the congregation. In his *Doctrine and Disciplines of the Azusa Street Mission,* Seymour not only laid out the foundational beliefs of the congregation and its founder, it also detailed liturgies and orders of worship. The doctrinal stances Seymour portrays in the work reflect his early Holiness affiliation, especially with the Evening Light Saints, while his liturgical formulations indicate an earlier tie to Methodism.[14] The breadth of the structure of these liturgies—replete with specific biblical passages, written prayers, and words of institution—show some exposure to, and appreciation of, traditions outside the Holiness or Pentecostal movement. The grammatical structure puts to bed the

---

[13] Walter Hollenweger, *The Pentecostals: The Charismatic Movement in the Churches*. Peabody, MA: Hendrickson Publishers, 1972, 24.

[14] For example, the polity outlined in *Doctrines and Disciplines of the Azusa Street Mission of Los Angeles*, clearly followed the structure used within the African Methodist Episcopal discipline.

lie that Seymour was largely illiterate. It portrays a man who valued education and had at least a rudimentary understanding of complex theological ideas. Within this document, he envisioned the establishment of educational institutions: primary and secondary schools, as well as colleges, universities, Bible schools, and seminaries to train ministers.[15]

While the revival continued, several who came and received their Pentecostal experience moved on to plant congregations that differed from Azusa Street in their more homogeneous racial makeup. As much as possible, Seymour continued a congenial fellowship with these pastors, preaching in their churches when asked and inviting them to preach at the Azusa Street Mission even during his absence. Seymour went as far as organizing a weekly meeting where these leaders could gather for prayer, mutual support, counsel, and Bible study. Many of their congregations grew and expanded at what appeared to be the Azusa Street mission's expense.

As important as Seymour's administrative and spiritual gifts may have been, an often-overlooked aspect of his leadership was his attempt at constructing a Pentecostal theological framework. Articles in *The Apostolic Faith*, as well as writings in *Doctrines and Disciplines*, show, however, that Seymour gradually moved away from insisting that speaking in tongues was the most valid initial visible evidence of Holy Spirit baptism or any insinuation that every Spirit-filled believer had to show such evidence.[16] Instead, he insisted that love was as sure sign of

---

[15] Seymour, *Doctrines and Disciplines*, 84.

[16] See for example, "Is the Speaking in Tongues the Standard of Fellowship with the Pentecost People?" *The Apostolic Faith* 1:12, (October 1907 - January 1908]. In an untitled article in the January 1907 issue of *The Apostolic Faith*, the editor declared. "We have seen missions and churches banded together to stop what they call a "tongues" salvation. But, dear ones, this is not a salvation of

Holy Spirit baptism as tongues, and that without such love tongues was an insufficient sign of the Spirit's indwelling of an individual.[17] Further, for him, the experience of Spirit baptism was not an essential element in conversion, but rather an added blessing or impartation of grace. According to Seymour, therefore,

> When we set up tongues to be the Bible evidence of baptism in the Holy Spirit and fire only, we have left the divine Word of God and have instituted our own teaching…While tongues [are] one of the signs that follows God's Spirit-filled children, they will have to know the truth and do the truth…all God's children… can pray… for an outpouring of the Spirit upon the holy sanctified life and can receive a great filling of the Holy Spirit and speak in tongues. But we don't put our faith on [the gift of tongues] as essential to our salvation[18]

Seymour fully expected that his stand might place him at odds with some Pentecostal brothers and sisters and wrote about that possibility. An article in *The Doctrines and Discipline of the Azusa Street Apostolic Faith Mission, Los Angeles, California* anticipated their objections by proclaiming,

---

tongues. It is in the Blood of Jesus Christ that cleanses from all sin." See also, Seymour, *Doctrines and Disciplines*, 51-53.

[17] Seymour said explicitly that "the baptism of the Holy Ghost means to be flooded with the love of God and power for service, and a love for the truth as it is in God's Word." *Doctrines and Disciplines*, 92. In an article in *The Apostolic Faith* 1:11 (October 1908 - January 1909), 2, entitled "Questions Answered," Seymour responded to the query of "What is the real evidence of that [one] has received the baptism with the Holy Ghost?" by asserting that it was "Divine love, which is charity."

[18] Seymour, *Doctrines and Disciplines*, 9.

> How does our doctrine differ from the other Pentecostal brethren? First, they claim that a man or woman has not the Holy Spirit, except that they speak in tongues… [T]hat is contrary to the teachings of Christ. If we would base our faith on tongues being the evidence of the Holy Ghost, it would knock out our faith in the blood of Christ and our inward witness of the Holy Spirit bearing witness with our Spirit.[19]

He was certain that many had settled for false hope in an outward physical sign without having an inward change in their spiritual condition, that he refuted by asking,

> How do you know when you have the gift of the Holy Ghost? He, the Spirit of Truth will guide you into all truth… The gift of the Holy Ghost is more than speaking in tongues. He is wisdom, power, truth, holiness. He is the person that teaches us the truth.[20]

Seymour's concern was, seemingly, tied to the outworking of Holy Spirit baptism rather than any mechanical, formulaic test of its reception. As Ithiel Clemmons asserts, at the heart of Seymour's pastoral vision w[ere] the principles of [h]oliness and [u]nity.[21]

Following the revival's three-year heyday, the spiritual fervor ebbed and waned for the next four years. Prominent ministers and everyday people visited, and schism and controversy fueled as much by personality conflicts and style as by doctrinal differences, continued

---

[19]Ibid., 51-53.
[20]Ibid., 51.
[21]Ithiel Clemmons, "New Life through New Community: The Prophetic Theological Praxis of Bishop William J. Seymour of the Azusa Street Revival," Address delivered at Regent University School of Divinity, April 18, 1996.

to plague the congregation. Each ensuing controversy took its toll until, in the end, the Azusa Street Mission was a small African American congregation that remained committed to the Pentecostal message but had lost its influence in the broader movement.

As the revival drew to an end, around 1914, there were more than twenty denominations and several hundred congregations in the United States identifying themselves as Pentecostal and holding the doctrine of tongues as the initial evidence of Holy Spirit baptism. Within twenty years after the close of the revival, the Pentecostal message had been heard all over the world.

For several years after the end of the revival, Seymour remained in demand as a speaker among a small circle of supporters. But as the years advanced, this circle became smaller and invitations fewer. One of his greatest hopes was that the unified movement never develop barriers of race, gender, class, or some insignificant theological distinction. He, previously, took steps to ensure this would be so, organizing a weekly meeting of pastors throughout the Los Angeles area to come together to pray, study Scripture, and share their struggles and triumphs. Using the Azusa Street Mission as a meeting site, men like Smale and Pendleton regularly joined with him for fellowship and succor and to promote a unified spirit among their disparate Pentecostal congregations.

In 1917, several years after the mission's revival fires waned, Seymour again called a meeting of Pentecostal leaders in or near Los Angeles to pray and fellowship. This time, the turnout was scandalously small considering his former prominence and the fact there had been no impropriety or heresy to discredit him as a leader of a movement that was barely eleven years old.

The Church of God Movement Tomlinson

After several years of affiliation with its leaders, W.F. Bryant and Robert Spurling, infrequent visits to worship services, visits in their homes, and invitations to preach for them, Tomlinson joined the Holiness Church[22] in 1903. He was quickly tapped to pastor the small Camp Creek, North Carolina congregation that had been led by the two men. In 1909, after proving himself to be a man of high spiritual integrity, astuteness, and preaching the Bible, and administrative skill, Tomlinson was selected to serve as the first general moderator.

While Tomlinson was at its helm, the Church of God went on to become one of the largest Pentecostal bodies not to have been formed directly out of the Azusa Street Revival. Though the body initially backed away from the experience of speaking in tongues, the Church of God would not go untouched by the fires of Azusa Street and that touch would accelerate the fire in the mountains. But Tomlinson's invitation to Cashwell would prove to be a pivotal point in the church's transformation from the Holiness to the Pentecostal camp.

Tomlinson, like Seymour, attempted to promote a more racially open climate within his adopted spiritual home. He appointed blacks as overseers of their own work. For example, he appointed Edmund Barr over black churches in Florida in 1915. W.R. Franks was appointed overseer of the Bahamas in 1920. James Richardson was appointed overseer of black churches in 1922. Further, in 1919, he created an opportunity for blacks who attended the General Assembly to hold their own worship service within the Assembly.

As early as the 1920s Tomlinson appointed a small number of black ministers to leadership positions beyond the local African

---

[22] The group that would later become the Church of God and spawn the Church of God of Prophecy.

American congregations, some as overseers of states that were not entirely black, and some on subcommittees of the General Assembly.

But, like Seymour, his efforts at reconciliation were not always successful. In 1922, after a large exodus of black ministers from the denomination occurred, when a delegation of blacks requested that one of their own be appointed to oversee their work, he responded that,

> I do not like any separations between nationalities and races, and yet, it is not always convenient, neither is it best, for different races to meet together regularly for worship.[23]

Though Tomlinson, at first, expressed an aversion to organization or church structure, he had his hand in almost every area of organization the early church undertook. Under his leadership, he established and gave oversight to a system of government, as well as a publishing house, a Bible training school, which became Lee University, and an orphanage.

In 1923, Tomlinson, who had been under fire from other church leaders, ostensibly partly because of his autocratic governing style and mishandling of finances, was ousted as general overseer. Some insist that part of the reason for his ouster was that his more progressive ideas regarding race were offensive to many of his white colleagues. With his departure, the apparent tenure of openness toward blacks in leadership positions declined. By the time Tomlinson left the denomination, there were more than 22,500 members in 740 churches served by 1,020 ministers.

---

[23] *Minutes of the Seventeenth General Assembly*, November 1-7, 1922, 26.

Tomlinson took several Church of God members with him to establish his new organization that kept the same name. In 1929, the faction adopted the name the Tomlinson Church of God. 1953 it permanently changed its name to the Church of God of Prophecy. Though the new body never grew to rival its parent it has generally evidenced a more substantial heritage or both racial equality and openness to the ministry of women.

The Cashwell Link

Though Tomlinson never visited Seymour's revival, neither he, Cleveland, or the Church of God would be without the influence of Azusa Street. Like the Olympic runner that carries the torch from station to station to leave a trail of light, the connection between Azusa Street and Cleveland, Tennessee would have such a torchbearer. The direct tie between the two groups was white former Methodist Southern minister, Gaston B. Cashwell.

His initial racial prejudice almost short-circuited his acceptance of the Pentecostal baptism. Yet, Cashwell, a Holiness evangelist from North Carolina came to Azusa Street and received the experience that would greatly impact the movement's early growth. Cashwell had previously been in mixed-race Holiness meetings, so these were not new to him. But he had not witnessed blacks at such important levels of leadership. A product of his time, Cashwell struggled to overcome racial prejudice that threatened to short circuit his participation in the revival and allow him to become the bridge between the two men and communities. After traveling to the West Coast to visit the Azusa Street Mission, the resident of Dunn, North Carolina only four hundred and sixty miles from Cleveland, was, at first, reluctant to take part in the revival. With initial misgivings about submitting himself for prayer at the hands of African Americans leaders and allowing them to touch him. he struggled for a time, before going forward to the altar to receive his impartation.[24] Once he broke through his cultural bias, he opened himself to the experience that would change his life and ministry for several years.

Like so many others, he stayed at Azusa Street only a brief time, leaving to conduct a succession of evangelistic. His openness would impact the early growth of the movement by drawing numerous of Holiness leaders and denominations into its sphere. Once Cashwell received Holy Spirit baptism, he left to conduct a succession of evangelistic services in Georgia and North Carolina, as well as Tennessee. In these meetings, leaders of several Holiness bodies heard his message of initial evidence of tongues, and several new Pentecostal bodies came into being.[25] Tomlinson was only one of the leaders of several Holiness bodies who heard the message of initial evidence of tongues at these services, and several new Pentecostal bodies moved from the Holiness camp including the Fire Baptized Holiness Church and the United Holy Church.

---

[24]Gaston B. Cashwell, "Came 3,000 Miles for His Pentecost" *Apostolic Faith* 1:4 (December 1906), 3.

[25]Along with Tomlinson, in one campaign in Dunn, North Carolina, J. H. King, who later became bishop of the Pentecostal Holiness Church, experienced speaking in tongues and was influential in getting that body to move into the Pentecostal camp. Also, because of his North Carolina campaign, the United Holy Church, a black Holiness body, adopted a statement of faith that placed the group in the Pentecostal family.

Seymour and Tomlinson Parallels

Most importantly for us today is the understanding that both Seymour and Tomlinson drank deeply from the well of the Wesleyan Holiness Movement with its emphasis on the radical equality of men and women of all races before God. Each man held to a three-step soteriology and understood sanctification as striving toward a state of perfection in which one is fully in love with God and with one's brother and sister. Each held a strong personal piety that exhibited itself in modesty in consumption and apparel, as well as abstinence from substances deemed injurious to the body. And each had an appreciation of a prophetic call to speak against injustice in the church and society and to live out just relationships within one's own context.

Both Seymour and Tomlinson envisioned a "glorious" church, unified by the power of the Spirit, without the ugly racial distinction that so marred the fabric of American society. They both worked to make that vision of the Church a reality within their disparate spheres of influence. They understood, intrinsically, that with such unity, the Church could be a better example of the love of Christ, and that without such unity the witness of the Church did not reflect the gospel that is preached. For the two men, racial unity was more than just a spiritual ideal. They saw it as an evangelistic tool that would aid the spread of the gospel.

At a time when racial segregation was the norm in American society, Tomlinson reached out to people of color to draw them into the Church of God, and Seymour reached out to whites and Hispanic as well as reluctant blacks to draw them into a more unified body of Christ. Both men pushed for racial unity within this body as a sign of the genuine outpouring of the Spirit. Echoing the Apostle Paul,

Seymour insisted that without love, even the language of tongues was as "sounding brass and tinkling cymbal."[26]

Seymour and his followers were early proponents of women's freedom to exercise their Spirit-empowered ministry fully and freely. Women were used in almost every aspect of the revival, as well as in the local congregation that housed it. They held important leadership positions and could be found up front exhorting the congregation in prayer, sermon, song, and testimony. But they also worked behind the scenes editing and publishing the newspaper as well as ensuring that temporal and spiritual needs were taken care of. As the embers of the revival began to wane, so did Seymour's, and the movement's, seemingly unbridled support of woman's ministry.

The teams that went out from the revival that Seymour led demonstrated racial unity as well as gender equality. Black women and men were as likely to lead the teams of evangelists and missionaries as were white men or women. Further, little attention was paid to race or class of recipients of their message. For the faithful were eager to win those who would listen to their urgent plea.

In its earliest days, the revivalers' push for unity was so evident that participant historian Frank Bartleman would report in his memoir that, "the color line was washed away in the blood."[27] But the line was being redrawn as little by little the Los Angeles Pentecostal community

---

[26] I Corinthians 13:1. However, after several failed attempts by some groups to wrestle leadership from Seymour left the mission as a primarily African American congregation, he largely abandoned his attempts at inter-racial inclusion and ultimately rejected having whites and Hispanics in leadership at Azusa Street.

[27] Frank Bartleman. *How Pentecost Came to Los Angeles. Republished as Azusa Street,* Los Angeles: F. Bartleman, 1925, 54.

and the groups that came out it drift into spiritually separate by equal camps.

Tomlinson would express this sentiment of the push for unity using the metaphor of a "Great Speckled Bird" that envisioned a movement of men and women of every race and culture as representing the Kingdom of God.[28] He adopted the words of a popular gospel song to express his sentiment that the true church should, "shelter men of all nations[, o]f earth's every color and race... gathered... in Her keeping to present to the Lord face to face."[29]

The ministry flowing out of the Azusa Street Revival never coalesced into a denomination. Though at times, it appeared that might happen through Seymour's aid, several white leaders, such as Florence Crawford and Frank Bartleman, broke off to start their own work. Though Bartleman's work was short lived, Crawford's Apostolic Faith Church, headquartered in Portland, Oregon, has several branches scattered throughout the United States.

Despite Tomlinson's efforts, in 1922, several black ministers exited the denomination. Subsequently, when a black delegation requested that a black person again be appointed to oversee their work, Tomlinson agreed to their request and the denomination's Committee on Better Government created an autonomous structure for the black churches, The Church of God Colored Work, appointing a black man, Thomas Richardson, as its first overseer. This group was not disbanded until 1966, when the General Assembly voted to disband it and

---

[28] R. G. Robins. *A. J. Tomlinson: Plainfolk Modernist.* New York: Oxford University Press, 2004, 227.

[29] "The Great Speckled Bird" in *Banner Hymns.* Cleveland, TN: White Wing Publishing House, 1957.

established the office of Black Liaison at its International Headquarters.

After Tomlinson was ousted from the Church of God and established his subsequent body, the latter denomination went on to establish branches that reach throughout the globe, though it never matched the breadth of the denomination he left. Even before his departure and for decades after, the former denomination still struggles to come to terms with the question of racial inclusion.

Shared Legacy

Parallels in the lives and ministries of Seymour and Tomlinson are evident. This legacy holds up the important, yet often forgotten, linkage between personal sanctification and social holiness. In retelling their history, neither the Church of God nor its direct offspring, the Church of God of Prophecy gives much attention to Seymour or the Azusa Street Revival as progenitors. Yet the unmistakable mark that Seymour left on, at least, one of their early leaders is undeniable.

Seymour contended that the gift of the Holy Spirit was poured out on a clean, sanctified heart. He saw this gift as a tool for "perfecting the saints for the work of the ministry."[30] And he saw an essential element of the work of the Spirit as unifying the body of Christ across racial, cultural, and gender lines. Ultimately, his insistence that such unity was a genuine indication as the Spirit poured out on all flesh would signal a starting point for Pentecostals who vigorously embrace social justice as a biblical mandate. Likewise, Tomlinson insisted that

---

[30] Ephesians 4:12

within his denomination should be found people of all nations—of every color and race.[31]

Tomlinson and Seymour differed in that the latter's vision also included the tearing down of barriers of class and gender. Laborers and household servants worked alongside seasoned more economically well-endowed members to accomplish whatever was needed to spread the news of what God was doing. And, at least in the earliest days of Seymour's ministry, women were free to answer their felt call to ministry and use their God-given and Spirit-empowered gifts at every level.

Within Tomlinson's context, class distinction was not an issue. Most members of his group were rural, working-class folk. Tomlinson's support for women's leadership in the Church of God movement was more problematic. During his tenure in various positions of leadership, women's role was constrained through repeated actions of the council. For though David Roebuck contends that the founders of the denomination included women, they were quickly relegated to a secondary role. The parent body would take decades to reach a semblance of equality, and women have yet to obtain full clergy rights.[32] Women have found more acceptance for their ministry in the subsequent body.

---

[31] "The Great Speckled Bird" in "Banner Hymns. Cleveland, TN: White Wing Publishing House, 1957.

[32] Women have received the title "Ordained Minister," but they are still held at the second of three tiers of ministry without the right to vote in the International General Council—the denomination's main legislative body. While as with the laity, women do have full voice and vote in the International General Assembly to ratify the Council's vote, they are prohibited from holding most administrative positions outside the local church, and are rarely appointed to senior pastorates. See David Roebuck, "Limiting Liberty: The Church of God and Women Ministers, 1886-1996." PhD dissertation, Vanderbilt University,

Seymour died in 1922, brokenhearted, not because he had failed to receive recognition from his brethren, nor because the demonstrative phenomena of the revival had subsided, nor because several colleagues whom he had thought of as loyal friends had betrayed him. Instead, he was disappointed that the unity for which he had fervently prayed and labored had not come to fruition.

A year later, Tomlinson was out of the Church of God, and by the time of his death in 1943, he was, like Seymour, disappointed that the reality of the vision of the speckled bird seemed far off. Sadly, both of their visions of the Body of Christ unified across racial lines have yet to materialize.

1997.

Without Form or Fashion: Liturgy in Non-Liturgical Classical Pentecostalism

A commonly held perception of Classical Pentecostal worship is that it is a free-form spiritual exercise, devoid of liturgical structure, ritual enactment, or symbolic presence. Commonly, Pentecostalism is characterized as a "Spirit" movement and its worship is assumed to be, an emotional religious expression centered around ecstatic experiences, and lacking any recognizable liturgical form. It is true that standard concepts of liturgy, ritual, and symbolism typically are not used by adherents of this movement to define what they are doing in worship. Because of the primarily oral tradition of the movement, its adherents often askew attempts to develop codified definitions or formulations for what is happening in their worship. However, Liturgy, ritual, and symbolism have been and continue to be consistently operable components of Pentecostal worship, even when adherents do not recognize them as such. Liturgical concepts and practices do have import for what goes on in Holiness-Pentecostal worship contexts.

I am especially familiar with two congregations that illustrate how liturgy, ritual, and symbolism operate in two different settings. The first is an urban, middle-class, African-American "oneness" congregation, which serves the mother church of a small denomination. The second is a suburban congregation with a multi-racial history that is part of a large Southern, Holiness-Pentecostal denomination. Finally, some conclusions about the liturgical elements of Classical Pentecostal worship and what this liturgical presence means will help set the movement squarely in line with the broader body of Christ.

Classical Pentecostalism

The most distinguishing feature of Classical Pentecostalism is the belief that the baptism or "outpouring" of the Holy Spirit on the believer is essential for the Christian experience. This outpouring is understood as the ultimate fulfilling the Old Testament prophecy of Joel 2:28-29 that, [a]fterwards, I will pour out my Spirit upon all flesh." Classical Pentecostals hold the Acts 2:4 depiction of the Day of Pentecost when "they were all filled with the Holy Ghost and began to speak in tongues as the Spirit gave them utterance" as foreshowing the contemporary outpouring. They see Peter's subsequent speech to the gathered crowd in Acts 2:38 is believed as confirming that "this is that which was spoken of by the prophet." For Pentecostals, this in-filling endows believers with supernatural empowerment to both live a holy life and to accomplish works of righteousness on behalf of the kingdom of God.

Secondly, adherents seek to establish a personal communion with God through ecstatic religious experience. For Pentecostals, this necessarily includes glossolalia or speaking in tongues as initial and objective evidence of that outpouring and in-filling and what is happening in their worship was biblically warranted.

Liturgy, Ritual, and Symbolism

Liturgy involves the collective actions of a gathered community of faith as it expresses its identity as a people of God and reaffirms a mediated experience of the presence of God. Within this context, ritual includes actions within the worship life of the gathered community at specifically designated times that articulate and impart meaning about the nature of the self, the Church, and of ultimate reality. Symbol relates to the special meanings that objects, language, gestures, and actions convey that is, explicitly or implicitly, shared by the worshiping community.

Studies of Holiness-Pentecostal Worship

Many scholars focus on the symbolic ritualization of the charismata (especially speaking in tongues) and other ecstatic expressions within Pentecostal worship,[1] attempting to identify liturgical parallels between worship within that context and the broader Christian Church. Over the last three decades, however, studies of Pentecostal liturgical elements have been undertaken from anthropological, sociological, theological, and ritual studies perspectives. One of the more salient findings of these studies is that the movement represents a primarily oral tradition. Any attempt to define what is happening in Holiness-Pentecostal worship must keep this in mind. As Walter Hollenweger points out:

> Oral liturgy might be expected to be among oral people, whose main medium of experience is the oral form-the story, the proverb, the parable, the joke, the dance, the song...[2]

Daniel Albrecht identified elements of Pentecostal worship that function as iconic symbols, correctly contending that, Pentecostal icons,

---

[1] See for example, Daniel E. Albrecht, "Pentecostal Spirituality: Looking through the Lens of Ritual" Pneuma 14 fall 1992 07-125; Charles Gaedes, Pentecost and Praise: A Pentecostal Ritual, Paraclete 22, Spring 1988; and Jonathan Alvarado, "Worship in the Spirit: Pentecostal Perspectives on Liturgical Theology and Praxis" *Journal of Pentecostal Theology* 21:1, January 2012, 135–151.

[2] Walter J. Hollenweger, "Social and Ecumenical Significance of Pentecostal Liturgy," *Studia Liturgica*, 8:4 (1973), 209.

are not painted altarpieces or works by pious artists... (but) a different sort, though (they) function within the ritual field similarly to icons of other Christians to (bring the congregation) to a sense of the Holy.[3]

Pentecostal iconography is exemplified in sound, sight, and movement.[4] Within this schema, music becomes an iconic sound, for, in Pentecostal worship, music is a constant. It not only accompanies individual and congregational singing, and is played during prayer or the collection of the offering, but it often punctuates and emphasizes strategic points in the sermon, and is an integral part of the altar ministry. As Hollenweger details, music is also a liturgical symbol, that moves the service from one point to another. Stressing the oral nature, most Pentecostals appear not aware of the liturgical function of musical icons. No formal sacramental theology exists that gives them articulated meaning. Even so, "their functions are clearly observable" and their primary function is to... "indicate the transition from one part to the other of the service... and everyone in the congregation understands the[m]."[5]

Though Albrecht also identifies iconic sight as important, the Pentecostal ritual space is usually "quite austere"[6] when compared to the ornate art that adorns Catholic edifices or many other Protestant churches. Ritual furnishings are minimal: the pulpit, altar rail, communion table, baptistery, and pews. Iconic sight comes from other sources. He suggests that the gathered people act as an iconic sight.

---

[3] Albrecht, "Pentecostal Spirituality" 111
[4] Ibid., 111-114.
[5] Hollenweger, *The Pentecostals*, 1972, 210-212.
[6] Albrecht, 112-113.

Kinesthetic icons are integral to the Pentecostal worship experience. Not to move, to raise one's hands, clap, sway, shout, or in some visible way indicate participation in the congregation's experience signals a lack of spirituality or that one is an outsider and a candidate for conversion.

Wilson and Clow confirm the importance of the body and body movements as symbols in Pentecostal worship.[7] Charismatic Catholic religious scholar, Kevin Ranaghan points out how the Pentecostal crisis experience of conversion and the ordinance of water baptism both function as rites of initiation involving the entire faith community. He specifically identifies these as "rites of public worship... celebrated in the midst of the congregation."[8] In doing so, he identifies the parallels among Pentecostal rituals and initiation rites and those in other settings.

Other works detail the social implications of ritual within these contexts. Bobby Alexander lifts up the anti-structural dimensions of Pentecostal ritual and its effectiveness in giving Pentecostal adherents the tools to express their feelings of social dislocation. He challenges the view of "the ecstatic ritual of socially disadvantaged Pentecostals as symbolic rebellion... functioning as a catharsis, a safety valve, accommodating them to their condition." Rather, he uses Victor Turner's concept of liminality to describe what happens in Pentecostal worship as "concretizing... opposition to the dominant society... [as the] embodiment of full humanity and personhood."[9]

---

[7] John Wilson and Harvey K. Clow, Themes of power and control in a Pentecostal Assembly" journal of the scientific study of religion 20, 1981, 242.

[8] Kevin Ranaghan, Conversion and Baptism: Personal Celebration and Ritual Experience in Pentecostal Churches," Studia Liturgica 10, 1974, 65-75.

[9] Bobby Alexander, "*Pentecostal Ritual Reconsidered: Anti Structural Dimensions of Possession, Journal of Ritual Studies* 3: 1973, 109-128.

Like Alexander, Wilson and Clow also discuss Pentecostal worship as a source of self-empowerment for its adherents, going on to identify distinct types of ritual within the worship experience and making assumptions about their symbolic meaning. They see the aim of Pentecostal worship as "receiving and retaining 'possession' of the Holy Spirit"[10] and they differentiate between initiation rituals that call down the Spirit and confirmatory rituals (such as speaking in tongues or dancing in the Spirit) that affirm spiritual power.[11]

Jon Michael Spencer pays attention to Pentecostal worship's kinesthetic elements, identifying such aspects as the shout, or holy dance, as ritual."[12] He also identifies its anti-structural dimensions, especially as they relate to the testimony service, as a rite of intensification. Spencer sees these dimensions as having an identifiable superstructure embodying communitas, coherence, and elements of musical liminality, marginality, and seminality.[13]

Others look at how Holiness-Pentecostals ritualize elements that they generally define as non-ritualistic ritualistic. Ruel Tyson, for instance, examines the structure of the testimony service and captures its significance as a rite of affirmation. In his analysis, Tyson discusses how the enactment of the testimony constitutes several levels of the speaker's and congregation's world. He characterizes that enactment as a "formalization of the religious practice and... understanding of the speaker," and looks at how words, and accompanying physical gestures symbolize transformative dimensions.[14]

---

[10] Wilson and Clow, 244.

[11] Ibid.

[12] Jon Michael Spencer, Isochronisms of Antistructure: Music in the Black Holiness-Pentecostal Testimony Service, Journal of Black Sacred Music, 5.

[13] Ibid., 5.

[14] Raul W. Tyson, Jr., "The Testimony of Sister Annie Mae," Journal of

Cheryl J. Sanders deals specifically with liturgical elements of African-American Holiness and Pentecostal worship. Though her description of a "typical Sunday morning worship service"[15] in a progressive inner-city congregation (such as the up-tempo beat of the processional hymn or the wearing of white by women "liturgical attendants" and the three-hour length of the service) are more common to the African-American context, several ingredients, including numerous prayers, the "praise and worship" portion of the service in which "several choruses and hymns are sung in succession" and the altar call, are recognizable in many Pentecostal settings, irrespective of cultural framework.[16]

Sanders draws on her familiarity with a typical congregation, as well as her knowledge of other works on African-American Pentecostal worship, to extract four schemas of the usual components of such worship. In comparing the four schemas (which average 12 elements each), seven recurring components were common to all four: a type of devotional; prayer, Scripture reading, congregational or special singing, the sermon, offering, and benediction. Additionally, three elements, the introit, announcements, and altar call, were found in three schemas. Though four elements, the recitation of a denominational creed, the holy dance, testimony service, and reading of the sick and shut-in lists were only found on one list each, other

---

Ritual Studies, 2, 1988, 163-144 and Melvin Williams, *Community in a Black Pentecostal Church.* Prospect Heights, IL: Waveland Press, 1974.

[15] Cheryl J. Sanders, Saints in Exile: The Holiness-Pentecostal Experience in African American Religion and Culture. New York: Oxford University Press, 1996. 42-46.

[16] Ibid. 68-69.

studies have shown that these are also common elements of Pentecostal worship.[17]

Richard Baer, a Charismatic Episcopalian scholar, makes a direct analogy between Pentecostal tongue-speaking and Catholic liturgy, seeing them as functionally equivalent. For him, although they and Quaker silence, might appear on the surface to be dissimilar, they share the same goal. All three practices "allow the analytical mind to rest... thus freeing the spirit for a deeper openness to divine reality." He refutes Wilson and Clow and other scholars who describe Pentecostal worship (specifically tongues) and Holy Spirit baptism as a type of "possession." Baer also refutes casual observers who characterize such worship as an uncontrollable expression of emotion, although he admits that the Pentecostal worshiper might be moved by deep emotion, as might the Quaker and the person engaged in liturgical worship. Baer contends that Pentecostal worship differs in form but not in substance from other Christian worship, so to define Pentecostal worship in terms of physical activity is "to substitute the form of praise for the substance of praise."[18]

Liturgy in Pentecostal Worship

From the start, Pentecostal adherents have often objected to the use of the terms such as liturgy, ritual, and symbolism. They have associated them with the "unspiritual" and "dead formalism." Early groups deliberately attempted to foster a sense of freedom from formalism and anything that smacked of "dead" structuralism. As

---

[17] Ibid., 49-51.
[18] Richard Baer. "Quaker Silence, Catholic Liturgy and Pentecostal Glossolalia." in Russell Spittler, *New Perspectives on Pentecostalism*. Grand Rapids, MI: Baker Book House, 1976, 152-153.

such, they understood ritual as ritualism-restrictive, repetitive ceremonialism that inhibits the movement of the' Holy Spirit in their worship experience. Indeed, these terms are not used extensively by Holiness-Pentecostal theologians who prefer "services," "distinctives," and "practices" for what they see happening in their worship.

However, such worship contains specific elements of liturgical, ritual, and symbolic presence. Further, Baer posits that they are present in almost every aspect, even those that each would declare "open" to the immediate move of the Holy Spirit-such as Holiness shouting or holy dancing or Pentecostal glossolalia or speaking in tongues.

There is a tacit, if not systematic, methodology for doing worship. As in other ecclesial contexts, that methodology evolves and changes, and has been adapted and modified as the movement and individual denominations and congregations have redefined themselves throughout their history. Essential elements, however, have remained in place, over the entire life of the movement, passed down primarily through its oral tradition.

One of the more salient characteristics of the Holiness-Pentecostalism to outside observers with little direct contact is the, seemingly, loose liturgical form of worship. From its inception, the movement has defined itself as bringing a return to apostolic simplicity, and as such, has continually proclaimed its disdain for anything that might, potentially, rob it of spiritual authenticity. Even so, as segments of the movement have moved from sect to church type institutions, they have incorporated more of the liturgical practices of their mainline and Evangelical counterparts, and contemporary worship styles often resemble those of their detractors.

Ranaghan agrees that "at the beginning… the order of Pentecostal meetings was one of complete spontaneity in an atmosphere of intense demonstrative worship."[19] But he concedes,

> As the Pentecostal churches emerged and became distinct ecclesial communities with their own buildings, clergy, etc., the free-form meeting began to be shaped into a definite order of service. This process; slow in some churches, rapid in others, has tended to regulate the elements of Pentecostal worship.[20]

Even within the worship of early "primitive" sect- type bodies, however, vestiges of liturgy, ritual, and symbolism were visible, especially when these terms carry their theologically broad meaning.

Contemporary Pentecostal worship is characterized by an openness that is easily adapted to various cultural and social milieus. A frequent prayer at the beginning Pentecostal worship services is for the Holy Spirit to "have Your way," and participants are repeatedly admonished to remain open to the "moving of the Holy Spirit" and "whatever He wants to do" in them. But, as Hollenweger has correctly noted, the openness is only within limits since, "the flexible oral tradition allows for variation within a framework of the whole liturgical structure, but only within that structure."[21]

---

[19] Ranaghan, "Conversion and Baptism," 68.
[20] Ibid.
[21] Hollenweger, *Pentecostalism: Origins and Developments Worldwide*, 271.

Limited Liturgical Calendar

In general, Pentecostals have little appreciation for the liturgical year and the church-year calendar. Though some seminary-trained ministers make limited use of lectionaries for sermon topics or themes, Pentecostal congregations rarely set a worship schedule based on a lectionary. Instead, preachers are expected to seek God through prayer for the specific needs of the congregation at any given time and to prepare a message specifically geared to meet those needs.

There are only four major events in the Pentecostal liturgical year that, with at least one major exception, are observed uniformly: Easter, Christmas, New Year's Eve, and Pentecost. The major holy day for Pentecostals is Easter Sunday. The most uniform rites of Easter are the Sunrise Service, the Easter cantata, and the Easter morning worship service.

Pentecostals do not, generally, observe an extended Easter season, and, specifically, do not observe Lent. Many Pentecostal congregations, however, observe Good Friday in some way. Where Good Friday is observed, the "Seven Last Words of Christ"—a service in which seven speakers deliver short sermonettes or homilies related to the last seven recorded statements of Jesus before his crucifixion—is one of the more often used thematic motifs. But this is not a uniquely Pentecostal form; many Protestant congregations, especially those within the Evangelical tradition, use this.

Christmas is the second most important event observed within most Pentecostal churches. There are some congregations and denominations, however, which do not hold Christmas as a significant holiday, arguing that, since no one knows the date of Jesus' birth, it should not be held as a Christian holiday. Some even forbid observance of the day, seeing it as a pagan holiday.[22] In both cases, this is the minority. For those congregations that celebrate Christmas, the main rituals may include a Christmas Eve service, a cantata, a Christmas play, and a congregational dinner or party that would include several elements of worship such as reading the Christmas story, a short Christmas homily or drama, and the singing of carols. Though the advent season is generally not observed, throughout December, in the regular worship services, Christmas hymns might be sung along with regular hymns and choruses.

New Year's Eve is generally commemorated with a Watch Night service during which the congregation watches in the new year in prayer, singing, and testifying about what God had done during the previous year, preaching and feasting. Most New Year's Eve services also include communion and many include foot washing. The central component of the New Year's Eve service for most congregations is the custom of all individuals kneeling and praying as the clock strikes midnight.

The day of Pentecost, coming seven weeks (49 days) after Easter is a special time for most Pentecostal congregations since it commemorates the event of the pouring out of the Holy Spirit on the Christians gathered in the Upper Room as the initiation of the Church. This is the event to which most Pentecostals point as the paradigm for their present mode of worship. However, it is observed with more or less formality within various Pentecostal settings. Some denominations convene special gatherings in which congregations come together for camp meetings style revivals. These Convocations are the highlight of

---

[22] For example, this was true in the Oneness Pentecostal denomination in which I was raised.

the church's year. Within denominations, individual congregations may commemorate that day or week with a special service or series of services emphasizing their "Pentecostal heritage." Some may make note of the day in passing remarks, but do not center the service around that theme. Others give it no significance at all, noting that every day is Pentecostal for the Spirit-filled believer.

Many contemporary Pentecostal congregations have started holding services to commemorate specific special occasions. For instance, the Church of God "Ministry Planning Calendar" is full of special days with a special preaching emphasis. These include events such as Ministry to the Military Day, Pastor's Appreciation Sunday, or Senior Adult Day. Denominational offices sometimes provide resource materials or suggest general worship formats, but individual congregations generally have complete freedom as to whether they participate and/or use the materials.

Limited Use of Liturgical Resources

On entering the Pentecostal ritual field, the absence of many usual liturgical resources is evident. With a few exceptions, there is no understanding or use of liturgical colors. They rarely adorn the worship space. They do play a part however, in ritual vestments.

Special celebrations often involve a color scheme and liturgical banners with highly stylized symbols or sophisticated artwork (though some storefront churches hang plaques or handmade banners with Bible verses). There, generally, are no stained-glass windows, neither are there fabric coverings for the altar railings or pulpit, and no large, strategically placed crosses.

Rarely do Classical Pentecostal congregations ornately adorned their places of worship (as they would designate the ritual field). As Albrecht states, these fields are relatively austere, though not completely stark and many are outfitted comfortably. However, many of the newer Pentecostal places of worship are quite elegant, though they usually exhibit a utilitarian rather than liturgical elegance. For, Pentecostals believe the ritual field should reflect a dignity befitting the nature of God. This utilitarian elegance would be reflected in components such as quality building materials (i.e., brick or stone facades, comfortable pews, or upgraded carpets), high-quality musical instruments, and the finest sound equipment. What Pentecostals would generally disdain is a ritual space decorated with what many consider liturgical "trappings" such as stain glass windows, liturgical art, or especially, statuary.

Within this primarily oral context; there is no written Pentecostal rite. There is no prayer book or missal. There are no liturgists or liturgical committees. There are no trained lay speakers or readers. Congregations rarely provide formal liturgical training for ministers. Instead, ministers generally learn how to preside over various rites and ordinances through hands-on training within the congregation. This learning starts at an early age, as children are, extemporaneously, called on to pray, read Scripture, lead a segment of the worship service such as the testimony service, or sing or play a song or chorus. New converts are quickly grafted into the ritual life of the community through incorporation into non-ministerial presiding functions such as praying for the offering, delivering the pulpit greeting to visitors, or duties similar to those of children.

Even within formal ministerial training programs that some denominations provide, the emphasis is on practical pastoral functions rather than liturgical form. This training primarily involves biblical scholarship and understanding, preaching techniques, and specific denominational history and administrative polity (i.e., how church government works, how to hold a church meeting, etc.). Formal courses in liturgy, liturgics, or even corporate worship theory or practice are negligible among offerings of Pentecostal seminaries. For example, the 1994-1996 course catalog of the Church of God School of Theology lists only one elective course related to this area, "Worship and Church Music." Essentially, as described below, the course accentuates the Pentecostal understanding of openness to the Holy Spirit in providing direction in worship:

> Sensitivity to the guidance of the Spirit is emphasized. Special attention is given to the crucial importance of music in Pentecostal Worship.[23]

A minister's service manuals, available from some denominational publishing houses, suggest general formats for special services such as weddings or funerals.[24] However, even here, none of these manuals published by Pentecostal denominations in America contain an order of service for regular congregational worship. The greatest proportion of the materials in these manuals consists of suggested Scripture readings and lists of elements that can be included, without any scripting or detailed instruction on how to conduct each rite. Ministers,

---

[23] Church of God School of Theology Bulletin, Vol. IX, 1994-1996. (Cleveland, TN: Church of God School of Theology, (1994), 81, emphasis added

[24] For example, see Clyde W. Buxton, *Minister's Service Manual*, Cleveland, TN: Pathway Press, 1985. Though the manual was published under the auspices of the denominational press, it represents the work of a single individual. Use of the manual in conducting ordinances is not mandatory.

however, are free to utilize any aids they want. While some ministers might use worship aids in their preparation for worship, many would decline their use in the pulpit for fear of appearing "unspiritual" to members of the congregation.

Though the practice is declining, the liturgical aid in Pentecostal worship most comparable to any found in more formal liturgical settings has been responsive Scripture readings found at the back of many hymnals. In actuality, these are primarily suggested Scripture passages that can be read responsively by the congregation on any given Sunday, as the minister determines. The presider reads the first verse of the Scripture alone, the next verse is read by the congregation in unison. They continue to alternate until the final verse, that is read in unison. In some cases, these are a single scriptural pericope, in others they are composites of two or more passages, generally following a theme. They are fairly limited in number and scope, but, since one of the primary "rules" of Pentecostal worship is that everyone brings his or her own Bible to public worship, this has not previously been seen as a problem. Before the introduction of newer translations into Pentecostal worship, responsive readings were generally read directly from the Bible. Because of the variety of translations now present in the worship service, responsive reading has been replaced in many cases with an individual reader.

Even where responsive reading is not employed, each member of the congregation is expected to follow along in a personal Bible whenever Scripture is read. This is generally done in at least two places in the service. There usually is at least one opening scriptural passage following the call to worship. The preacher will also read the specific passage related to his or her message just before preaching. Additionally, the sermon itself is often interspersed with short passages and the congregation is usually directed to turn to the respective passage and read along. Scriptural passages may also be introduced into worship in conjunction with other elements of the service such as raising the offering, communion, or baptism. Sometimes individual members of the congregation will read a Scripture passage as part of their testimony.

The use of hymnals in Pentecostal worship is relatively limited. Though many Pentecostal denominations publish at least one hymnal, many congregations (especially since the influence of the Charismatic renewal) use hymnals only sparingly. Much of the singing is by rote. People generally know, by heart, the words of choruses and even complicated hymns.

Limited Sacramental Identification

The idea of sacrament is foreign to the Pentecostal self-understanding, either in the Wesleyan idea of an outward sign of an invisible grace that is already present in the believer or the Catholic tradition of sacraments as having transformational quality. Instead, rites are viewed as ordinances.[25] In this sense, they are understood as not having "self-contained efficacy" as conveyors of grace in any dimension.[26]

Rather, these rites are defined as obedient responses to biblical commands of Christ as relating to the life of the individual and the church. But, just as with a sacramental understanding of these elements, these ritual ordinances are public, participatory affairs. There are primarily two ordinances that all Pentecostal churches regularly

---

[25] Duffield and Van Cleave, 436.
[26] Burgess, et. al., *Dictionary of Pentecostal and Charismatic Movements*, 653.

observe: water baptism and communion. Baptism does not take place in a private place. Communion involves all the gathered church.

Water baptism is reserved for converts (whether children or adults). Most Pentecostal congregations observe baptism by immersion only.[27] However, nowhere is an understanding of the symbolic nature of rites more evident within the Pentecostal milieu than in the language of the following entry concerning baptism from a denominational statement of faith:

> We believe that water baptism... according to the command of our Lord, is a blessed outward sign of an inward work, a beautiful and solemn emblem...[28]

At First Church, baptismal candidates wear special white garments designed specifically for the baptism ritual. The women wear long white bloomers with robes over them and white swimming caps to keep their hair from getting wet. At Harvest Temple, the ritual is no less public, if less formal. In keeping with its less formal atmosphere, no special clothing is worn. People dress in casual clothing and bring a change of clothing from home. In both cases, baptism is held as part of the regular worship service. Singing is an essential element, and the choir or congregation intones a variety of baptismal hymns and choruses as each candidate is immersed, stopping only long enough for the minister to ask the candidate for confirmation of faith and to pronounce the words of enactment.

---

[27] The exception is the Pentecostal Holiness Church which allows converts to choose between immersion, sprinkling and pouring.

[28] Declaration of Faith, International Church of the Foursquare Gospel.

In the Pentecostal tradition, communion also called the Lord's Supper is observed strictly as an ordinance, an act of obedience to the command of God. It is a time of remembering the sacrifice Jesus made on the cross and looking forward to His return and reunion with Him in heaven. As Ranaghan states:

> The overwhelming majority of American Pentecostals adhere to a Zwinglian theology of Christ's presence in the Eucharist, espousing the bread and the wine only as tokens of a past event and only as symbols of a separate spiritual reality. Yet the universally deep experiences of the presence of the Risen Christ and the power of his Spirit... tend to infuse their Eucharist with an intense awareness of the actual presence of Christ in the sharing of the bread and cup.[29]

Individual pastors set the schedule for communion. It is not rare to find a wide disparity in the frequency of communion, even within a single denomination. Church of God (Cleveland, TN) pastors, for instance, vary to the extent that some serve communion monthly, some serve it quarterly, some serve it at no regular interval. But it is rare to encounter a Pentecostal church that serves communion weekly. There is also divergence on when communion is served. While some congregations serve it as part of a Sunday morning worship service, others serve it on Sunday evenings, and some set aside a weeknight for the observance. For some, it is conducted as a separate worship service, for others, it is a part of a standard worship service. Many

---

[29] Kevin Ranaghan, Liturgical Renewal at Oral Roberts University, *Studia Liturgica*, 8, 1973. 122.

congregations also incorporate communion into special occasions such as Christmas or New Year's Eve or Good Friday.

The observance of foot washing is considered to be the third ordinance by some denominations and is practiced at various times and intervals within local congregations. In the foot washing service, participants are seated in chairs set aside for the purpose, and basins of water are placed at their feet. Another individual kneels before a basin and proceeds to ritually pour water over the person's feet, using their hands to bathe them. They might also quietly pronounce some blessing or prayer for the one whose feet they are washing. Then they dry the feet with a clean towel. They then switch places and repeat the ritual. This process is done until everyone in the congregation who elects to has participated. Many churches incorporate foot washing as a regular part of their communion services. Some only incorporate it into special services such as—New Year's Eve and Good Friday. Other congregations rarely practice the rite at all. There is also wide diversity as to whether participation is expected of all members or left to the member's election. Within some denominations, all baptized believers, regardless of age, are expected to participate in foot washing. In others, participation is completely optional, out is open to everyone who wants to participate.[30]

In addition to these ordinances, several other rites are regularly practiced by Holiness-Pentecostal congregations. Dedication of babies replaces baptism or confirmation as the major rite for children.

---

[30] For an understanding of the rite of foot washing, see Ray H. Hughes, "Prediluvian Distinctive," in *Church of God Distinctives*, Cleveland, TN: Pathway Press, or Gary B. Magee, "Ordinances in Burgess, Frank, Gary McGee and Patrick Alexander, eds. *Dictionary and Pentecostal and Charismatic Movemen*ts. Grand Rapids, MI: Zondervan Publishers, 1988, 654.

Children-usually, but not necessarily infants, are presented to the church by their parents or a responsible adult to receive a special prayer of dedication and blessing by the pastor. At the same time, the parents, grandparents, and the entire church are charged with the responsibility for the well-being and religious nurturing of the child.

The "Right Hand of Fellowship" is centered around accepting of candidates into congregational membership. This generally involves some form of public reading and accepting of the doctrines of the church by the new members, an official motion, an informal congregational vote of acceptance of candidates (raising of the right hand) into membership and a ritual greeting of new members by ministers and leaders of the congregation or the entire congregation.

Two Pentecostal Worship Expressions

Pentecostalism is a diverse movement characterized by the variety of its expressions. Many of the distinctions noted between the two congregations highlighted in this work can be explained by the two different points in time covered by this paper. However, when I initially moved from one congregation to the other in a short space of time, some differences were already apparent. The communion and baptismal rituals, as well as their modes of praying for the baptism of the Holy Spirit, are perhaps the most distinctive; the musical competency and variety were also generally more pronounced at First Church.

High Church Holiness-Pentecostalism: First Church.

Many large urban and suburban Pentecostal congregations, especially those whose members have attained some degree of educational and economic upward mobility or those whose leaders migrated into the Pentecostal movement from more upwardly mobile traditions, tend to practice a style of worship that is a mixture of "Old Time Religion" and more traditional Christian worship. Within these congregations, hymns, anthems, and organ music are mixed with impromptu choruses and the electronic keyboard. A robed choir fills the choir loft and the choir director may either have some musical training or is at least "gifted" in music.

The First Church of Jesus Christ is a part of a small African-American denomination that operates primarily within an urban context. Because the congregation has generally used spaces purchased from existing congregations of other denominations, Albrecht's description of the liturgical space as austere does not apply here. For example, during the more than twenty-year-period that I attended United Church (from 1956 to 1978), its worship space was an edifice built for a Greek Orthodox congregation, St. Sophia's. The sanctuary was adorned with stained glass windows. Brass pipes for a pipe organ lined the front wall.

When urban renewal forced the congregation to relocate, it did not attempt to build a new structure around its worship style. It located and purchased a facility vacated by a Methodist congregation. The building was all brick, with a large sanctuary, a rear balcony, a rolling green lawn, and stained-glass windows. The critical issues for the church were not liturgical presence, but whether the facility was large enough and whether they would have to move out of the city, since many older members lived in the city and depended on public transportation or carpools to get to and from church. It also had to be ample enough to reflect the middle-class status of the congregation and the quality of graciousness that was apparent in the former facility.

The worship service at First Church, during the years I attended, was a mixture of Pentecostal fervor (with spirited preaching, exuberant singing, extemporaneous prayers, and the characteristic ecstatic expression) and Methodist order—represented by a robed minister and choir, a processional, and responsive readings. Both the Sunday morning and evening worship services began with a processional of the pastor, other ministers, and the choir. The processional litanies included reciting Psalm 1 for the Sunday morning worship service and Psalm 37:1-11 for the evening worship service, both of which every regular member of the congregation could recite by heart. Additionally, the morning worship service always ended with the same hymn.

> God be with you til we meet again;
> By his counsel guide, uphold you,
> Neath his wings securely fold you;
> God be with you, til we meet again.
> Til we meet, til we meet,
> til we meet at Jesus' feet;
> Til we meet, til we meet,
> God be with you til we meet again. [31]

Likewise, the evening worship service had its specific format and always started with the same hymn:

> If I have wounded any soul today,
> If I have caused one foot to go astray,

---

[31] Jeremiah Rankin, "God be with You Til We Meet Again" music by William G. Tomer, s.l.: s.n., 1880.

If I have walked in my own willful way;
Dear Lord, forgive.

Forgive the sins I have confessed to Thee;
Forgive the secret sins I do not see;
O guide me, love me and my keeper be,
Dear Lord, forgive. [32]

At the close of the evening worship service, just before the benediction was prayed, the same closing chorus was sung:

God be with you, God be with you
God be with you til we meet again.

May God bless you, May God bless you,
May God bless you, til we meet again.[33]

One of the most liturgical memories of First Church is the communion service. The celebration of communion was held every fourth Thursday evening since a regular worship service was scheduled for that night each week. Even when Thanksgiving or Christmas or some secular holiday fell on this day, it was still reserved for communion, and most people attended faithfully, not to take communion was a sign that there was something seriously wrong spiritually. Attendance at communion usually rivaled that of Sunday morning worship. However, this was never understood to be an open

---

[32] Charles H. Gabriel, "An Evening Prayer" 1911.
[33] Author Unknown. Public Domain.

table. Only "baptized believers"[34] could receive communion at First Church. Young children were excluded unless they had been baptized. People from other congregations were allowed to partake only if they professed to be "saved," and this was made explicitly clear from the pulpit as the service started.

Communion was a solemn occasion, not a celebration. People were expected to have confessed to God and repented of all known sin in their lives and could not approach the communion table unless such confession and repentance had been made. So there were some in the congregation, on any given occasion, who did not partake, though they attended the service. In fact, just before the actual serving of the elements, people were instructed to "examine yourself to see if there is any 'hidden' sin in your heart" and to make it right. This was the understanding of "eating and drinking unworthily and eating and drinking damnation to oneself."[35]

Communion was a major occasion and required a great deal of preparation. As the service began, all of the pulpit furnishings had been draped in white. The altar, the communion table, the podium, and the minister's chairs were all draped with white muslin sheets. The elements had been prepared beforehand and were in the front center of the sanctuary on the communion table. They, too, had a single white muslin' clothe covering them. All the females of the church were expected to wear white. Since women were expected to wear some type of head covering, most also wore white hats or chapel caps, and many had on white stocking and white shoes. The men wore dark-colored

---

[34] Meaning those who had been baptized in Jesus' name.
[35] This understanding is based on a literal appropriation of Paul's admonition to the Corinthian church in I Corinthians 11:28-29.

suits. This is the one setting in which color becomes a liturgical icon, signifying the purifying virtue of the blood of Christ.

Though some question may be raised as to why only women wore white, in a conservative congregation such as First Church, it might have been considered "worldly" or flashy for men to wear white. In many contemporary Pentecostal congregations that maintain this symbolism, however, men also dress in white shirts and white trousers or suits, and sometimes even white shoes.

A regular worship service preceded communion with the singing of hymns, testimony, and maybe a short sermon. But the serving of communion was the highlight of this service. It took up the greatest portion of the time.

As communion began to be served, the white-robed minister approached the back of the communion table from the pulpit area. Two "mothers" of the church approached the table with him and lifted the white covering that had been draped over the elements. They held this panel between the minister and the congregation (as if to preserve the mystery), and the minister ritually washed and dried his hands, using a neatly folded linen towel from the table. Once this ritual cleansing was completed, the minister signaled the choir to begin singing, and the serving of communion commenced.

Starting with the ministers seated on the rostrum, followed, in order, by the deacons and the mothers, seated at the front of the sanctuary, then the rest of the congregation, each row of pews was invited to the altar railing. Each individual knelt, waited, and held the elements until each person at the altar railing was served. As they waited, the choir sang one of the hymns designated in one of the church's four hymn books under the subheading of communion. It would be a hymn such as,

> There is a fountain filled with blood,
> Drawn from Emmanuel's veins
> And sinners plunged beneath the flood
> Lose all their guilty stain.[36]

Then they all partook of the elements together as the minister intoned the words,

> This is my body that was broken for you and my blood that was shed for you. Take, eat ye all of it. As often as you do this, you show forth my death, burial, and resurrection until I come. This do in remembrance of me.[37]

As he did, the choir continued singing softly in the background. Possibly they had changed to another chorus such as,

> What can wash away my sin?
> Nothing but the blood of Jesus;
> What can make me whole again?
> Nothing but the blood of Jesus.
>
> O! precious is that flow
> That makes me white as snow;

---

[36] William Cowper, "There is a fountain filled with Blood," music by Lowell Mason, s.l., s.n., 1772.
[37] I Corinthians 11:24.

No other fount I know;

Nothing but the blood of Jesus.[38]

After all the kneelers had been served, a short extemporaneous prayer was said.

This same ritual was repeated again and again until the entire congregation had been served. The process of serving communion usually took forty-five minutes or longer, depending on how many were in attendance. During this entire period, the choir and congregation continued to sing, changing hymns after every two or three pews were served. At the end of the service, after the pastor had made any special remarks he deemed necessary, the same special hymn, "Blest be the tie that Binds," was sung and the same ritual performed:

Blest be the tie that binds, our hearts in Christian love;

A fellowship of kindred minds, is like to that above.

As the first verse was sung, members of the congregation clasped their hands over their heads.

We share our mutual woes; our mutual burdens bear;

And often for each other flows a sympathizing tear.

Everyone would sing the second verse as they moved from person to person, shaking hands or hugging each other, but never ceasing to sing.

When we asunder part, it gives us inward pain;

---

[38] Robert Lowry, "Nothing but the blood of Jesus" (1876).

But we shall still be joined in heart, and hope to meet again.[39]

The final verse would be sung as people in the individual rows of pews throughout the congregation stretched across the aisles to link hands. Each time the service ended with the same words from Scripture: "And when they had sung a hymn, they went out..."[40] The pattern never varied.

Low-Church Pentecostalism: Harvest Church
Liturgy within low-church Pentecostal churches is somewhat less obvious and more loosely structured. This is the form in which Pentecostalism is generally practiced. Here the disdain for anything that, seemingly, smacks of ritual will be the greatest. Many of these congregations and their leaders are fiercely independent. They rely on "nothing but the Bible" as their guide for every aspect of life and worship. Everyone in the congregation is expected to have a Bible with them. If not, there will be plenty of Bibles in the pews. These serve as more than sources for the preaching text. People often turn to a Scripture passage and read it in the midst of whatever else they are responsible for doing in the service. Often simple choruses come directly from Scripture and are put to simple tunes.

Many pastors and ministers within this segment of Pentecostalism have little formal theological training. While some ministers use Bible study aids such as concordances and commentaries extensively, and many avail themselves of opportunities such as church training, correspondence courses, or Bible schools, many eschew higher

---

[39] John Fawcett. "Blest be the tie that Binds" 1782
[40] Matthew 26:30

education. Despite this, Pentecostal ministers frequently can quote long passages of Scripture and can expound on them with detail. Within this context, the truly oral nature of Pentecostal liturgy is most evident.

These same "unlearned" ministers have generally internalized almost every segment of the Pentecostal worship service. They can be and often are called on to preside over a segment of the worship service with literally a moment's notice, and do so quite willingly, "depending on the Holy Spirit" to provide whatever is needed for the occasion. If there is a choir, instead of robes, they may wear specified colors or styles of dress such as white blouses and dark skirts for the women and white shirts and dark pants for the men. The pastor usually will wear a suit and tie if the person is male, or a suit or dress if it is a woman.

But a type of storefront Pentecostalism is operable in many congregations that are housed in less revealing structures. Many of the congregations have contemporary, and even sophisticated, structures and equipment, and the worship ritual is more refined than that found in true storefront buildings. And though these congregations may represent a somewhat higher social class than in a storefront congregation, even here the disdain for anything that smacks of ritualism is evident. It is enunciated in remarks by the ministers and presiders, as well as reiterated in congregants' testimonies and exhortations. This disdain for what is perceived to be ritualism is also apparent in the way many Pentecostal services are conducted. There is a struggle to maintain "decency and order" while not losing any of the spiritual energy that makes Pentecostalism "Pentecostalism." Growing or transitional congregations struggle to maintain balance.

In many ways, Harvest Church is engaged in such a struggle. When I first began worshipping with the congregation in 1978, it was housed in a structure that had been built some thirty years earlier. The plans, obtained from the denomination, had the simple style evident in many of the denomination's churches that I have visited. It was a simple clapboard country church structure. It had no stained-glass windows and simple wooden pews. Even as the church was renovated to accommodate the growth that had forced it to hold two separate Sunday morning worship services, the new space had a simple, though much more contemporary, design. The lines of the worship space were stark. The walls were white and unadorned. Lacking were any liturgical accouterments besides the pulpit, communion table, altar railings, baptistery, and the pews. Along with these were several musical instruments including an organ, piano, electric keyboard, and drum set.

Harvest Church is a middle-class congregation located in a suburban community within a large metropolitan area. Over the last 18 years, the congregation has seen a complete metamorphosis from an all-white, working-class congregation to an almost completely African American lower-middle-class congregation. Although now it is predominantly Black, it is part of a denomination with a primarily Southern white heritage. So, while the congregation and its style of worship have changed considerably, the Southern white influence is reflected in many ways in the congregation's worship style. As Walter Hollenweger explains:

> In the structure of the Pentecostal "liturgy," one might find most of the elements of historical liturgies. Invocation, Kyrie, Confession, Gloria, Eucharist, Canon, and Benediction. Yet, these parts are hardly

ever so named and for most observers not recognized as such, since the element which structure the different parts of the service are not the rubrics and techniques, but the choruses, the short spontaneous songs known by heart by the whole congregation. [41]

The elements that Hollenweger identifies as Pentecostal liturgical presence are most evident in the program bulletin, or "Order of Worship" for each service. Such orders have been evident in almost every Sunday morning or evening Pentecostal worship service that I have visited (except in the smallest, most primitive storefronts). They are also provided for many special services such as revival meetings or regional fellowships involving more than one congregation. Some are crudely composed on electric typewriters or personal computers with minimal software. Others are professionally composed using the latest desktop publishing techniques. All of them, however, represent an attempt to impose some order on Pentecostal. worship,

The order of worship generally lists the elements of the worship service in chronological order, as well as who will lead or be in charge of each element. The basic liturgical format for the Pentecostal worship service is contained in the order of worship: the call to worship, the pastoral prayer, the Scripture reading(s), intercessory prayer, congregational and special music, the sermon, testimony, and altar ministry (individual prayer and laying on of hands). Whether the biblical readings are incorporated into the program varies from congregation to congregation. If the church does not have hymn

---

[41] Walter J. Hollenweger, "Social and Ecumenical Significance of Pentecostal Liturgy", 210.

books for everyone and a specific hymn is to be sung, it is usually photocopied or the words are neatly typed out in the program.

The spontaneous response to the perceived presence of the Holy Spirit would be the characteristic that most identifies storefront Pentecostal worship. This element certainly is present at Harvest Church. In such a climate, the order of worship serves as a guideline for conducting the service. Often, interspersed between these formal elements are extemporaneous testimonies, impromptu solos or congregational songs, prayers, and exhortations "as the Spirit leads." At all costs, Pentecostals believe that God's Spirit must have the freedom and the final say to direct the worship service in any direction.

What one would not find in the program or order of worship, but would be equally a part of a Pentecostal worship service, is the opportunity and expectation of the experience of the dynamic in-breaking of the Spirit of God at some point in the service. This is the time when congregants are most open to the experience of the direct presence of God through tongues speaking and/or ecstatic worship. If the singing is exceptionally lively or exceptionally devout, or if the prayer is exceptionally fervent or moving, there is likely to be an extended period when several people "break out in a shout" or "holy dance." Also, the presider (usually a minister or elder) will sense a special need among the people (sickness, grief, a financial difficulty, emotional distress, or "someone in need of salvation") and will break with the written order of the service, call for a time or prayer, and invite people to come to the altar. The pastor and/or several of the ministers might gather around those in need and proceed to anoint them with oil and pray for them individually or as a group. These moments are never seen as interruptions in the service. For, as Wilson and Clow point out, "they are experienced as opportunities for the congregation and the individual to reaffirm spiritual power."[42]

One Sunday morning at Harvest Church, during the time I was researching this paper, the congregational singing (designated "Praise and Worship") was proceeding. Several people were moved by the Spirit. A prolonged session of dancing or "shouting" broke out. The congregation continued to sing chorus after chorus of up-tempo worship songs. Though the pastor had a prepared message, he did not attempt to interrupt, but joined in the worship celebration and sang, clapped, and danced with the rest of the congregation. After about forty-five minutes, punctuated with a crescendo of raising and falling exuberance, the pastor moved to the podium to announce that, though he was prepared to preach, the Spirit had something else in mind and was leading the service another way. He did not mind yielding to the Spirit. At this point, the celebration became even livelier and continued for several more minutes. Eventually, a message was given in tongues. This was followed by an interpretation. When the interpretation was completed, the people stood for a moment in reverence, then the celebration and praise began again with some praising God in English, some in tongues. No one was shocked by this occurrence; it is expected. As Wilson and Clow observe:

> Pentecostal believers understand the Spirit as being imminently present in the worship service, and more importantly, imminently present within each individual believer who has been baptized in the Spirit.[43]

---

[42] Wilson and Clow, 244.
[43] Ibid.

Testimony as Liturgy

In a primarily oral tradition, oral means will be the primary carriers of the tradition. Certain rituals will become highly developed instruments for carrying out this function. Several scholars, including Spencer, Williams, and Tyson, have identified the testimony as such an instrument.

To an outsider, the testimony service may seem like a free-for-all event. On the signal of the presider, individuals stand and exhort each other about their experiences of faith. If you listen carefully, however, a definite, collective pattern is discernable in the individual testimonies. Although these testimonies are specific to the individual, certain themes are repeated, and these themes generally change and evolve as do other liturgical patterns.

The testimony generally starts with a greeting (or salutation) to the other members of the congregation and to the ministers: "First giving honor to the pastor, pulpit associates, saints, and friends." This is almost always followed by an affirmation that attests to the individual's right to be included in the community based on specific; shared spiritual experience: "Thank the Lord, that I'm still saved, sanctified, and filled with the Holy Ghost."[74] There are regional and cultural varieties to the patterns of testimonies and definite racial patterns that can be discerned in the language and style of testimonies. Even so, the basic elements of the individual testimonies have remained the same over several generations.

Whatever the formula for the body of the testimony, they all share an important final element, an invitation to assent by the faith community. These testimonies are not solo spiritual journeys the speaker details for detached spectators. Instead, the victory of the testifier becomes the victory of the congregation. Individual loss becomes group loss. Nowhere is this more evident than in the closing admonition to the listeners, that, "those who know the words of prayer, pray my strength in the Lord" or "I desire your prayers" or "pray much for me."[80]

Prayer and Conversion as Liturgy

Knowing the words of prayer is almost indispensable to participants in Pentecostal worship. These words are not known in the precise sense; they do not represent a formed, written prayer or learned formulations. Rather, they are the individual's contribution to the concert of extemporaneous congregational supplication. These words provide a sense of what is appropriate to say to God on behalf of the desired spiritual or material results. The sheer number of prayers offered during the typical worship service gives credence to the important role prayer plays in Pentecostal worship. Ranaghan's composite worship order, from research on several congregations, identified five prayer rituals interspersed throughout other elements of the service:

(1) the opening prayer of invocation,

(2) prayers first by the pastor and then by the congregation (pastoral or intercessory prayer),

(3) prayer for the Spirit to anoint the preacher,

(4) the altar call with congregational prayer and music in the background, and;

(5) the altar service; and (6) the benediction.[44]

---

[44] Ranaghan, "Conversion and Baptism," 88-69.

Most, if not all, of these prayers are extemporaneous.[45] In many congregations, everyone is expected to take part by praying together, simultaneously, but in their own words, out loud. Most worshipers will be praying in the vernacular of the congregation, but some may be praying in tongues. Others may be only offering sporadic "hallelujahs," "amens," "thank you, Jesus" or other mantras. A few may be just raising their hands in praise or waving their arms, weeping softly or clapping. But everyone is somehow engaged.

Even in the "altar service" the congregation participates in a major way when "seekers meet at the altar railing to pray. Often, ministers will impose hands, altar workers from the congregation will counsel and pray, the congregation or part of it may come forward to surround the seekers with praise and intercession, the choir may sing, or music may be played in the background."[46] Altar ministry is a vital part of many Holiness-Pentecostal worship services and is included at the end of many written orders of worship. The fluidity of these worship services allows the altar service to take place at any point as the Spirit directs. In some instances, there is more than one altar service in a single time of worship as the presider or minister senses is appropriate.

At First Church, the extended altar call was usually relegated to the end of the worship service and often became a mini-sermon. This was a prolonged appeal, often taking as long as ten to twenty minutes.

---

[45] Some Pentecostal congregations do use formal benedictions, however, these are usually familiar biblical passages such as : May the Lord watch between me and thee while we are absent one from another (Gen 31:49) or "The Lord bless thee, and keep thee; the Lord make his face shine upon thee, and be gracious unto thee; the Lord lift up his countenance upon thee, and give thee peace (Numbers 6:24-26). And, these are generally from the King James Version of Scripture.

[46] Ranaghan, 68.

The choir sang a hymn from the section of the hymn book under the salvation or conversion headings, as the pastor reiterated parts of the sermon that had just taken at least an hour to preach. He pleaded with those in the congregation who did not "know Jesus as your personal Savior" or needed to repent of some sin committed the previous week. They were urged to come to the altar and pray for salvation or forgiveness (in essence to "get right with God").

At Harvest Church, the intent of the altar call was the same, but the appeal was more general and considerably shorter. People are instructed that "whatever you need from the Lord" will be found at the altar. Here again, the altar service was generally at the end of the service, but, in keeping with the more free form, it also was a setting in which the altar service could be inserted extemporaneously into other portions of the worship service, "as the Spirit leads."

Another special prayer emphasis central to the Pentecostal self-definition is the prayer for receiving the baptism of the Holy Spirit. The mode for this type of prayer differs greatly from denomination to denomination and often between congregations within a denomination. The emphasis at First Church was on "tarrying" for the baptism of the Holy Spirit. "Tarrying meetings" were designated prayer services for seekers praying to "receive" the baptism of the Holy Spirit. Much of the misunderstanding of Spirit baptism as possession might derive from the chanting style of the prayer reminiscent of a mantra. The seeker repeatedly invokes the name "Jesus" or the word "hallelujah" or a phrase like "thank you Jesus" in an attempt to free one's mind and spirit from earthly concerns and become completely open to the divine.

Generally, seekers participated in several of these services before they, actually, spoke in tongues as a demonstration of the "initial evidence" that they had truly received or been baptized in the Spirit. Prayer for Holy Spirit baptism at Harvest Church is a much less formal undertaking and occurs as part of the regular altar service. There is no tarrying. There are no special prayer meetings set aside for this.

Conclusion

Two indispensable concepts are necessary for understanding how liturgy and ritual are present within Holiness and Pentecostal worship. The first is the self-definition of worship as non-liturgical. The second and equally important is the primarily oral tradition of these related movements. Despite this, several scholars have been able to document through ethnographic studies and theological reflection a distinct liturgical presence within Pentecostal worship.

The self-definition of these groups as non-liturgical does not speak to the reality of their worship. Pentecostal ministers are reluctant to admit that their services follow a planned (liturgical) order, and such elements as vestments and hymnology often have been dismissed as remnants of a dead faith and void of any signs of spiritual fervor. However, the foregoing gives some indication of the wealth and variety of liturgical presence in Pentecostal worship.

Within the primarily oral tradition, liturgical elements, ritual, and symbolism are not always written, and even when written sources are available, they are not always used. Hymns, choruses, and gospel songs are learned by heart and passed on by repetition. Entire scriptural passages are committed to memory. Their meaning is internalized and take on a shared symbolic significance for all who regularly participate in them.

No definition of liturgy, ritual, or symbolism used here indicates that participants must define what they are doing as such. Neither do they incorporate a distinction between written and oral modes. Yet, Pentecostalism's oral nature does not in any way preclude it from a liturgical definition. As Hollenweger indicates, adherents "demonstrate that their alternative to written liturgy is not chaos, but a flexible oral tradition that allows for variation within a framework..."[47] As Baer contends, this happens in much the same way as Quaker silence and Episcopalian or Catholic liturgy. For example, there is shared meaning among all Catholics about meanings ritual and symbolism, and there is a shared consensus among most Methodists about the meaning of Wesleyan rituals and symbolism. Yet, each Catholic and Methodist believer appropriates these in a personal way. Likewise, Pentecostal believers share meanings regarding ritual and symbolism. Each believer appropriates these shared understandings in a way that is particularly meaningful to their social, theological, and ethical contexts.

Hollenweger states correctly that the Pentecostal worship service is a "liturgy continually in the making."[48] As a congregation grows from sect to church type or its membership gradually moves into the middle class, the presence of liturgical form becomes even more obvious. However, even within the most high-church setting, the hand-clapping, shouts of "Praise the Lord," or quiet lifting of the hands in a reverent pose continue to be interspersed throughout the structured elements and serve as' the kind of iconic sights and sounds that Albrecht identifies as so important to Pentecostal worship. For he insists that:

---

[47] Hollenweger, "Social and Ecumenical Significance of Pentecostal Liturgy," 210.
[48] Ibid., 207.

> The vitality of Pentecostal ritual has less to do with the structure of the ritual than with the embodied attitudes, or the orientation which the congregants engage in the rites as structured. Salient sensibilities appropriately applied can help to produce living, breathing, moving ritual performance rather than lifeless acts of ritual.[49]

The two congregations that served as my models exhibited liturgical presence in different ways. Yet each considers itself thoroughly Pentecostal. What they share is a mode of spirituality in worship, with no loss of vitality. In coming to terms with the liturgical presence of what they are doing in worship; they will be able to understand that order and form are not synonymous with deadness, but with what the Bible calls "decency and order."

The emphasis of the broader church's understanding of the Spirit's person and place has been enriched by encounters with Pentecostal spirituality. Renewal groups now can be found in almost every Christian denomination and such encounters have focused renewed emphasis on the work of the Holy Spirit in the everyday life of the believer and congregation.

If it is to gain an appreciation for liturgical presence in worship, the Pentecostal movement must proceed from the broader ecclesiological understanding that has been unfolding over two thousand years of church history. Burgess suggests such a starting point with the possibility of "adopting a broader definition of sacrament as a rite directed by Scripture and observed by the gathered

---

[49] Albrecht, 120.

people of God"⁵⁰ Adopting such a definition and lifting up elements of their worship held common wider church, further enhances the opportunity for ecumenical dialog.

As Cecil Robeck asserts, we need to change those (understandings) that stand between us and that which is truly spiritual. Anything that divides the church and disrupts its true catholicity must be discarded. Otherwise, Pentecostalism will continue to be viewed as an anomaly or oddity.

What makes such change difficult, however, is that the tradition's oral nature brings with it a historical disconnectedness with the broader church. Even when the language is similar, the understandings often are different from those held throughout the Church's life and history. Yet, what is at stake in Pentecostal worship is not more or less spiritual ways of experiencing God. What Robeck asserts about Pentecostal spirituality, that it is "no different from other forms of spirituality," is essentially true of Pentecostal worship. As he affirms, the object of these symbols and rituals is the same.[51]

---

[50] Burgess and McGee, 653.
[51] Cecil M. Robeck The Nature of Pentecostal Spirituality," *Pneuma,* 14: Fall, 1992, 105.

Revisiting the "New Issue:" Toward a Broader Conversation on the Godhead[1]

All orthodox Christian traditions essentially hold the unity (monarchia) of the Godhead to be a fundamental doctrine. This foundational, non-negotiable tenet of faith, is what many theologians through the centuries have seen as a central theological issue of the Christian faith. Yet, within the unfolding history of the Contemporary Pentecostal movement, wrestling with the outworking of the nature of God's unity caused one of the most visible expressions of Evangelical Christianity to splinter into two contentious camps (Trinitarian or Oneness) nearly a century ago—within less than a decade of the birth of the movement. While there were other fissures within the early movement—the schism over Wesleyan Holiness understandings of salvation, the conception of the "finished work" of Calvary by William Durham, or the evolving racial fissure that has plagued much of its history—none has proven to be as deep or as serious, or as difficult to resolve.

Trinitarian Christians have historically and globally made, up the vast majority of the tradition, representing approximately 99% of all Christians, and not a significantly smaller proportion of Pentecostals. Conversely, there are an estimated 17,000,000 Oneness Pentecostal adherents out of 600,000,000 million Pentecostals globally, with 2.2 million of them within the United States. This represents only one-half to one percent of all Pentecostals and an even smaller proportion of all Christians or Evangelicals.

---

[1] This paper was originally presented at the 42nd Annual Meeting of the Society for Pentecostal Studies.

Significantly, the Oneness theological understanding has primarily been limited to the Pentecostal tradition.[2] Further, outside of the context of Pentecostalism, this theology is largely unknown or roundly rejected as heretical.

Theoretically, then, one might suggest that such a small faction could have no significant impact on its common witness. Yet, Oneness Pentecostal have been persistent in their vehement insistence that they have an essential contribution to make to the Pentecostal theological project and that they offer an important revelatory insight without which the broader faith tradition remains off course. They further insist that failure to take this contribution seriously is detrimental to God's salvific project. In opposition, Trinitarian believers dismiss such inference as merely coming from another, heretical group of discontents who rightly have been locked out of the broader theological conversation—not unlike the Mormons or Jehovah's Witnesses.

Some leaders within either faction attach unfortunate connotations such as "artificial Pentecostals," to the other. They often entirely shun or vilify them, or most disturbingly, offer official condemnation of each other's doctrinal stances. Adherents on either side regularly attempt to convert the other to what each considers "authentic Christian faith." In some instances, family relationships of professing Christians are destroyed over the issue. In a division that parallels the liberal and conservative Christian gulf—though both groups are found in either camp—individuals are denied employment in "Christian" organizations and locked out of pulpits and lecture halls,

---

[2] Though there is at least one Baptist group, Emmanuel Tabernacle Baptist Church of the Apostolic Faith, and several Non-denominational group that embrace this doctrinal understanding.

or otherwise discredited. All of this comes about simply because opposing group members don't correctly pronounce what is a shibboleth regarding the appropriate understanding of the nature of the Godhead. A Oneness colleague pointed out to me, for example, that it is unfortunate that Trinitarian believers (even Trinitarian Pentecostals) are Christians, "but are not saved."

Interestingly, however, this level of division does not occur at the grassroots of the movement. Trinitarian and Oneness Pentecostals laypersons regularly attend each other's worship services, work on ministry projects together, or enjoy fellowship with each other. Often they do not know, or at least understand the distinctions in the others' doctrines. In fact, many Oneness and Trinitarian Pentecostal laypeople worship together under the assumption that they share the same doctrine of God.

The majority of Evangelical Christians (including Pentecostals) hold the word "Trinity" in the same sacred esteem as the people of Israel held the name YAHWEH. In some instances, Trinitarians act as if the terminology and conception were handed down by God himself with the commandments at Mt. Sinai. For them, it is as if the word was the name forbidden to be taken in vain instead of Jehovah. Trinitarians define God as three persons coexisting consubstantially as one in being. Some Adherents contend that the formulation is "the most foundational doctrine of the Christian faith."[3] Moreover, for many, the terms Trinity and Godhead are interchangeable, as if they were no other way to conceive of the Divine Being.

---

[3] Michael Foust, "T. D. Jakes Embraces Doctrine of the Trinity, Moves Away from 'Oneness' View," *Christianity Today,* https://www.christianitytoday.com/news/2012/january/td-jakes-embraces-doctrine-of-trinity-moves-away-from.html.

At the opposite end, Oneness believers (primarily, but not exclusively within the Pentecostal tradition),[4] understand that, yes, there is one God, but that this God exists as a singular Divine Spirit, who manifests himself in varying temporal and soteriological contexts as either Father, Son, or Holy Spirit. Oneness Pentecostals reject the Trinitarian doctrine of the distinct existence of eternally co-equal persons in one triune Godhead as an extra-Biblical invention with no foundation in Scripture. In essence, Oneness theology teaches that there is only one numerically singular God and that this God is Jesus Christ in whom "dwells the fullness of the Godhead bodily."[5]

Having been raised within the Oneness tradition, and still maintaining relations with several Oneness colleagues, I easily moved into a Trinitarian congregation several decades ago. I saw little difference in the worship. Jesus was still at the center. We still pray for new believers to receive the Pentecostal Holy Spirit baptism with the initial evidence of speaking in tongues. We still baptized them by immersion in water, though these baptisms were scheduled rather than spontaneous.

After that move, however, my Oneness community practically declared me anathema much as ancient Jewish families disowned a child who became a Christian believer. And the dividing line for some of them remains as rigidly drawn as forty years ago. While it is understandable that I am not invited to preach in their pulpits or teach in their conferences, the division goes far beyond that. Some Oneness brothers and sisters distance themselves socially, not allowing for any extended fellowship.

---

[4] For example, Emmanuel Tabernacle Baptist Church of the Apostolic Faith was founded in 1917 by Martin Rawleigh Gregory.
[5] Colossians 2:9.

For some Oneness faithful, I have been grandfathered in because I grew in the tradition and was baptized in the "name of the Lord Jesus Christ" as a child. But, often in my conversation with them, I sense that they assume that, in my heart, I know "the truth," but have chosen to worship with Trinitarian congregations within Trinitarian denominations simply for logistical or practical reasons.

My Trinitarian colleagues, on the other hand, imposed a test of faith to ascertain the orthodoxy of my understandings of God. This juxtaposition was manifested when I applied for ministerial credentials within the denomination with which I have been affiliated for several years. I was required to be re-baptized with the Trinitarian formula, as my previous baptism was considered invalid. During denominational ministerial training, it was pointed out to our class that though Oneness Pentecostals spoke in tongues, it was not by the power of God, but by "some other spirit" since they were not Christian.

Religionist, J. Lee Grady refers to this unfortunate fissure as a "family split" that involves "hateful name-calling" and often leads those on each side to "condemn each other to hell."[6] Indeed, the issues between the two camps have become so sensitive that among the scholarly colleagues within the Society for Pentecostal Studies,[7] any official dialog related to the issue has been carried out behind closed doors with a select number of participants chosen by its leadership to speak for each side. Grassroots members of the Society (themselves academics and other intellectuals) had only limited access to the proceedings through official reports.

---

[6] J. Lee Grady, "The Other Pentecostals" *Charisma* (June 1997)."

[7] See, Frank Machia, "The Oneness-Trinitarian Pentecostal Dialogue: Exploring the Diversity of Apostolic Faith" *The Harvard Theological Review* 103:3 (July 2010), 329-349.

My failure to endorse or anathematize either posture as the singularly correct understanding of the Godhead has left me squarely in the middle of a feud between the two camps. Yet, castigation or vilification of the opposing group defies God's self-disclosure as uniquely mystery and beyond our finite understanding. While, with both groups, I hold the orthodox understand that God had revealed Godself as eternally existing as one in three persons (or revelations), I contend that God has not revealed how this true. Further, the ability to articulate the correct formulation is not a valid test or who is or is not Christian.

Historical Division

Both streams of contemporary classical Pentecostalism have a common beginning point in the 1906 Azusa Street revival. As the fervor of that revival began to wane, the enthusiasm for Pentecostal worship was spreading

One of those events, the Apostolic Faith Worldwide Camp Meeting, convened in the spring of 1913 in Arroyo Seco, California, with acclaimed evangelist Maria Woodworth-Etter as one of its main preachers.

At the same meeting, Canadian evangelist, Robert McAlister, administered baptisms to new converts. McAlister stunned the crowd when he proclaimed that the apostles never used the Trinitarian formula —in the name of the Father, and of the Son, and of the Holy Spirit, outlined in the Matthew 28:19 passage. Instead, the apostles baptized converts in the name of Jesus as outlined in Acts 2:38, that McAlister contended was preferable. After hearing McAlister's sermon and staying up all night praying, John G. Scheppe ran through the camp the next morning, shouting that he had received a new revelation from God about the name of Jesus.

Importantly, for this conversation, many of the early Oneness proponents such as Frank J. Ewart, Glenn Cook, and William and Maggie Bowdan were prominently involved in and received their Pentecostal Holy Spirit baptism at the Azusa Street Revival. They were also among the earliest emissaries of the movement that flowed from Seymour's mission. Further, their involvement in a movement that appreciated continuing subordinate revelation allowed them to appropriate Oneness doctrine into their theology.

For the sake of unity, Seymour never inserted himself into the middle of the fray. In his 1915 publication, *The Doctrines and Discipline of the Azusa Street Apostolic Faith Mission, Los Angeles, California*. However, the Azusa Street revival leader referred to the practice of baptism in Jesus' name as unbiblical.[8]

Over time, as Pentecostal bodies took on more structure, denominational statements were used to solidify the official doctrinal positions. The largest Oneness denomination, the United Pentecostal Church International, and the Assemblies of God, one of the largest Trinitarian Pentecostal denominations in the United States have officially condemned each other's doctrines within published faith statements.

What Trinitarian and Oneness Pentecostals Share

Might it be, however, that Oneness and Trinitarian Pentecostals have more in common than the issues separating them? And, might

---

[8] Talmadge French, *Early Interracial Oneness Pentecostalism: G. T. Haywood and the Pentecostal Assemblies of the World (1901-1931)*. Eugene, OR: Wipf and Stock Publishers, 2014. 58.

these common points serve as a beginning location for a mutually richer dialog and common witness of Pentecostal unity. In the least, might it be a framework for what I have previously called an "ecumenism of the Spirit" that acknowledges, but makes way for divergence on theological themes that are difficult to understand, more or less, resolve.

As a starting point, in the main, both Oneness and Trinitarian traditions hold to a broad "orthodox" Evangelical theological stance. Both sides affirm a high view of the authority of Scripture, the unique divinity of Christ, His atoning work on the Cross, and the necessity of personal faith for salvation. These affirmations bind them in a common heritage with all Evangelical Christians as over against such groups as the Church of Jesus Christ of the Latter Day Saints (Mormons) or Jehovah's Witnesses,[9] or even what might be considered liberal Christians. These affirmations also place them in opposition to those who are less likely to hold these propositions as central to Christian faith. For, Mormons and Jehovah's Witnesses are not considered non-Christian because they deny the Trinity, but because they deny the deity of Christ and his exclusive atoning work on the cross.

However, it is this commitment to the authority of Scripture that is often the crux for any stumbling block in forging the division. Against those who contend that Oneness Pentecostals employ a rigid hermeneutic, Kenneth Archer explains,

---

[9] While the Church of Jesus Christ of the Latter Day Saints hold that Jesus Christ is divine, they also hold that his divinity is not unique in that we may all become God through the process of exaltation. On the other hand, Jehovah's Witnesses hold that was a perfect man, and that he is a person distinct from God the Father.

> Oneness Pentecostalism was not the result of an unbending literalism, but... an unwillingness to embrace doctrinal statements like Trinity that were not directly supported by exact words or phrases in the New Testament, especially from the book of Acts. Hence, Oneness Pentecostals were unbending in their consistent rejection of the philosophical language of man-made creeds which did not express a biblical understanding and/or language.[10]

Yet, these divided brethren and sisters have an even closer affinity in their common heritage of the Azusa Street Revival that birth the movement they both claim as their own. Both embrace its emphasis on immediate access to the Holy Spirit and the Spirit's empowerment of the believer for righteousness, acts of service, and supernatural manifestation within the individual's and community's life. And many within both groups insist that speaking in tongues is the initial evidence of Holy Spirit baptism. Further, the majority of both groups hold generally conservative theological views that work themselves out in an ethic of personal and social holiness. It was not until seven years after the Azusa Street Revival had gotten underway, that the "new issue" as Oneness theology came to be known, exploded on the scene.

Theologically, both Oneness and Trinitarian believers resolve the issue of distinction of monotheistic consciousness in the Godhead by attributing ontological oneness of being to the Father, the Son, and the Holy Spirit. They both affirm that the three are co-equally and eternally God. The discrepancy lies within their understandings of the way the

---

[10] Kenneth J. Archer, *A Pentecostal Hermeneutic: Spirit, Scripture and Community*. Cleveland, TN: CPT Press, 2009, 92.

three are distinct and in what way they are one. Trinitarians maintain that each of the three is a discrete individual member of the Godhead who has maintained that distinction throughout eternity. Oneness Pentecostals maintain that neither the Father, the Son, or the Holy Spirit are singular persons, but rather are distinct modes, or manifestations, of the One divine being.

Neither tradition negates the deity and lordship of Christ nor the exclusive salvific effectiveness of his atoning work on the Cross. Neither violates the understanding of the requirement of belief on Christ for salvation. And, undeniably, protecting the deity of Christ is part and parcel of both Trinitarian and Oneness Pentecostal projects. In neither case is Jesus either simply a moral exemplar or the victim of unfortunate circumstances that led to his crucifixion. For both, instead, he is eternally God, creator of heaven and earth, who from the foundation of the world was determined to be the only acceptable sacrifice for the sins of humankind.

Essentially, it is the belief in the existence of the three persons as divine beings, not the separation or unity of the three persons, that distinguishes Christianity from the two other monotheistic religions—Judaism and Islam. And, both Oneness and Trinitarian Pentecostal traditions hold that all three members of the Godhead equally share in that divine reality. Neither holds a subordinate view of the Son that attributes a lesser degree of divinity to Him. Within both traditions, neither, the Father, the Son, nor the Holy Spirit is less God.

What both camps struggle with (as does much of the Christian tradition) is a way to explain how God can be, at the same time, both three and one. For none of the traditional illustrations have proven adequate.

Both camps refute the Arian understanding of subordinationism that concludes the Son, although divine, was a creature and, therefore, less than God the Father. Unlike Arianism, both Oneness and Trinitarian Pentecostals hold to an ontological oneness (union) between the Father and Son. Although unapologetically modalistic, Oneness Pentecostals, resemble their Trinitarian brethren in their divergence from a Sabellian view that claims that the trinitarian names refer to three modes or manifestations of the one single divine being successively revealing Godself in history.

What can be gained or lost?

In making headway in our discussion, we must recognize that all theology is political. In every dogmatic argument, some substantial ground can be gained as well as some important footage may be lost by either side. Each party has some interest that they feel bound to protect, and over which they are continually tempted to break fellowship with other Christians.

On the one hand, Oneness Pentecostals attempt to protect the deity of the Son as the co-equal, co-eternal member of the Godhead. For them, Jesus, the second person of the Godhead, is the singular focus of Christian faith. Alternatively, Trinitarian Pentecostals seek to ensure that subordinationist conceptions of the Godhead do not seep into their understanding.

Often when Trinitarians move into the Oneness camp or vice versa, they give up their understandings of propositions they formerly held sacred to insist that they have, finally, found "the" truth. Many new convert senses that they are compelled to refute previously held doctrinal understandings. Moreover, like the sinner who converts to

Christian faith later in life, they often become the most vehement proponents of their newfound reality.

This project of protecting one's truth makes this enterprise of coming to a commonly understood middle position so difficult. Both sides ardently feel that they are doing God's bidding in defending a vital orthodoxy within an authentic Christian faith.

Given these critical self-interests, the question still must be raised regarding what each side stands to gain or lose if they come to appreciate, if not adopt, a middle way position. The issue both sides must respond to is whether continued fissure within the movement is warranted or sustainable, and what the cost might be for maintaining their staunch postures.

Possible Gains

Within the ecumenical context, settling on a middle way position jointly held by all Evangelical, Spirit-empowered believers, would, obviously, bring about greater unity within the Pentecostal segment of the body of Christ as well as with other Christian faith traditions. Further, it would preserve the affirmation of the understanding that the Godhead is a mystery that theologians have wrestled with for two thousand years. Contrary to the contention of either side, it is not a settled issue.

And some of the greatest ancient and contemporary theologians have been hard-pressed to find a convincing solution. For even the most esteemed theologians found difficulty in discussing the unique situation of the Godhead. Reformed theologian Karl Barth, for example, used the terminology, "one divine subject in three different modes of being." Karl Rahner, on the other hand, insisted on the language of "modes of subsistence." In the end, the rethinking of positions requires the humble consideration that no aspect of the infinite God is completely knowable by the finite human mind. One of the most prominent forerunners of the Evangelical tradition, John Wesley, believed strongly in the doctrine of the Trinity, but he did not insist on belief in it for recognizing someone as a Christian.[11]

Historically, Pentecostals have been reluctant to rely on assistance from formal, academic theologians to clarify doctrinal stances. Rather, they have been disposed to assert that the same direct, continuing revelation that birth this understanding of the new issue is a surer aid in understanding the unknowable. Adopting a middle way posture, however, would deliver both camps from any insistence of claims of an exclusively correct understanding of the nature of the Godhead—which is idolatry.

An initial step might be acknowledging that any baptism that recognizes and affirms the lordship of Jesus Christ is valid. This would eliminate the necessity of rebaptism for believers who, subsequently, affiliate with the other tradition. While this overture might be considered anathema to denominational leaders, such practical solutions are already in place among pastoral colleagues within local congregations who adjust baptismal formulas to accommodate this broader understanding. I have also been present at baptismal rituals in classical Pentecostal, Trinitarian congregations that have invoked the formula, "[i]n the name of the father, the Son—the Lord Jesus Christ and the Holy Spirit," so that members with differing understandings could be accommodated.

---

[11] Olson, Roger E. How Important Is the Doctrine of the Trinity? *Patheos* (April 29, 2013). http://www.patheos.com/blogs/rogereolson/2013/04/1807, viewed 1/21/17.

Such accommodations are also in place among non-denominational Charismatic bodies who adjust their statements of faith to include a broader understanding. For example, the prominent televangelist, T. D. Jakes has managed to keep his theologically varied following by adopting the position that there is,

> one God, Creator of all things, infinitely perfect, and eternally existing in three manifestations: Father, Son, and Holy Spirit. [12]

Another example of this accommodation is seen in the statement of faith of Joseph Garlington, a former Oneness megachurch pastor who has gained some prominence in broader Evangelical circles, that there is,

> one true God who has revealed Himself as existing in three persons; Father, Son, and Holy Spirit; distinguishable but indivisible. (Matthew 28:19, Luke 3:21-22)[13]

Both formulations differ decidedly from the adamant sentiment expressed in the hymnody prominent within bodies in which either of these former Oneness Pentecostals were raised, that there is "one, one, one way to God—Baptize in Jesus name."[14] But it also moves away

---

[12] "Belief Statement" of The Potter's House, viewed on 10/23/16 at http://thepottershouse.org/explore/belief-statement/.

[13] "Our Beliefs, Covenant Church Pittsburg viewed on 10/23/16 at http://ccop.org/our-belief/.

[14] This is the lyric a popular Oneness Pentecostal baptismal chorus. Though its authorship is uncertain, is was popularized by Sherrod C. Johnson, founding bishop of the Church of The Lord Jesus Christ of the Apostolic Faith, as the theme song of his weekly radio broadcast.

from the insistence of words of the stalwart Trinitarian hymn, "God in three persons, blessed Trinity."[15]

Possible Losses

By adopting rigid stances, both sides stand in danger of erasing the mystery of the Godhead and reducing the unfathomable nature of the Divine Being to a formulation that must be held, if not fully understood and believed, much like Catholic dogmatic pronouncements. The exclusive insistence by either side that their position is the only possible biblical revelation of the nature of the Godhead is both problematic and dangerously divisive. Instead, each side is called to abandon their insistence that the opposing view is spiritually deficient up and that either understanding is unequivocally right to the absolute exclusion of the other.

What we know for sure from Scripture is that there is only one God and by inference, only one Godhead who has existed throughout eternity as an indivisible unity. Yet how that Divine reality operates in God's essence does and should remain a mystery that protects the sovereign lordship of God. Christian humility requires proponents, as well as opponents of either stance to confess the limit of human finitude for understanding the depth of such mysteries.

Our contemporary individualistic worldview conceives of personhood differently from the understanding held by the Church Fathers. Unlike these Fathers, who consistently envisioned personhood within community, within this modern worldview, the human conception of this Divine Reality could easily lead either the unsophisticated Trinitarian believer to hold a tri-theistic conception of

---

[15] Reginald Heber, "Holy, Holy, Holy! Lord God Almighty!" s.l.: s.n., 1826.

God or the Oneness believer to hold a solitary conception of God. A crucial step in appropriating a middle position is relinquishing individualistic understandings of personhood to engage an understanding of the Godhead that more closely resembles the unity it represents.

Yet, the debate is more than simply semantics as the Charismatic religionist, Grady would contend.[16] It essential that one not be forced to espouse a nonchalant either/or position, as if the conversation does not matter, or place oneself at either end of the furthest poles of the theological continuum, distancing oneself from the other. But rather, for the sake of a common witness of the deity and salvific significance of Christ, what must be worked out is a both/and position that makes room for the possibility of both positions and allows a broader understanding. For, most importantly, through an ecumenical lens, what is lost when this does not happen is the opportunity for such a common, unified witness to the transforming power of the Holy Spirit to offer grace and build community, within the midst of theological diversity.

For such a project to work, both camps must rethink their, largely uninformed, exegetical projects that support their claim of reading relevant scriptural texts as the only appropriate rendering. Oneness Pentecostals are correct in insisting that the baptismal formula of Matthew 28:19 "in the name of the Father, and of the Son, and of the Holy Spirit" is never again mentioned in Scripture, while references are made to baptism in the name of Jesus.[17] Might it be, however, that the literal importance attached to this point is overstated? Could

---

[16] Grady, "The Other Pentecostals," *Charisma Magazine* (June 1997), 62-68.

[17] Such as in Acts 10:48, 8:16 or 19:5.

Trinitarians also be correct in posturing that the early disciples operated within a context that made it necessary to invoke the literal name of Jesus within a culture that had explicitly denied His deity? On the other hand, could it be that the Trinitarian insistence on this point also might be overstated? Could it be that both formulas were used by the New Testament and Patristic church depending on the cultural context in which they found themselves (e.g., whether their audience was Hellenistic or Jewish)?

Further, could we affirm that the exact relationship between the Father, Son, and Holy Spirit was not explicitly defined in the New Testament or the writings of Ante-Nicene Fathers? And, might we concede that the earliest formulation of Trinitarian doctrine came about three hundred years after Church's birth in response to the controversy regarding Christ's deity, that both sides hold as absolute?[18] And this critical turn is part of what Pentecostals have come to value as non-negotiable, ongoing subordinate revelation on which both sides, in part, base their arguments.

Starting Ground for a Middle Position

Less this project of finding a practical middle ground seems impossible to envision, core common beliefs hold Oneness and Trinitarians together on solid footing for a higher level of dialog. Again, they agree that there is only one God. Secondly, both hold that the Father, Son, and Spirit are all and equally God. Third, each agrees that Scripture makes a distinction between Father, Son, and Spirit. And, finally, both hold that only Jesus Christ, the begotten Son of God—and not the Father—died on the cross.

---

[18] Originally defined during the First Council of Nicaea in 325 and refined at the First Council of Constantinople in 381.

However, significant divergence in their understandings of these this common foundation makes efforts at rapprochement somewhat rocky. First, Trinitarians hold that the one God consists of three eternal persons, while Oneness adherents believe the one God is only one person. Secondly, Trinitarians insist that the second person of the Trinity became incarnate, while Oneness adherents believe YHWH, the lone person of the Godhead, became incarnate. Third Trinitarians hold that the Son is an eternal person in the Godhead, while Oneness adherents believe the Son is a term referring to YHWH's temporal human existence. Lastly, Trinitarians understand the biblical distinction between Father and Son to be a distinction between two divine persons. On the other hand, Oneness adherents understand the Father-Son distinction as relating to the way God exists in Godself (Father), the way God came to exist as man (Son), or the way God expresses Godself in salvation history.

As relates to the authority of Scripture, both camps hold that the Bible, as the word of God, is uniquely revelatory. Still, despite the mixed witness in the literal text, both sides insist that Scripture, as the final authority, clearly supports their respective positions. Both insist that the biblical witness, given to the church by Divine revelation provides the exclusive disclosure by which the Godhead is to be represented; for each, any other representations are heresy. Further, for each, their unique exposition represents the authoritative biblical position.

Again, in looking to the actual text, it cannot be denied that the biblical witness is that the disciples baptized their converts "in the name of Jesus." Further, Oneness adherents are correct that the word, "Trinity," is absent from the biblical text. However, their insistence that specific inferences to the reality of the existence of the three persons in either Hebrew Scripture or the New Testament is overly ambitious.[19]

Furthermore, both traditions appreciate continuing, subordinate revelation through which the mystery of Godself clarifies the ongoing work of the Spirit. And both hold that appropriation of their truth—their version of continuing revelation—is critical for salvation. It is through this appreciation for such continuing revelation that both formulations achieved prominence in their respective camps.

While Trinitarians contend that their official doctrine was established by early Church councils through the clarification provided through such revelation, Oneness Pentecostals, contend that it was through such subordinate revelation that their position unfolded. Several months after the Azusa Street Revival was birthed, Canadian evangelist, Robert McAlister preached a message that signaled a turning point in Pentecostal history. In it, he identified the name of Jesus as the formula that had been revealed to him as appropriate for Christian baptism.[20]

Despite a history of unbroken continuing revelation, might it be unreasonable for Oneness Pentecostals to believe that for most of the 2000 years of church history, almost the entire church got it completely wrong? Could it be untenable to believe that, therefore, the bulk of those identifying themselves as believers during that period were not only deficient in faith but were not Christian? For Oneness Pentecostals label the Trinitarian formula, and the baptismal ritual in

---

[19] See for example, plural references to God within the Creation narrative (i.e., Gen 1:1 and 1:26). The clearest biblical statement of plurality in God is seen in Isaiah 48:16-17.

[20] See Steve Studebaker "Baptism among Pentecostals" in Gordon L. Heath, ed., *Baptism: Historical, Theological, and Pastoral Perspectives.* Eugene, OR: Wipf & Stock Publisher, 2011, 201-224.

which it is used, as Catholic error forced on the church with the Nicene Creed. That suggestion mirrors the arrogance some in both camps exhibit in insinuating that only those who speak in tongues are baptized in the Holy Spirit, that Christians who do not exhibit this initial evidence are not filled with God's Spirit, or that only those who exhibit this evidence are saved.

Perhaps, for Pentecostals in both camps, however, the principal issue is the spaces where we can find harmony. One way beyond the impasse is to discuss the work of the Holy Spirit in the life of the worshipping community.[21]

A Way Forward–The Perichoretic Godhead

A fruitful proposal suggests a turn to the concept of the perichoretic Godhead as a way to protect both investments and move forward. This conception, as put forth by liberation theologian, Leonardo Boff contends that a proper understanding of the Godhead requires that we see it as the interpersonal, interdependent relationship of the three persons to one another. This understanding insists on the complete, co-indwelling, co-inhering, and interdependence of the three members of the Godhead such that neither can be extracted from, or act independently of, the other.[22] It combines Threeness and Oneness is a way that precludes the danger of either modalism or tri-theism.[23]

---

[21] Jason Oliver Evans *Taking the Doctrine of God off the Table: A Necessary Theological Dialogue Between Black Oneness and Trinitarian Pentecostals*. Master's Thesis, Duke University Divinity School, 2001, 29.

[22] For a full discussion of the Perichoretic Trinity see Leonardo Boff, *Holy Trinity, Perfect Community*. Maryknoll, NY: Orbis Books, 2000.

[23] Bingaman, Brock. *All Things New: The Trinitarian Nature of the Human Calling in Maximus the Confessor and Jürgen Moltmann*. Eugene, OR: Pickwick Publications, 2014, 22.

Within this understanding, we can openly speak of God's trinity in unity as "Trinity in Oneness." A cogent representation of this idea can be seen in a three-sided prism. Each side is distinct and each has a separate, recognizable face. Yet it is only when they are strategically attached that they make up the three-sided prism. To take either side away is to destroy the structural integrity of the whole. Yet while no side is ever out of place, not all sides can be viewed at the same time—from a single vantage point.

Alister McGrath assists us with this understanding of the Godhead when he asserts that the perichoretic Trinity, "allows the individuality of the persons to be maintained while insisting that each person partakes in the life of the other two. An image often used to express this idea is that of a 'community of being,' in which each person, while maintaining their distinctive identity, penetrates the others and is penetrated by them."[24]

Again, at a practical level, Oneness Pentecostals are as ethnically diverse as are Trinitarians, with a strong representation from the black community. However, the broader Pentecostal tradition can take some cues from its African American constituency. For, accept at the farthest extreme, the issue that is so divisive to the broader movement is less problematic among black Pentecostals, especially in North America. Though each camp still maintains its doctrinal position, leaders often trade pulpits and participate in cooperative ecumenical and community building projects. For them, at least at the practical level, the experiential evidence of salvation and holiness of life exceeds doctrinal difference.

---

[24] McGrath, Alister. *Christian Theology: An Introduction,* 3rd ed. Malden, MA: Wiley, Blackwell, 2001, 325.

Another clue could come from the willingness of the Pentecostal academy to tackle other issues that are ignored or taboo within the broader movement. Within Pentecostal Bible and theological schools, would it be possible to open our doors to students (as well as faculty and/or staff) who hold—but do not forcefully promulgate—opposing views? Might theological classrooms become safe places to interrogate divergent conceptions that neither negate a particular stance nor vilify the opposing understanding as heretical or demonic? In this way, we could invite critical thinking that opens future Pentecostal leaders to fruitful dialog and the possibility of greater unity.

Finally, though Pentecostals repeatedly castigate other Evangelicals for their propositional approach to theology, they often mirror this approach, keeping the shibboleth of correct understanding as the door into fellowship with one another. Might a more profitable approach be found in intentionally seeking to develop a solid fellowship that allows our common experience of the Spirit to guide our theological interactions in such a way that we come to understand the other as a full brother or sister in the faith? From there, we can begin to listen to each other's testimonies of experiences in the Spirit to discern common ground on which to begin deeper dialog regarding our common witness.

What Doth the Lord Require: Toward a Pentecostal Theology of Justice

Since its dramatic early 20th century beginnings and despite the ruminations of a few progressive black Pentecostal leaders, the modern Pentecostal movement has continued to draw criticism from a number of both internal and external arenas, for a variety of reasons. Two areas of critique particularly interest me as an African-American Pentecostal woman scholar serving in the urban context with its full range of social problems and need for relevancy. First, Pentecostalism has been castigated as a "Spirit" or "tongues" movement—a totally emotive religious expression lacking a clearly articulated, cohesive theological foundation. Secondly, it has been criticized for the perception that Pentecostal individuals, congregations, and denominations are seemingly preoccupied with other-worldly sensibilities and personal piety to the almost utter neglect of social realities facing our communities.

To what extent are the criticisms of lack of involvement in social justice and a clearly articulated theology valid? Moreover, to the extent that they are true, to what extent are contemporary Pentecostals moving to rectify these shortcomings while holding to their important theological distinctives? Ultimately, however, are Pentecostals willing to subject our theological self-understanding to the critical reflection required to identify blind spots that hinder a full understanding of the biblical mandate for the justice God desires for humankind?

Again, despite these seeming weaknesses, Pentecostal spirituality remains the fastest-growing segment of the Christian tradition. With growth has come inescapable institutionalization. Pentecostal congregations in the Western hemisphere—especially the Northern portion of that hemisphere—increasingly resemble the congregations of their mainline or Evangelical detractors in their socio-economic mix, political attitudes, and styles of worship. Pentecostal congregations have also historically exhibited a full range of responses to social justice depending, as in other traditions, on the prophetic vision of their leaders and the particular political proclivity and social consciousness of their membership.

Some individuals and congregations have provided progressive practical approaches for the communities they serve, involving themselves in true social justice as well as social action and benevolence. Innovative programs combine preaching of the gospel and ministry to spiritual, emotional, and material needs with advocacy, education, and social empowerment.[25] Other segments of the movement have maintained status quo, 'quasi-biblical', interpretations of contemporary problems such as race relations, urban violence, family and community disassociation, and gender issues without making any meaningful contributions.

We can make the same type of comparison regarding the theological maturity of the movement. Some segments of the movement, primarily larger, more progressive congregations, and denominations have begun to take the tasks of theological reflection and articulation seriously have begun the process of developing cohesive, systematic doctrinal statements and theological treatises. This group has broken rank with their peers by refuting biblical literalism and reconsidering the nature of biblical authority. At the same time,

---

[25] Herbert Daughtry's House of the Lord Pentecostal Church in Brooklyn, New York, Arthur Brazier's Apostolic Faith Church in Chicago, and Eugene Rivers' Azusa Community in Boston are excellent examples of this type of "Progressive Pentecostalism." See, for example, Sammie M. Dortch, *When God Calls: A Biography of Artur M. Brazier*. Grand Rapids, MI: Wm. B. Eerdmans Publishing Co., 1996.

they have attempted to respond to contemporary issues such as racism, gender equity, poverty and economic injustice, homosexuality, HIV/AIDS with more compassionate and nuanced strategies than would have previously been considered.

Other segments of the movement have preferred to maintain an essentially oral and eclectic theological tradition that eschews any genuine engagement with the contemporary situation. They see the tendencies of more progressive siblings as spiritual compromise and a threat to its integrity and unity. For them, such compromise stifles the opportunity for dynamic revelation by the Holy Spirit and is synonymous with retreat. They maintain their historical disdain for "man-made" theologies, often preferring to see the Bible as their only frame of reference. What makes the difference regarding justice issues? What is the impetus for the two approaches to the theological task? Several questions related to these issues serve as a starting point for developing a Pentecostal theology that is both systematic and comprehensive, as well as sensitive to the issues of social justice in the society of which Pentecostals are—willingly or not—a part. Importantly, how can a salient twenty-first-century theology retain a distinctively Pentecostal ethos while addressing biblical and contextual justice mandates in our congregations, denominations, communities, and world? Such theology must take seriously the Pentecostal self-understanding of a movement that is ever open to the Spirit of God for revelation and empowerment of individuals and congregations to act on God's behalf while mediating God's concern for the world He so loved.

Biblical Framework

Within the theological quadrilateral of Scripture, tradition, reason, and experience, critiques of Pentecostalism would place its emphasis on experience, specifically the experience of the baptism of the Holy Spirit. What is not always obvious to the casual observer, however, is that concepts of Word and Spirit are integrally related in the life of the Pentecostal individual and movement. Pentecostals consider themselves "people of the Word" as much as "people of the Spirit." The movement sees itself as an obedient response to New Testament imperatives for Christian life and worship. Scripture reading and Bible study are deemed essential to Christian formation and discipleship.

While Pentecostals see all Scripture as divinely inspired, the New Testament is normative as a paradigm for God's relating to the modern world and the church. The Acts depiction of Pentecost and subsequent episodes of persons being filled with the Spirit through the Apostles' ministry are viewed as cogent models for today's church. Further, the unfolding New Testament church life as characterized in the epistles becomes a workable paradigm for present-day Christian practice.

Major Pentecostal hermeneutics and preaching revolve around a personal salvation or "born-again" experience, a personal relationship with Christ, sanctification or growth toward holiness, and the ongoing manifestation of spiritual gifts (especially healing) as necessary for effective ministry to the Body of Christ and the world. Other themes include growth in Christian virtues characterized by self-giving action or "good works" and moral and ethical purity, evangelism and discipleship of others, the sovereignty and all-sufficiency of God, and the deity and authority of Christ.

Contemporary socio-political implications of Old Testament prophecy are de-emphasized, except as they relate to a messianic vision of an eschatological outworking of God's Kingdom. Emphasis is given, of course, to Joel's discourse of the latter-day outpouring of the Holy Spirit "on all flesh." And, importantly, a distinction is made between Old Testament law and New Testament grace. As such, the law is represented as being only a guide to Christian morality. Ironically, however, emphasis on piety in hermeneutics and preaching quickly aligns itself with legalistic, Old Testament prophetic standards for personal morality.

The lack of a detailed theological framework does not preclude Pentecostals from having a strong, sometimes very personal, ethical foundation. Specific "biblical" injunctions against such perceived ethical failings as smoking, use of alcoholic beverages, sexual sin, and immodest dress have been staples within Pentecostal spirituality. When shifted to a New Testament context, the concept of sinfulness remains primarily centered on personal morality and ethics and the need for salvation from personal sin is deemed most critical. Jesus' ministry is seen as a ministry to individuals, with limited social implications, except how individual members of the body of Christ should treat their fellow human beings in chiefly personal relationships. Even here, the emphasis is on maintaining relationships with other Christians as, for many, hospitality and assistance to non-believers is, simply, an evangelistic tool.

What, often, has been lacking in this paradigm is an understanding of the corporate implications of sinfulness, leaving Pentecostal hermeneutics and the preaching and teaching that emanate from it neglectful of the "weightier matters of the law"[26] concerning justice and compassion for the stranger, servants and oppressed. Eldin Villafañe's

---

[26] Matt 23:23.

assertion in *The Liberating Spirit: Toward an Hispanic American Pentecostal Social Ethic*, that the (Pentecostal) understanding of sin must be broadened, has credence in this context. What he says about Hispanic Pentecostals is generally true of the movement as a whole:

> There is a need to extend this...understanding of the Spirit's... struggle with the flesh, the world, and the devil, within their social correlates - sinful social structures, the 'world (cosmos) and principalities and powers - if a social ethic is to emerge.[27]

The Pentecostal emphasis on the Kingdom of God might prove to be a fruitful point for entering a conversation regarding developing a cogent theology of social justice. Expansion of the understanding of that Kingdom, as not only crucial for the eschaton, but requiring a practical outworking in the here and now, is imperative. Such an understanding involves cooperating with the Spirit in holding the Kingdom values of justice and righteousness in tension with each other. A conversation centered on this understanding requires an affirmation of each human being—male and female, and regardless of distinctions of race, ethnicity, physical ability, or class—as created fully in the image of God as a salient beginning.

Though, again, much of Pentecostal theological discourse about the Kingdom centers on an eschatological hope to which adherents already hold, promise rest in new discussions of the already-but-not-yet dimension of the Kingdom emerging within nascent Pentecostal

---

[27]Eldin Villafañe, *The Liberating Spirit: Toward an Hispanic American Pentecostal Social Ethic*. Grand Rapids, MI: Wm. B. Erdmann's Publishing Co., 1993, 164.

theology. This discourse takes seriously the prophetic witness of New Testament texts regarding justice, especially Jesus' proclamation of his mission in setting free the captives and liberating those who are bound.[28] It provides a beginning place for seeing this liberty not only as freedom from bondage to personal habits, but from social ideologies, structures, and systems that, in any way, degrade the image of God within the individual. Though not naming it as such, early Pentecostals saw themselves as living in this dimension and sought to model its reality in their worship, ministry, and the egalitarian communities to which they gave allegiance.

Historical Framework

Since the Pentecostal movement comes directly out of the 19th century Wesleyan Methodist Holiness Movement, its belief system is built upon the Wesleyan doctrine of entire sanctification and the theological notion of a second act of grace available to the earnest seeker following conversion. The practical out-workings of early Pentecostal spirituality emerged from the Great Awakenings, the Holiness camp meetings, and Higher Life movements that began to adopt the language of Holy Spirit baptism and looked for ways to verify the experience within the believer.

While many historians still date the beginning of the movement with Parham's formulation of the initial evidence doctrine, his efforts to promote widespread acceptance of his formulation failed. The movement received its most significant early notoriety and impetus for growth under the leadership of Seymour, whose Azusa Street Revival received widespread media attention. It was this revival and this

---

[28] Luke 4:17-19.

attention that helped launch Pentecostalism into a world-wide movement. Importantly, primal beginnings of the social justice implications of Pentecostalism were woven into the fabric of that revival and its leader. That revival was multi-cultural and gender-inclusive in a time when rigid social conventions and understandings of race and women's place were embedded within American culture.

Holiness roots brought a marked affinity for social justice causes, so many early Pentecostal leaders vigorously took on a variety of social causes. Seymour championed racial reconciliation, believing that unity among all Spirit-baptized believers, regardless of race, was the "more sure" indication of God's presence.[29] Frank Bartleman, an eyewitness and early participant in the revival, was an outspoken critic of militarism, and an ardent supporter of programs for the poor. The racial unity he observed in the Azusa Street Revival, for example, led to his premature characterization.[30]

George and Carrie Judd Montgomery, who made a fortune in mining, were involved in a variety of social causes including setting up an orphanage and donating land to the Salvation Army for a rescue home for girls. A. J. Tomlinson, one of the earliest leaders and the first General Overseer of the Church of God (Cleveland, TN), ministered to the poor in Appalachia and pursued racial harmony and justice within the young body when segregation and discrimination were norms in the church and society.

Aimee Simple McPherson, the founder of the International Church of the Foursquare Gospel, founded Temple Commissary to aid the poor of all races and religious affiliations, fighting against organized crime, and involving her congregation in earthquake relief.

---

[29] *Apostolic Faith,* (September 1906), 3.
[30] Frank Bartleman, *How Pentecost Came to Los Angeles,* 54.

Social reformer and faith preacher, Finis Yoakum, a wealthy former surgeon, aligned himself with Pentecostal tenets after being healed following a near-fatal car accident. He set up the Pisgah Home movement to help the poor and other social outcasts.

Such visible activism appeared to have failed to survive the movement's initial stages for several reasons. First, Pentecostalism arose at the same time as such movements as Darwinism, higher criticism, the social gospel, and ecumenism. Threatened by the perceived potential of these movements to destabilize biblical Christianity, Pentecostals joined other Evangelicals in protesting against these "modernist" tendencies and "false doctrine." A primary fear was that the social gospel movement would substitute social work for grace and social transformation for personal salvation. Secondly, early adherents suffered heavy persecutions including taunting and bearing such derogatory names as "holy rollers," and being shunned by "respectable" religious folks who often considered them demon-possessed. Physical beatings and arson against members were not uncommon during the early years. In turn, Pentecostals often shunned the outside world, seeing most outsiders as hostile, hopelessly lost, and worldly.

Finally, there was also a shift in the Holiness Movement from post-millennial to pre-millennial interpretations of eschatology that saw a parallel shift in the Pentecostal movement. With this change, the earlier Holiness optimism about bringing about structural change in the surrounding society gave way to a pessimism that changed the character of the movement forever vis-à-vis that society. The greatest hope was to rescue those few who would place their faith in Christ's return and the founding of the new Kingdom.

In its early years, leaders and most adherents came from the lower classes. The uneducated, the undereducated, African Americans, Hispanics, and other minorities had a higher representation in the movement than did the middle- and upper classes, the highly educated or whites. With age has come a degree of dialogue with other Christian traditions and some movement toward ecumenism. Though still considered an oddity in some circles, modern Pentecostalism draws its rank from a broader segment of society than the "disinherited"[31] members among whom it was first popular and so has gained a semblance of respectability and acceptance. Second and third-generation Pentecostals have moved increasingly into the social and economic mainstream, and Pentecostal spirituality is infiltrating mainline congregations via the Charismatic and Neo-Pentecostal movements. According to Vinson Synan,

> ... By the 1930s it became clear that the great appeal of the... movement would be to the lower classes and that once these classes rose up the economic scale, the socio-cultural character of the movement would rise with it.[32]

In recent years, several Pentecostal denominations have relaxed personal piety codes and injunctions against such activities as movie-going, secular music, dancing, participation, and attendance at sporting events, the wearing of certain colors, or types of clothing or jewelry. Additionally, most have changed their stances on such pursuits as higher education, with some larger Pentecostal denominations having

---

[31] A characterization used by Robert Mapes Anderson in *Vision of the Disinherited: The Making of American Pentecostalism.* Peabody, MA: Hendrickson Publications, 1992.

[32] Vinson Synan, *The Holiness-Pentecostal Movement,* Plainfield, NJ; Logos International; 1975, 200.

at least one accredited institution of higher education.[33] With this has come a new emphasis on training clergy either formally or informally. Still, even larger numbers of Pentecostal youths are pursuing secular education, and many are going into professions such as law, secular writing, and theater—areas that were previously labeled "unspiritual" or "sinful."

At the same time, the Pentecostal church is undergoing a moral crisis with many of the behaviors the church historically deplored are becoming increasingly evident within its congregations. Within the last twenty years, the social behavior of Pentecostal youths and adults has grown to exhibit the same range of problems as do members of other denominations. Teenage premarital sex and pregnancy have increased dramatically within the movement. Though still lower than the general population or among mainline denominations, the divorce rate among Pentecostals is rising faster than among any other Christian tradition. And, more divorced persons are remarrying, an action once prohibited and punishable by disfellowship. Though drug and alcohol use and abuse are still lower than among other populations, they are on the rise among people who consider themselves Pentecostal, though probably less so among active adherents. These currents of increased assimilation and experience of social problems have heightened the awareness among some Pentecostals that a pro-active stance on social issues and social justice must be forthcoming.

---

[33] The Assemblies of God for example has fifteen accredited institutions in the United States and several in foreign countries, as well as an ATS accredited seminary. The Church of God has Lee College and the Pentecostal Theological Seminary. The Pentecostal Holiness Church has two institutions: Emmanuel College and Southwestern Christian University. The Church of God in Christ has C. H. Mason Seminary as part of the Interdenominational Theological Seminary.

Pentecostals and Social Justice

The dearth of popular, doctrinal, and scholarly discourse surrounding social justice does not indicate that Pentecostals are socially unconcerned or immune to these issues. Pentecostal praxis, especially at the local congregation level, has often been integrally involved in social action within their immediately surrounding communities. Pentecostal Congregations are generally quick to respond to evident material need, and benevolence has always been a high priority. Such benevolence is seen as an obedient response to Jesus' injunction to minister to "the least of these."[34] Clothes closets, food pantries, and emergency financial help for those within and outside of the congregation are a staple of most Pentecostal churches. Individual members or groups within these congregations might also involve themselves in activities such as prison ministry (visitation and holding worship services) and hospital visitation.

Often, however, Pentecostal social action has been incidental rather than intentional, and reactive rather than pro-active. They do not fit the definition of what Donald Miller has termed, "progressive Pentecostalism," that applies to "Christians who, inspired by the Holy Spirit and the life of Jesus, seek to holistically address the spiritual, physical, and social needs of people in their community."[35] These authors suggest that this definition applies to less than fifteen percent (15%) of all Pentecostal churches and believers.[36] Another important

---

[34] Matt: 25:40.

[35] Donald E. Miller and Tetsunao Yamamori, Global Pentecostalism: *The New Face of Christian Social Engagement.* Berkeley: University of California Press, 2007, 2-3.

[36] Donald E. Miller "Progressive Pentecostals: The New Face of Christian Social Engagement" 2006 Presidential Address *Journal of the Scientific Study of Religion*, 46:4 (2007)), 439.

element of a definition of Progressive Pentecostals is that their social ministries are available to everyone in the community and, therefore, even though conversion may be a byproduct of the church's commitment to follow the teachings of Jesus.[37] Though, as Miller suggests, this segment of Pentecostalism may have historically been small, it has never been absent, and evidence suggests that it is growing.

Historically, Pentecostal responses to injustice often remain at the level of benevolence. Congregations within its ranks are generally less likely than mainline or Evangelical congregations to seek out justice causes or potential areas of ministry that have not made themselves manifestly evident. They are generally less likely to be involved in advocacy, community organization, or prevention programs for issues such as HIV/AIDS or drug abuse. They are also less likely to provide religious education on practical concerns such as these issues.

One rarely finds visible activist movements in any arena of the Church that are heavily populated by Pentecostals. Rarely do Pentecostal leaders make public political statements regarding community issues or even the gravest injustices within society. Political concerns are seldom addressed directly from Pentecostal pulpits. Sermons rarely have a direct tie-in to current social themes, unless they reflect some specific category of sin such as high rates of teen pregnancy related to the high rate of sexual involvement or what some perceive as the "gay agenda." This is especially true when the injustice does not directly affect the immediately surrounding community. An excellent example of this is the almost complete ignoring of the implications of such community trauma by many pulpits and periodical publications within Pentecostal denominations. This distancing from

---

[37] Ibid.

political involvement is often true, however, even on an issue as closely tied to doctrinal beliefs as anti-abortion and right-to-life groups.

Some deviation from the pattern renders African American Pentecostals generally more justice-oriented than their white counterparts (because of the struggle for the civil rights struggle). And, conservative white congregations may involve themselves in activities such as letter-writing campaigns on "family values" issues, such as the recent push against homosexual unions. Even in these cases, however, individual involvement is low when contrasted with other Christian bodies.

Though Pentecostal leaders and adherents would describe themselves as more politically and socially involved than most casual observers suppose, the priority remains on evangelism. Social transformation is often seen as a vehicle for evangelism and not the end goal. That evangelism, however, allows impacting the lives of socially disadvantaged persons and communities in positive ways. The nature and structure of Pentecostalism have implications for bringing about social change among those won to the movement. Often dramatic change can be seen in the lives and conduct of previously "disinherited" converts imbibe the community's emphasis on forsaking old lifestyles and adopting a strict personal moral/ethical code.

For, involvement in Pentecostalism spirituality and community often fosters a personal revolution within individuals that changes their world view, helps them deal effectively with their situation, and provides a compassionate base for dealing with other individuals. This changed world view, the resulting changed personal moral code, and the support system that generally characterizes most Pentecostal congregations imbue the individual with the coping skills necessary to move upward in society. As Grant McClung states,

> Pentecostalism... did not develop a social ethic which would encourage participation... in labor unions or political organizations, which promote social change. This does not mean that Pentecostalism failed to have any social impact. Rather...the Pentecostal communities meant a powerful offering of life-meaning for wide sectors excluded from our societies.[38]

The rigid personal moral standard, emphasis on cohesive family structures, and adherence to a strong work ethic drive individuals and families to exhibit behavior that often leads to the upward mobility of both. For them, then, rather than serving simply as a refuge in the face of economic deprivation, Pentecostalism becomes as a launching pad into higher socio-economic class. A proponent of the movement describes it this way:

> What is overlooked is that Pentecostals have quietly gone about social renewal in unobtrusive ways, working with the poor of the world in unheralded corners.[39]

This emphasis, however, does little to change the contributing factors in the surrounding society. Neither does it foster a social justice consciousness among those individuals not already sensitive to those issues, even if they have reaped the benefit of this Pentecostal ethos. In too many cases, individuals who have escaped the ravages of poverty or discrimination see themselves as somehow more deserving than

---

[38]Grant McClung, "Pentecostal Charismatic Perspectives on a Missiology for the Twenty First Century" *Pneuma* 16 (Spring 1994), 15.
[39]William Menzies, "Current Pentecostal Theology of the End Times," *The Pentecostal Minister* 8 (Fall 1988), 9.

those who are unable to do so. More dangerously, spiritual sanction is accorded the disparity between their situation, and those who are not as fortunate in escaping are demonized.

Signs of Movement Toward Engagement Injustice

Hopeful signs have loomed on the Pentecostal horizon. The October 1994, gathering of leaders of African American and white Pentecostal bodies to begin to bring about racial reconciliation in the movement is an example of a nascent move toward broader social involvement. As an outgrowth of this meeting, the Pentecostal Fellowship of North America that had an almost exclusive representation from predominantly white bodies was dissolved. In its place, a new bi-racial organization, the Pentecostal and Charismatic Churches of North America, was created. Its first elected president, Ithiel Clemmons, of the Church of God in Christ, was African American. Its twelve-member leadership board also included an African American woman, Bishop Barbara Amos of Norfolk, Virginia.

Another such sign is the current trend at the popular level of denominational and independent Pentecostal and Charismatic media such as magazines, books, articles, television, and radio programs to begin to pay attention to social justice issues. These media have broadened their focus and include a much more socio-economically and culturally diverse pool of contributors. For example, one recurring theme in Charismatic and Pentecostal magazines during 1994 was racial reconciliation. Several media also dealt with the issues of homelessness and AIDS more thoroughly than had ever previously been done. Since such media is often at the avant-garde of information on social change, it is hoped that this is a genuine signal of the beginning of stirring within the movement.

A further sign of movement is the recent trend of electing more progressive leadership to head many of the Pentecostal denominations. Through the mid to late 1980s, these bodies have historically been headed by old-liners—generally white men, and there has been little place for the inclusion of people of color, women, or people with adequate theological training. As these leaders move on, denominations increasingly opt to not replace them with similar leadership. They choose, rather, to tap a new genre of secularly and theologically educated talent who remain committed to Pentecostal distinctives but are willing to change outdated cultural responses. One hopeful sign, within the last two decades, is the inclusion of people of color and, increasingly, women in some of the most visible positions in Pentecostal denominational leadership.[40]

Despite these beginnings, we can say much for the concerns included and excluded from the movement's social consciousness. The move toward racial reconciliation, for example, falls short of inclusiveness of all races and has focused almost exclusively on healing wounds between blacks and whites. Hispanics and Asians, who have a relatively high proportional representation among Pentecostals, are rarely found within the leadership or faculties of Pentecostal institutions and are excluded from the discussions of racial reconciliation almost entirely, as are Native Americans. Additionally, the attention of the Memphis racial reconciliation conference was almost entirely on healing racial wounds among Pentecostals. The issue

---

[40] For example, in 2009, the Assemblies of God elected a woman as one of its General Presbyters and the International Church of the Foursquare Gospel returned the social witness of its earlier roots by elected a woman as president of the denomination and selected two women, an African American and a Latino to fill six of its ten district supervisor slots.

of the need for racial justice within the wider society was largely untouched.41

Again, while these signs indicate progress among more progressive Pentecostals, there does not seem to be the same level of concern for institutional justice at the congregational level. Too often, there is no bridge between progressive Pentecostal thinkers and rank-and-file adherents, or between these thinkers and church leaders. Few, if any, major Pentecostal denominations include women in church leadership in a meaningful way or provide parity for women clergy in credentialing or ministry placement. In these areas, the Pentecostal movement, that is the baby on the American denominational scene lags several years behind its elder mainline and Evangelical siblings.

The task of formulating a Pentecostal theology of social justice will not be an easy one. However, impetus might come from the realization that the same issues touching the lives within the broader society are increasingly touching the lives of Pentecostal individuals, families, and the communities in which they live and serve. Drug abuse, alcoholism, teenage pregnancy, AIDS, disintegrating families, spousal and child abuse were once "not mentioned among us," at least not publicly. Today, though, Pentecostal pastors deal with the full range of these and other evidence of societal injustice and disorganization, both within the congregation and right outside the church doors. Racism, classism, and sexism are as much a problem for the church as for the rest of society. They may not voice this, because to do so might appear somehow less spiritual. However, within themselves, and more often now vocally, they are asking questions that require seasoned, theologically sound responses that are relevant to their social context.

---

[41] This conference led to the disbanding of the all-white Pentecostal Fellowship of North America

Contemporary Pentecostals are more upwardly mobile, more educated, and more economically well off than their predecessors. They are also more independent in their response to church dogma, and less likely to accept the status quo answers to the questions that touch their lives.

From Engagement to Theology

In attempting to develop a relevant, yet distinctively Pentecostal, theology of justice, several issues deserve consideration. The first is Pentecostal's theological self-understanding. Second, is the Pentecostal movement's highly sectarian nature with its many divisions and subdivisions. Third, are ongoing tensions between competing theological streams within the movement. Fourth, is the continued sociological, historical, ecclesiological, and theological disconnectedness of the movement from the broader faith community. Fifth, is the limited appropriation of the meaning of prophetic ministry. The movement's relative infancy compared to the rest of the Christian tradition also contributes to a lack of theological sophistication and clarity. Separately, each issue has implications for critical, ethical theological reflection. Collectively, they make this task a difficult one. Each must be resolved to some extent before the movement can make real progress toward framing a socially just theological stance.

Yet, while little exists in the way of a cohesive written theology, a Pentecostal theology does exist. Or, more correctly, Pentecostal theologies exist. These are primarily oral, stemming from the largely oral traditions of first- and second-generation Pentecostalism. They are not generally composed of exhaustive creeds and tomes; but given the movement's non-creedal position, this is expected. More often, they exist in tracts, pamphlets, periodicals, sermons, Sunday school commentaries, denominational polities, and a small number of textbooks on Pentecostal faith confessions.

The Pentecostal movement exists as a response to a theological understanding of the place and work of the Holy Spirit in the present world. Those within it, see it as representing a twentieth-century reformation that re- expresses the first-century outpouring of the Holy Spirit. They see the purpose of this reformation as empowering the church to engage itself in God's last-days redemptive mission. Generally, Pentecostals see this mission as largely, and sometimes almost entirely, related to evangelism and personal salvation.

An integral part of this theological self-understanding is that Pentecostal theology is largely a biblical theology. The conviction that the whole Bible is the inspired word of God is at the center of Pentecostal hermeneutics and praxis. Some disagreement exists about the exact definition of "inspired" and how that inspiration came about. However, Pentecostals essentially see the Bible in its totality as "a reliable revelation of God, stating the exact truth that the Holy Spirit intends to convey."[42]

Some Pentecostals would go so far as to declare the entire Bible as the ultimate systematic theology. They maintain, therefore, that no further refinement or restatement is necessary. "To understand God and God's redemptive purposes" they would say, "read, study and understand the Bible." This unfortunate oversimplification sometimes deters those progressive Pentecostals from attempting to develop a codified theology because they fear fellow believers may consider them "unfaithful" or "unspiritual."

Despite this, several attempts have been made by scholars to

---

[42] French L. Arrington, "The Use of the Bible by Pentecostal," *Pneuma*, 16 (Spring 1994), 101-107.

develop theological statements for their respective bodies. These works are explicitly sectarian and highlight the highly factional nature of the movement, while further complicating efforts to develop a representative Pentecostalism systematic theology. Rather, these are often apologetics that highlight minute distinctions of one faction from another as well as the broader body of Christ. Such works, for example, deal with topics such as the baptism formula, the "oneness" nature of the Godhead, or the initial evidence controversies.[43] Other scholars have taken on certain theological aspects such as Christology or soteriology, pneumatology, or missions. More recently, progressive Pentecostal scholars have dealt with Pentecostal responses to social issues. A body of works related to these topics is in place.

Since its beginning in the 1960s, the Charismatic movement has sparked new interest in Pentecostalism generating a prolific body of popular Pentecostal/Charismatic theology. And, though much of this material deals with sensational or shallow issues, some have tackled hard theological and social justice issues with honesty and compassion, if not thoroughness.[44]

---

[43] See, Myer Pearlman, *Knowing the Doctrines of the Bible*. Springfield, MO: Gospel Publishing House, 1937 *and* J. Rodman Williams, *Renewal Theology: Systematic Theology from a Charismatic Perspective Vols. I-III*. Grand Rapids, MI: Zondervan Publications, 1996.

[44] For example see such works as Cheryl Bridges-Johns, *Pentecostal Formation: A Pedagogy of the Oppressed*. Sheffield, England: Sheffield Academic Press, 1993 or "Pentecostals and the Praxis of Liberation: A Proposal for Subversive Theological Education," *Transformation* 11 (Jan-Mar 1994), 11-15; Murray Dempster, "Pentecostal and Charismatic Scholars call for an End to Apartheid"; Sharon L. Georgianna, "The American Assemblies of God: Spiritual Emphasis and Social Activism," in Paul Elbert, ed. *Faces of Renewal*, (Peabody, MA: Hendrickson Publishers, 1988), 265-277, Frank Macchia, *The Spirit and the Kingdom: Implications of the Message of the Blumhardts for Pentecostal Social Spirituality,* Metuchen, NJ: The Scarecrow Press, 1993. "Pentecostals and Social

Promising work has begun to emerge from Pentecostal scholars, including the fruitful area work by members of the Society for Pentecostal Studies in its quarterly journal, *Pneuma,* and presentations at its annual conferences. Such scholars as Eldin Villafañe, Vinson Synan, Peter Paris, Larry Christiansen, Murray Dempster, Leonard Lovett, Margaret Poloma, and Cheryl Bridges-Johns have purposely set out to address issues of social justice with honesty and clarity. Another fruitful area is the work of the *Journal of Pentecostal Theology.* Here again, scholars from both within and outside the movement have undertaken the theological task with rigor and seriousness. But, often, as with Villafañe's *The Liberating Spirit,* addressing Hispanic Pentecostals, these efforts are limited to a sectarian or sub-cultural focus.

Beyond these initial attempts, however, Walter Hollenweger's criticism of Pentecostalism as having "made no contribution to the theme of ethical rigorism"[45] demands consideration. What is missing, is a substantial body of systematic Pentecostal theology that spans its depth and breadth. What is needed is for inside interpreters within these traditions to articulate a written, cohesive, and inclusive self-definition. It remains to be seen whether this is possible, given the importance placed on seemingly insignificant divisions.

These divisions ensure that a major problem hampering the formation of a systematic Pentecostal theology of social justice is the movement's apparent failure to resolve competing theological tensions. Among these is an ongoing tension about the nature of the

---

Ethics," *Pneuma*: 9 (Fall 1987), 129-153 and Eldin Villafañe, "The Contours of a Pentecostal Social Ethic: A North American Hispanic Perspective," *Transformation* 11 (Jan-Mar 1994), 6-10.
　　[45]Walter J. Hollenweger, *The Pentecostals: the Charismatic Movement in the Churches*. Peabody, MA: Hendrickson Publishers, 1972, 3.

Holy Spirit's working out God's purposes in a world that is overtly secular and sinful. Does the Spirit work only through the life of a "Spirit-filled" Christian and only on behalf of the church? Or, conversely, is the Spirit hovering over and concerned for all the world that God created and so loved? Is Holy Spirit empowerment that is received only for personal transformation and piety or also to equip the believer for service where he or she is placed?

Related tension revolves around the need to be "separate" from the world while also being "salt and light;" to be "in" but not "of the world." These tensions are both practical and eschatological, involving every element of Pentecostal self-understanding and praxis. Adherents attempt to balance a pre-millennial hope in the hereafter with a life lived in the present sinful world in a way that appropriates God's Kingdom principals to make a difference in their everyday life.

On the one hand, the question is: "Why work to bring about social justice in a world on the verge of supernatural interruption?" On the other hand, the question might be more: "How can a people supernaturally transformed and empowered by the Holy Spirit involve themselves in bringing about the Kingdom of God and a more just world while not acclimating themselves to its sinful social order?"

Since just after its early beginnings, Pentecostalism has been and remains, at its core, pre-millennial. A major tenet of Pentecostal doctrine is the belief that Jesus Christ will return to earth and rapture away the body of Christ—the church—before setting up a thousand-year reign of peace. Pentecostals see his reign as preceding the final destruction of the world as we know it. They further see the redeemed as living forever with God in heaven and the wicked being cast into eternal hell. Out of this pre-millennial belief system come Pentecostalism's strong missiological and evangelistic thrusts. The primary mission, then, is to get as many people saved and ready for the rapture as possible. Everything else is secondary.

This imminent return of Christ is the same hope that the early church held. Two thousand years have passed, and Pentecostals still hold to this belief. But, with the passing of two millennia, they realize that "God's timing is not our timing," and "imminent" might not necessarily be tomorrow. The question then becomes, "what do we do today, in our lives, our congregations, and the communities we serve that make them more like the Kingdom of God in practical and tangible ways?" Often, this question remains unanswered. Too often, however, it is not asked.

Tension exists around the question of the nature of revelation. Caught mid-way between fundamentalism and liberalism, Pentecostals believe two, diametrically opposed, truths regarding the scope of revelation. First, they contend that the canon of Scripture—the Bible—as we have it today, in its totality, represents the complete, inspired, infallible and inerrant Word of God. Yet, they also believe in continuing revelation; that the Spirit is still revealing Himself and God's nature, purposes, and will in new and empowering ways.

The question is how to reconcile the notion of the Bible as containing God's entire revelation with the notion of the Holy Spirit's ongoing revelation to the modern church. The first notion is implied in the doctrines of inerrancy and inspiration that make up a central focus of Pentecostal dogma. The second stems from understanding the perpetuity of spiritual gifts (including the gift of prophecy) as necessary for maintaining the life, vitality, and ministry of the body.[46]

---

[46] John Christopher Thomas. "Women, Pentecostals and the Bible: An Experiment in Pentecostal Hermeneutics," *Journal of Pentecostal Theology* 5 (1994), 41-56.

Finally, there still exists a tension between the perceived validity of theological scholarship as opposed to spiritual revelation. Within this tension, the rational understanding of faith and its implications for the individual believer's life and society is juxtaposed against lived faith. The lingering lack of appreciation for theological education within many local congregations exists to some extent in all facets of modern conservative Protestantism. Despite some strides of the Evangelicals toward openness to such education in some segments, resistance is still probably most pronounced among Pentecostals. The joke from Pentecostal pulpits about seminaries being spiritual "cemeteries" is longstanding and pervasive. Though many younger Pentecostal leaders recognize the need and legitimacy of higher theological education, this gap will not close quickly.

Taken together, these tensions represent theological wrestling points with which the movement must grapple to be relevant within the modern spiritual and social context. Tackling them head-on will require the "ethical rigorism" that Hollenweger found lacking. Evidence of the beginning of such wrestling is apparent in works such as Villafañe's *Liberating Spirit*.[47] Miraslov Volf's *Exclusion and Embrace*[48] and works by scholars such as Amos Yong, and Clifton Clarke. Yet, much more is needed before a Pentecostal scholarship can, collectively, be taken seriously by the wider theological community and make a meaningful contribution to the broader theological discourse.

Another major impediment to constructing a socially just theology, or any systematic Pentecostal theology, is an inherent sense

---

[47] See Eldin Villafañe, *The Liberating Spirit: Toward an Hispanic American Pentecostal Social Ethic*, 2.

[48] Miraslov Volf, *Exclusion and Embrace: Theological Exploration of Identity, Otherness, and Reconciliation*. Nashville: Abingdon Press, 1996.

of disconnectedness. This sense manifests itself in both doctrine and praxis. Careful examination discloses four areas of disconnectedness—sociological, historical, ecclesiological, and theological—that have existed since the movement's inception and are only now beginning to be mitigated.

Sociological disconnectedness exists as Pentecostalism has, in many ways, been a separatist movement. Again, adherents see themselves as distinctly "in" but not "of" the world. For them, one is are either "saved" or "unsaved." Life in the Spirit is considered a life detached from the "sinful" cares and concerns of this present life. The implications permeate Pentecostal believers' and congregations' mindsets, often stunting efforts to find helpful solutions to genuine community problems and concerns.

Historically, many Pentecostals understand the movement to be God's completely new undertaking to reintroduce the work and person of the Holy Spirit into the church. They see nineteen hundred years of Christian history between the first-century church and the modern Pentecostal revival as, somehow, a period when the Holy Spirit was essentially absent from the church. This view does not appreciate the movement as a part of the ongoing revelation of God through the Holy Spirit. It neglects evidence of the Spirit's dynamic movement within preceding periods of the Church's life, disregarding the many ways the Holy Spirit has continued to reform and empower it.

While Pentecostals have been relatively uneasy givers, they often have been equally unwilling to take elements from the broader church that could help them develop into a mature faith community. Such elements as liturgical order, creeds, vestments, formal hymnody, and the like have often been dismissed out-of-hand as remnants of a dead faith and void of any signs of spiritual vitality or vital spirituality.

This historical and ecclesiological disconnectedness results in a theological disconnectedness that makes it difficult for the movement to place itself within the broader context of systematic theology. For many Pentecostals, then, the task is difficult because of a felt need to re-invent the theological wheel rather than build upon the understandings of the Holy Spirit and ecclesiology that have unfolded over two thousand years of church history. What makes it more difficult is that often such disconnectedness is not obvious. The language may be similar, but the understandings are often totally different from understandings developed and accepted throughout the life and history of the church.

Such theological disconnectedness contributes to the failure to engage and codify social justice dialogue. Relatedly, many Pentecostals have been unwilling to salvage principles from higher criticism, anthropology, and sociology that could enhance its theological self-understanding. They reject this entire body of work as, blatantly, secular and worldly, disdaining discourse that takes these into account as irrelevant for the spiritual maturity of the church. Again, for many, such discourse is seen as an impediment to the dynamic movement of the Holy Spirit.

Another impediment is the understanding of the prophetic role that discounts the Old Testament model of the socio-cultural prophet as irrelevant for the New Testament church. Among more charismatic segments of the movement, prophecy is understood as a spiritual gift more aligned with foretelling and discerning corporate direction than a vehicle for individual, corporate, and societal correction.

The recent rediscovery of Old Testament prophetic models is encouraging. Yet, while Pentecostal scholars and leaders are beginning to appropriate these models, development of a systematic, biblical theology of social justice must take the entire Scripture seriously, including the Old Testament canon, as normative or, at least, informative for shaping the life and conduct of the individual, congregation, and entire body of Christ.

This is facilitated by rediscovering the larger milieu of prophetic ministry, including its socio-critical attributes. Such rediscovery calls us to understand the mind and heart of God so that we share compassion for the entire world that God so loved. It requires recognition of the innate worth of human beings of all races, genders, socio-economic classes, nationalities, and spiritual conditions (not just regenerated believers) as created in God's image and fully carrying the Imago Dei. It mandates seeing the peculiar dignity and unique worth of each person as an image-bearer of the divine. In this context, our understanding of prophetic ministry must include addressing social structures that, in any way, degrade or demean any member or segment of the human community or attempt to rob them of their inherent, God-given dignity.

Within this broader understanding of prophetic witness is an expanded understanding of Holy Spirit empowerment. This goes beyond empowerment for godly living and accomplishing the personally salvific work of God, to the understanding of the empowerment for action. To be relevant, Pentecostal theology must confess that the Old Testament prophets, empowered by the Spirit for ecstatic expression, made no distinction between the requirement for righteousness and the requirement for doing justice. These two have always stood side by side in the mind of God and the mouth of Old Testament prophets. They both, therefore, must be integral components of the proclamation of the already-but-not-yet Kingdom by the church that was established by the Spirit. For Pentecostals, especially, this understanding comes by seeing that the first mention of the promised outpouring of the Spirit by Joel falls squarely within this prophetic stream.

Given the dating of its beginnings, the modern Pentecostal movement is a century old. As such, it is still in its theological and sociological adolescence as compared to older, more established denominations. Since theology generally lags behind reformation and revival, we should not be surprised that Pentecostalism is only recently beginning to take the task of theological reflection seriously. However, the time has come for the community to put away the "childish things"[49] that hamper the fresh move of the Spirit in truly revitalizing ways, and begin its journey toward becoming a spiritual adult, able to tackle the "deep things" of God.[50]

The catalog of inherent, structural impediments to the theological task within Pentecostalism are numerous and long-standing. These will not easily fall to the demands of modern life and culture. But, some appreciation for a different way of doing the Pentecostal church's ministry must develop if it is to be at all relevant to the demands of twenty-first-century life. The Holy Spirit dynamically moves God's people toward any goal we honestly attempt in the name of Christ. So it is not entirely impossible to envision a socially just response to the theological task within the Pentecostal realm.

Conclusion

Consideration of the requisites for the construction of a Pentecostal theology of social justice opens as many issues as it provides answers. The question is "Where do we begin building such a theology?"

---

[49] I Cor 13:11.
[50] I Cor 2:10.

Indeed, some existing infrastructure is in place as starting points that represent the strengths of the modern movement throughout its first century. These points are often obscured by the more sensational caricatures of a movement growing faster than its theology can keep up. Yet, they have remained essential components over its lifetime

One such entry point is an appreciation for Scripture as the Word of God and an attempt to live out what is understood as an authentic of a biblical worldview. Broadening this understanding from its narrow concentration on New Testament paradigms to an appreciation for all of Scripture would be beneficial. Such appreciation would provide more complete understanding of the revelation of God's nature and God's interaction with the world in this present age, and a greater appreciation for the biblical mandate for social as well as personal holiness.

A second entry point is an appreciation of the Holy Spirit's dynamic work in the believer, congregation, and community. Until now, this was understood, primarily, as enabling individuals to live a life of personal holiness, withdrawn from the sinful world. But it must broaden to reflect an appreciation of the Spirit's work throughout the body of Christ, in particular, and throughout the world, in general. Such understandings must appreciate God's desire to empower and enlist believers to work on behalf of God's mandate for justice.

Additionally, while the Bible, as the Word of God, must remain the central foundation of theological reflection, and Pentecostal experience is a relevant starting, the Wesleyan tools of tradition and reason are useful for developing a well-rounded theological framework. This broader framework could serve as a footing for a consistent, comprehensive systematic theology and as a model for Christian praxis and participation in the larger society. For the self-understanding, all faith communities are colored by their traditions and experience, and since Pentecostals quickly acknowledge the prominent place their experience of God plays in spirituality, gaining an appreciation for these other resources would not be a far leap.

A final starting point is a long-standing heritage of social ministry (much of it non-institutionalized) within Pentecostal communities. These efforts have been an integral part of the movement since its inception, not as do-good activities for bored Christians, but as active responses to immediate, perceived needs within the faith community and the surrounding culture. Broadening their efforts, again, calls for including a prophetic understanding of the need to dissolve structures exploit those created in the image of God. There must be a willingness to see, understand, and participate with the Holy Spirit's work in confronting those structures and actively seeking to bring about reformation.

Beginning the development of this understanding with reflection on the what is going on in existing benevolence and social outreach efforts allows us to lift up the relationship between service and social justice—between personal and social holiness—in a manner that views such service as more than an evangelistic tool or such personal holiness as more than a way to secure a spot in heaven. It permits us to locate these actions within the individual's and church's participation with God in loving response to the world God so loved. Secondly, any such efforts should reflect an honest attempt to grapple with existing tensions with the various factions within this dynamic movement. It arms Pentecostal believers with the ability to go beyond stock responses and seriously consider the divergent perspectives that have always been part of the movement. It also forces us to acknowledge our dynamic connection to the rest of the faith community.

Further, grappling with the necessity to reach outside our narrow theological enclave without capitulating to an unbiblical worldview, forces us to acknowledge our own sinfulness. It also requires us to address a need for individual redemption that discloses itself in more than personal piety but also includes loving, moral, and ethical responses to people, communities, and structures that are part of God's world.

It is impossible to complete the construction of a socially just Pentecostal theology within the limited scope of this discussion. Yet, setting some parameters for further work is an important first step. Whatever the final product, to be distinctively Pentecostal such a theology must affirm the place of the Holy Spirit in the life and ministry of the individual believer, the congregation, and the church at large. At the same time, this understanding will need to be broadened to reflect the myriad ways the Spirit works.

After prolonged disengagement from the social justice implications of the systematic theological task, initial efforts will reflect a degree of immaturity. But, we must begin. Otherwise, another one hundred years will past with the Pentecostal church failing to respond prophetically. With such failure, the movement will either dies out or become increasingly ineffective in responding to present-world realities.

Unfortunately, the Pentecostal church has often been unwilling to grant its scholars and leaders freedom to wrestle with hard issues for which there are no easy answers. To make headway, it must trust that the intellect within those who hold Pentecostal distinctives as important, claim for themselves supernatural endowment of Holy Spirit baptism, and want desperately to see the church align itself with what the Lord requires–justice, mercy, and humility–will work to bring this about. Then this same church and these same leaders must be willing to hear and act upon "what the Spirit is saying to the Church" through the gift of a spirit empowered intellect.

Bibliography

Albrecht, Daniel E. "Pentecostal Spirituality: Looking Through the Lens of Ritual," *Pneuma* 14 (Fall, 1992),107-125.

Alexander, Bobby. "Pentecostal Ritual Reconsidered: Anti-Structural Dimensions of Possession," *Journal of Ritual Studies*, 3 (1973), 109-128.

_____. "Correcting Misinterpretations of Turner's Theory: An African-American Pentecostal Illustration," *Journal for the Scientific Study of Religion*, 30 (March 1991), 26-44.

Alexander, Estrelda. *Black Fire: One Hundred Years of African American Pentecostalism*. Downers Grove, IL: InterVarsity Press, 2011.

_____. *Limited Liberty: The Legacy of Four Pentecostal Women Pioneers*. Cleveland, Ohio: Pilgrim Press, 2008.

_____. *The Women of Azusa Street*. Lanham, MD: Seymour Press, 2012.

Alvarado, Jonathan. "Worship in the Spirit: Pentecostal Perspectives on Liturgical Theology and Praxis" *Journal of Pentecostal Theology* 21:1 (January 2012), 135–151.

Anderson, Robert M. *Vision of the Disinherited: The Making of American Pentecostalism*. Peabody, MA: Hendrickson Publishers, 1992.

Archer, Kenneth J. *A Pentecostal Hermeneutic: Spirit, Scripture and Community*. Cleveland, TN: CPT Press, 2009.

Arrington, French L. "The Use of the Bible by Pentecostals" *Pneuma*, 16:1 (Spring, 1994),101-107.

Babcock, Neil. *Search for Charismatic Reality: One Man's Pilgrimage*, Portland, OR: Multnomah Press, 1985.

Bach, Marcus. *The Inner Ecstasy*. New York: The World Publishing Co., 1969.

Baer, Richard "Quaker Silence, Catholic Liturgy and Pentecostal Glossolalia" in Russell Spittler, *New Perspectives on Pentecostalism*. Grand Rapids, MI: Baker Book House, 1976, 150-164.

Barnett, Donald L. and Jeffrey McGregor. *Speaking in Tongues: A Scholarly Defense*. Seattle, WA: Community Chapel Publications, 1986.

Bartleman, Frank. *How Pentecost Came to Los Angeles*. Los Angeles, s.n.: 1925.

Bernard, David K. *Oneness and Trinity, A.D. 100-300: The Doctrine of God in Ancient Christian Writings*. Hazelwood, MO: Word Aflame Press, 1991.

Best, Ernest. "Interpretation of Tongue" in *Speaking in Tongues: A Guide to Research on Glossolalia*. Grand Rapids, MI: Wm. B. Eerdmans Publishing Co., 1986, 295-312.

Bigger, Nigel. "The Church's Witness in Evangelism and Social Action," *Evangelical Review of Theology*, 16 (July 1992), 296-309.

Bingaman, Brock. *All Things New: The Trinitarian Nature of the Human Calling in Maximus the Confessor and Jürgen Moltmann*. Eugene, OR: Pickwick Publications, 2014.

Boff, Leonardo. *Trinity and Society*. London: Burns & Oates, 1988.

Boyd, Gregory A. *Oneness Pentecostals and the Trinity*. Waco, TX: Baker Book House, 1992.

Bridges-Johns, Cheryl. "Pentecostals and the Praxis of Liberation: A Proposal for Subversive Theological Education" *Transformation* 11 (Jan-Mar 1994), 11-15.

_____ *Pentecostal Formation: A Pedagogy of the Oppressed*. Sheffield, England; Sheffield Academic Press; 1993.

Burgess, Frank, and Gary McGee. *Dictionary and Pentecostal and Charismatic Movements*. Grand Rapids, MI: Zondervan Publishers, 1987.

_____ and Eduard M. van der Maas. New International *Dictionary and Pentecostal and Charismatic Movements, Expanded and Revise Edition*. Grand Rapids, MI: Zondervan Publishers, 2002.

Buxton, Clyde W. *Minister's Service Manual*. Cleveland, TN: Pathway Press, 1985.

Cashwell, Gaston B. "Came 3,000 Miles for His Pentecost" *Apostolic Faith* 1:4 (December 1906), 3.

Church of God School of Theology Bulletin, IX, 1994-1996. Cleveland, TN: Church of God School of Theology, 1994.

Christenson, Larry. *Speaking in Tongues and Its Significance for the Church*. Minneapolis: Bethany Fellowship, 1968.

Clemmons, Ithiel. *Charles Harrison Mason and the Church of God in Christ*. Los Angeles: Pneuma Life Publishers, 1996.

_____. "New Life through New Community: The Prophetic Theological Praxis of Bishop William J. Seymour of the Azusa Street Revival," Address delivered at Regent University School of Divinity, April 18, 1996.

Cutten, George. *Speaking in Tongues: Historically and Psychologically Considered*. New Haven: Yale University Press, 1927.

Dayton, Donald W. *The Theological Roots of Pentecostalism*; Peabody, MA; Hendrickson Publishers; 1987.

Delattre, Roland. "Ritual Resourcefulness and Cultural Pluralism," *Soundings*, 61 (1978), 281-301.

Dempster, Murray. "Pentecostal Social Concerns and the Biblical Mandate for Social Justice," *Pneuma* 9 (Fall 1987), 129-153.

Duffield, Guy and Nathaniel VanCleave. *Foundations of Pentecostal Theology*. Los Angeles: L.I.F.E. Bible College. 1983.

Ervin, Howard. *Spirit Baptism: A Biblical Investigation*. Peabody. MA: Hendrickson Publishers, 1987.

Evans, Jason Oliver. *Taking the Doctrine of God off the Table: A Necessary Theological Dialogue Between Black Oneness and Trinitarian Pentecostals*. Master's Thesis, Duke University Divinity School, 2001.

Ford, Josephine Massyngberde. "Toward a Theology of Speaking in Tongues," *Theological Studies* (January 1, 1971), 3-39.

Gaede, Charles S. "Pentecost and Praise: A Pentecostal Ritual?" *Paraclete*, 2:2 (Spring 1988), 5-8.

Georgianna, Sharon L. "The American Assemblies of God: Spiritual Emphasis and Social Activism" in P. Elbert, ed. *Faces of Renewal*, Peabody, MA: Hendrickson Publishers, 1988, 265-277.

Gerlach, Luther P. "Pentecostalism: Revolution or Counter-Revolution," in Irving Zaretsky and Mark Leone, eds., *Religious Movements in Contemporary America*. Princeton, NJ: Princeton University Press, 1974.

Gerlach, Luther P. and Virginia H. Hines. *People, Power, Change; Movements of Social Transformation*. Indianapolis: Bobbs-Merrills, 1970.

Goodman, Felicitas. *Speaking in Tongues: A Cross-Cultural Study of Glossolalia*. Chicago: University of Chicago Press, 1972.

Grady, J. Lee. "The Other Pentecostals" *Charisma* (June 1997), 62-68.

Granaiwic C, Helen. *Towards a Classical Pentecostal Hermeneutic: A Bibliographic Investigation*. Lanham, MD: University of America Press, 1988.

Grimes, Ronald L. *Beginnings in Ritual Studies*. Washington, D.C.: The University Press of America, 1982.

_____. "Defining Nascent Ritual," *Journal of the American Academy of Religion*, 50 (December 1982), 539-550.

Gromacki, Robert. *The Modern Tongues Movement*. Philadelphia: Presbyterian and Reformed Pub. Co., 1967.

Hall, Connor B., ed. *Hymns of the Spirit*. Cleveland, TN: Pathway Press, 1969.

Hesser, Garry, and Weigert, Andrew J. "Comparative Dimensions of Liturgy: A Conceptual Framework and Feasibility Application" *Sociological Analysis*, 41 (Fall 1980), 215-219.

Higgins, John, Michael Dusing, and Frank Tallman. *An Introduction to Theology: A Classical Pentecostal Perspective*. Dubuque, IA: Kendall/Hunt Pub., 1993.

Hocken, Peter J. *The Glory and the Shame The Glory and the Shame: Reflections on the 20th-Century Outpouring of the Holy Spirit*. Gildford, UK: Eagle, 1994.

Hollenweger, Walter J. *Pentecostalism: Origins and Developments Worldwide*. Peabody, MA: Hendrickson Publishers, 1997.

_____. *The Pentecostals the Charismatic Movement in the Churches*. Minneapolis, MN: Ausburg Press; 1972.

_____. "Social and Ecumenical Significance of Pentecostal Liturgy," *Studia Liturgica*, 8 (1973), 207-215.

Hannagraff, Hank. "Oneness Pentecostalism: Heresy, Not Hairsplitting" *Christian Research Report*, 11:1 (1998), https://www.equip.org/article/oneness-pentecostalism-heresy-not-hairsplitting/.

Howell, Joseph H. People of the Name: Oneness Pentecostalism in the United States. Ph.D. Dissertation, Florida State University, 1985.

Hughes, Ray H. Church of God Distinctives, Revised edition. Cleveland, TN: Pathway Press; 1968.

Hunter, James. *American Evangelicalism: Conservative Religion and the Quandary of Modernity*. New Brunswick, NJ: Rutgers University Press, 1983.

Kelleher, Margaret M. "Liturgy, An Ecclesial Act of Meaning" *Worship*, 59 (1985), 482-497.

Kelsey, Morton. *Tongues Speaking: An Experiment in Spiritual Experience*. Garden City, NY: Doubleday, 1968.

Komonchak, Joseph. *Tongues Speaking: The History and Meaning of Charismatic Experience*. New York: Crossroad, 1981.

Komonchak, Joseph, ed. *The New Dictionary of Theology*. Wilmington, DE: Michael Glacier, 1986.

Land, Steven J. *Pentecostal Spirituality: A Passion for the Kingdom*. Sheffield, England: Sheffield Academic Press, 1993.

Laurentin, Rene. *Catholic Pentecostalism*, Translated by Matthew J. O'Connell. Garden City, New York: Doubleday, 1972.

Lawless, Elaine. *God's Peculiar People: Women's Voices and Folk Tradition in a Pentecostal Church*. Lexington, Ky.: University of Kentucky Press, 1988.

McGrath, Alister. *Christian Theology: An Introduction*, 3rd ed. Cambridge, MA: Blackwell, 2001.

Macchia, Frank D. "Pentecostals and Social Ethics," Pneuma: 9 (Fall 1987), 129-153.

_____. *The Spirit and the Kingdom: Implications of the Message of the Blumhardts for Pentecostal Social Spirituality, Metuchen, NJ: The Scarecrow Press, 1993*.

_____. "The Tongues of Pentecost: The Promise and Challenge of Pentecostal/Roman Catholic Dialogue" Paper delivered to the 25th Annual Meeting of the Society for Pentecostal Studies. March 1996, Toronto, Canada.

Marston, George W. *Tongues Then and Now*. Phillipsburg, TN: Presbyterian and Reformed Publishing Co., 1983.

McCone, Clyde R. *Culture and Controversy: Investigating the Tongues of Pentecost*. Philadelphia: Torrance and Co., 1978.

McDonnell, Kilian. *Charismatic Renewal and the Churches*. New York: Seabury Press, 1976.

_____. *Toward A New Pentecost for a New Evangelization*. Collegeville, MN: The Liturgical Press, 1974.

_____ and Montague, George. *Christian Initiation and Baptism in the Holy Spirit: The Evidence of the First Eight Centuries*. Collegeville, MN: The Liturgical Press, 1991.

McGee, Gary, ed. *Initial Evidence: Historical and Biblical Perspectives on the Pentecostal Doctrine of Spirit Baptism*. Peabody, MA: Hendrickson Publishers, 1991.

_____ and Stanley Burgess. *The Dictionary of Pentecostal and Charismatic Movements*. Grand Rapids, MI: Zondervan Publications., 1988.

McClung, Grant. *Azusa Street and Beyond: Pentecostal Missions and Church Growth in the Twentieth Century*. South Plainfield, NJ: Bridge Publishing, Inc., 1986.

_____. "Pentecostal/Charismatic Perspectives on a Missiology for the Twenty-first Century," *Pneuma* 16.1 (Spring 1994), 11-14.

Macchia, Frank. "The Spirit and the Kingdom: Implications of the Message of the Blumhardts for Pentecostal Social Spirituality," *Transformation* 11:1 (January-March 1994), 1:1-5.

Menzies, William; "Current Pentecostal Theology of the End Times" *The Pentecostal Minister*, 8 (Fall, 1988), 1-9.

Michel, David *Telling the Story: Black Pentecostals in the Church of God (Cleveland, Tennessee).* Cleveland, TN: Pathway Press, 2000.

Miller, Donald E. "Progressive Pentecostals: The New Face of Christian Social Engagement" 2006 Presidential Address *Journal of the Scientific Study of Religion*, 46:4 (2007), 435-445.

Miller, Donald E. and Tetsunao Yamamori. *Global Pentecostalism: The New Face of Christian Social Engagement.* Berkeley: University of California Press, 2007.

Mills, Watson E. *Glossolalia: Studies in the Bible and Early Christianity with a Bibliography.* New York, The Edwin Miller Press, 1985.

_____. *Speaking in Tongues: A Guide to Research on Glossolalia.* Grand Rapids, MI: Wm. B. Eerdmans Publishing Co., 1986.

_____. *A Theoretical/Exegetical Approach to Glossolalia.* Lanham, MD: University Press of America, 1985.

_____. *Understanding Speaking in Tongues.* Grand Rapids, MI: Wm. B. Eerdmans Publishing Co., 1972.

Moltmann, Jürgen. *The Church in the Power of the Spirit. A Contribution to Messianic Ecclesiology.* Trans. By. Margaret Kohl. Minneapolis, MN: Fortress Press, 1993.

_____. *The Spirit of Life: A Universal Affirmation.* Translated by Margaret Kohl. Minneapolis, MN: Fortress Press, 1992.

Montague, George T. *The Spirit and His Gifts: The Biblical Background of Spirit-Baptism, Tongues-Speaking, and Prophecy.* New York: Paulist Press, 1974.

Murphy, Larry G., J. Gordon Melton, et al., eds. *Encyclopedia of African American Religions.* New York: Routledge, 1993.

Olson, Roger E. How Important Is the Doctrine of the Trinity? *Patheos* (April 29, 2013). https://www.patheos.com/blogs/rogereolson/2013/04/1807/

Pearlman, Myer. *Knowing the Doctrines of the Bible*, Springfield, MO: Gospel Publishing House, 1937.

Poloma, Margaret. The Charismatic Movement: Is There a New Pentecost? Boston: Twayne Publishers, 1982.

Ranaghan, Kevin and Dorothy Ranaghan. *Catholic Pentecostals.* New York: Paulist Press, 1969.

Ranaghan, Kevin M. "Conversion and Baptism: Personal Experience and Ritual Celebration in Pentecostal Churches," *Studia Liturgica*, 10 (1974), 65-75.

_____. "Liturgical Renewal at Oral Roberts University," *Studia Liturgica*, 8: (1973), 122-136.

Rappaport, Roy. "Verocity, Verity and Verium in Liturgy," *Studia Liturgica*, 23 (1993), 35-50.
Ricoeur, Paul. *The Conflict of Interpretations: Essays in Hermeneutics*. Evanston, IL: Northwestern University Press, 1974.
Robeck, Cecil M., Jr. "The Nature of Pentecostal Spirituality," *Pneuma* 14 (Fall, 1992), 103-106.
_____ ed.; "Pentecostals and Social Ethics" *Pneuma* 9 (Fall 1987) 103-193.
Robins, R. G. *A. J. Tomlinson: Plainfolk Modernist*. New York: Oxford University Press, 2004.
David Roebuck, *Limiting Liberty: The Church of God and Women Ministers, 1886-1996*, Doctoral Dissertation for Vanderbilt University, Nashville, TN, 1999.
_____. "Loose the Women" *Christian History* Issue 58, 17:2 (1998).
Samarin, William J. *Tongues of Men and Angels: The Religious Language of Pentecostalism*. New York: MacMillan, 1972.
Sanders, Cheryl J. *Saints in Exile: The Holiness-Pentecostal Experience in African American Religion and Culture*. New York: Oxford University Press, 1996.
Scanzoni, Letha and Susan Setta. "Women in Evangelical, Holiness and Pentecostal Traditions" in Rosemary Ruether and Rosemary Keller, eds., *Women in Religion in America*, Vol 3, 1900-1968. Cambridge, MA: Harper and Row Publishers, 1981.
Schussler-Fiorenza, Elizabeth. *In Memory of Her: A Feminist Theological Reconstruction of Christian Origins*. New York: Crossroad Publishing Company, 1990.
Seymour, William J. *Doctrines and Disciplines of the Apostolic Faith Mission of Los Angeles*, edited Larry Martin. Joplin, MO: Christian Life Books (January 1, 2000
_____. "Questions Answered," *Apostolic Faith* 1:11 (October 1908-January 1909), 2.
Spencer, Jon Michael. "Isochronism of Anti-Structure in the Black Holiness-Pentecostal Testimony Service," *Journal of Black Sacred Music*, 2 (Fall 1988), 1-18.
Studebaker, Steve. "Baptism among Pentecostals" in Gordon L. Heath, ed., *Baptism: Historical, Theological, and Pastoral Perspectives*. Eugene, OR: Wipf & Stock Publisher, 2011, 201-224.
Suenens, Leo Joseph Cardinal. *Ecumenism and Charismatic Renewal: Theological and Pastoral Orientation*. South Bend, IN: Servant Books, 1978.
Synan, Vinson. *The Holiness-Pentecostal Movement*. Plainfield, NJ: Logos International; 1975.
Thomas, John Christopher. "Women, Pentecostals and the Bible: An Experiment in Pentecostal Hermeneutics" *Journal of Pentecostal Theology*, 5 (1994), 41-56.
Tomlinson, A. J. The Annual Address to the Twenty-Seventh Annual Assembly—September 7-13, Cleveland, TN, in the *General Assembly Annual Addresses, 1928-1943*. Cleveland, TN: The White Wing Publishing House, 2012, 142.
Tomlinson, Ambrose J. *Last Great Conflict*. Cleveland, TN: Press of Walter E. Rodgers, 1913.
Tugwell, Simon. *Did You Receive the Holy Spirit?* New York: Paulist Press, 1972.

Tyson, Ruel W., Jr. "The Testimony of Sister Annie Mae," *Journal of Ritual Studies*, 2 (Summer, 1988), 163-184.
Unger, Merrill. *New Testament Teaching on Tongues*. Grand Rapids, MI: Kregel Publications, 1971.
Villafañe, Eldin. "The Contours of a Pentecostal Social Ethic: A North American Hispanic Perspective," *Transformation* 11 (Jan-Mar 1994), 6-10.
_____. *The Liberating Spirit: Toward an Hispanic American Pentecostal Social Ethic;* Lanham, MD: University Press of America; 1994.
Williams, Cyril G. *"Strange Gifts" Speaking in Tongues: A Guide to Research on Glossolalia*. Grand Rapids, MI: Wm. B. Eerdmans Publishing Co., 1986.
_____. *Tongues of the Spirit: A Study in Pentecostal Glossolalia and Related Phenomena*. Cardiff: University of Wales Press, 1981.
Williams, J. Rodman. "The Phenomenon of Tongues." in *Renewal Theology: Vol 2- Salvation, the Holy Spirit and Christian Living*. Grand Rapids, MI: Zondervan Publishing House, 1990.
_____. *Renewal Theology: Systematic Theology from a Charismatic Perspective Vols. I-III*. Grand Rapids, MI: Zondervan Publications, 1996.
Williams, Melvin. *Community in a Black Pentecostal Church: An Anthropological Study*. Prospect Heights, IL: Waveland Press, Inc., 1974.
Wilson, John, and Harvey K. Clow. "Themes of Power and Control in a Pentecostal Assembly," *Journal for the Scientific Study of Religion*, 20 (1981), 241-250.

Index

African Methodist Episcopal
   Church, 33, 312
African Traditional Religion, 17, 19-
   26, 56, 57, 59, 60
Africanisms, 15, 39-55, 79
Albigensians *see* Cathari, 101
Allen, Richard, 33
Apostolic Faith Worldwide Camp
   Meeting, 252
Apostolic Overcoming Holy
   Church, 45
Assemblies of God, 146, 161 n. 55,
   164-165, 170, 253, 281 n. 33,
   287 n. 40
Azusa Street Revival, 1, 9, 15.40-58,
   81-85, 163-175, 180-181, 199-
   230, 291-292, 321-322

Baer, Richard , 104, 121 n. 14, 131,
   210-211, 242
Baptists, 32, 33, 69, 88, 162, 174,
   135 n 110, 162 n 57, 181, 248
   n. 2,
Barth, 258
Bartleman, Frank, 73, 157, 159, -
   186-187, 191, 198- 278,
Batman, G.W. and Daisy, 150

Blassingame, John, 32
Boddy, Alexander, 177
Boff, Leonardo, 266
Bowdan, William and Maggie, 253
Bridges-Johns, Cheryl, 291 n. 4, 292
Bryant, W. F., 192

Camisards, 101
Cashwell, Gaston Barnabas (G.B.),
   177, 183, 192, 194-195
Cathari, 101
Catholicism, ix, 6, 94, 95, 99, 101,
   130, 131, 132, 181,
   206,207210, 219, 207, 210, ,
   242, 261, 266
Charismatic Movement, 2, 3, 4, 8 ,
   9, 102 n. 26, 123, 128-136
   135, 219, 260, 280, 286, 291
Christian, William, 45, 69
Christiansen, Larry, 292
Church of Christ (Holiness), 71
Church of God in Christ, 45, 76,
   162-164, 177, 286
Church of Jesus Christ of Latter-
   Day Saints, see Mormons
Church of Our Lord Jesus Christ of
   the Apostolic Faith, 84

Church of the Living God (Christian Workers for Fellowship), 45, 69-71
Church of the Living God Pillar and Ground of the Truth, 153, 312
Clark, Elmer, 17
Clarke, Clifton, 295
Clemmons, Ithiel, 44, 79 n. 24, 90, 163-164, 190, 285
Colson, Charles, 129
Cones, James, 65
Contomblé, 18
Cook, Glenn, 177, 253
Crawford, Florence. 145, 147-148, 153, 177, 198

Dempster, Murray, 292
Doctrines and Discipline of the Azusa Street Apostolic Faith Mission, Los Angeles, California, 151, 189, 253

Ecumenism, 93-136
Episcopalian liturgy, 94, 113, 219, 242
Evangelicals/Evangelicalism, 6, 140, 141, 155, 160, 182, 211, 213, 247, 249, 254, 258, 259, 260, 268, 272, 279, 283, 288, 295
Evening Light Saints, 75, 180-182, 187
Ewart, Frank J., 253
Farrow, Lucy, 40, 144-147, 179, 189
Frazier, E. Franklin, 31
Fundamentalism, 6-7, 16, 107, 135, 141, 247, 294

Garlington, Joseph, Jr., 260
Garr, Alfred Garrison (A. G.), 177
Gerloff, Roswith, 61, 37-38 n. 46
Glossolalia, 3, 4, 11, 44, 95-136, *see also* speaking in tongues
Goss, Howard, 146-147
Grant, Jacqueline, 65
Great Awakenings, 17, 102, 277

Haywood, Garfield T., 83-84
Herskovits, Melville J, 18 n. 17, 31-32
Hocken, Peter, 185-1869
Holiness Movement, 44, 68, 102, 180, 181, 196, 277, 279

Hollenweger, Walter, 41n., 43, 236-237, 244, 269-270, 279-289, 339, 342

Holy Spirit, iv, 2, 3, 4, 5, 8, 11, 16, 45, 57, 58, 75, 92, 98, 106, 109, 112, 116, 118, 120, 122, 123, 124, 129. 130, 143, 146,173, 185, 189, 190, 199, 208, 212, 214, 217, 232, 235, 240, 243, 250, 255, 273, 274, 282, 290, 293, 294, 296, 297, 298, 299, 300, 301, 302

Baptism in, 11, 15, 55, 56, 58, 60, 73, 93, 96, 106, 107, 108, 112-113, 130, 132, 134, 135 n. 10, 142, 144, 145, 146, 147, 149, 150, 151, 152, 156, 160, 175, 176, 177, 179, 183, 188-189, 190, 191, 195, 210, 211, 223, 240, 241, 250, 253, 255, 262, 277

Homosexuality, 273, 284
Huguenots, 101
Hurston, Zora Neal, 47-48, 52, 60
Hutchins, Julia, 40, 145, 150

International Church of the Foursquare Gospel 153-154, 278
Irving, Edward, 101

Jakes, Thomas Dexter (T.D.), 260
Jansenists, 101
Jones, Charles Price (C.P.), 44-45, 71-72
Jones, Major, 65

Ku Klux Klan, 83

Lambert, Eva, 153
Lawson, Robert Clarence (R.C.), 83-89
Liberation Theology, 65, 266
Liturgy, 12, 105, 131-132, 151, 203-244
Lopez, Abundio and Rosa, 150
Leonard Lovett, 31, 292

Macchia, Frank, 133
MacRoberts, Iain, 39
Mason, Charles Harrison, iv, 44, 45, 47, 48, 76, 78-79, 81, 163, 177
Massyngberde Ford, Josephine, 119-120

Mbiti, John, 32
McDonnell, Kilian, 99, 117, 132
McGrath, Alister, 267
McPherson, Aimee Semple, 153-154, 169-170, 278
Mead, Samuel and Ardell, 151
Moore, Jennie Evans, 148-149, 179
Mormons, 102, 248, 254
Mount Sinai Holy Church, 80, 153, 171

Neo-Pentecostalism, 2, 3, 4, 8 ,9, 128-129, 135, 280

Oneness Pentecostalism, iv, v, vii, 84, 117, 203, 247-268,

Parham, Charles, 15-16, 41, 45, 52, 60, 73, 141-143, 144-145, 162, 179, 181, 185, 277
Paris, Peter, 28, 292
Payne, Daniel, 33
Pentecostal Assemblies of the World, 83
Pentecostal Holiness Church, 154
Perichoretic Trinity, 266-267
Phillips, William, 45
Poloma, Margaret, 114

praying in tongues, 58, 239

Quakers, 120, 131,182-183, 210, 242

racism, 68, 74, 82-91, 182, 273
Ranaghan, Kevin, 117 n. 71, 207, 212, 221, 238-239
Roberts, J. Deotis, 66, 91
Robinson, Ida Bell, iv, 6, 79-83, 153, 155, 171
Ricoeur, Paul ,110, 128
ring shout, 33, 41, 47, 52

Santeria, 18
Sargent, Phoebe, 146
Scandrett-Leatherman, Craig, 46, 48-49, 54
Schussler-Fiorenza, Elizabeth, 123
Seymour, Jennie Evans, 149, 152, *see also* Jennie Evans Moore
Seymour, William Joseph, iii. iv, v, 15, 37-38, 40, 72-76, 85, 113, 142, 162, 174, 177, 179-181, 185-191, 195-201,277, 278
Shearer Schoolhouse Revival, 174, 178, 179
singing in tongues, 42

slave Christianity, 26-36
Smith, Elias Dempsey, 55-46, 76-77
Society of Friends, 82, see also Quakers
speaking in tongues, 3, 4, 7, 11, 15, 16, 41, 44, 55, 58, 61, 73, 74, 93-136, 142, 144, 145, 146-147, 149, 150, 175, 176, 177, 178, 179, 181, 183, 186, 188, 189, 190, 192, 204, 205, 208, 210, 211, 235, 236, 240-41, 250, 266, see also Glossolalia as initial evidence of Holy Spirit Baptism, 75, 15, 240-241, 250, 255
Spittler, Russell, 109
Spurling, Robert, 192
Suenens, Cardinal Leo Joseph, 123, 130, 135
Synan, Vinson, 280, 292

tarrying, 50, 52, 53, 240-241
Tate, Mary Magdalena, 69, 153-154, 169, 170 n
Terry, Neely, 144-145
The Apostolic Faith, 58, 59, 147, 148, 177, 181, 188

Tomlinson, Ambrose Jessup (A. J.), 11, 173-201

Triumph the Church and Kingdom of God, 46, 76-78

Unger, Merrill, 107-108
United Holy Church, 79, 154-155, 195
United Pentecostal Church, 253

Villafañe, Eldin, 275, 292, 295
Vodun, 18

Waldenses, 101
Waldo, Peter, 101
Welsh Revival, 101-102
Wesley, John, 38, 102, 259
Wesleyan Methodism, 9, 38, 68, 102, 178, 195, 219, 242, 247, 277, 300
Wiley, Ophelia, 146, 148
women, vi, vii, 4,7,11, 19, 25, 26, 31, 37, 45-46, 49, 51, 55,68-69, 79-80, 88, 139-171, 181, 194, 197, 200, 209, 220, 227, 278, 287

Yong, Amos, 65, 295

www.ingramcontent.com/pod-product-compliance
Lightning Source LLC
Chambersburg PA
CBHW050311120526
44592CB00014B/1865